The Complete Book of Bible Promises

God makes wonderful
promises to us if
we only follow him
in our lives. We can
go so far from him as we
want to but if we turn
around and look for him
again he is right there.
Don't forget that.
　　　　　Love
　　　　　Nan

　　　　　　　1999

PS In your reading,
check out the writings
of C.S. Lewis.

"Mere Christianity"
"The Screwtape letters"
also Pilgrims Progress etc
for enlightenment

THE COMPLETE BOOK
of Bible
Promises

J. STEPHEN LANG

Tyndale House Publishers, Inc.
WHEATON, ILLINOIS

Visit Tyndale's exciting Web site at www.tyndale.com

Library of Congress Cataloging-in-Publication Data

Lang, J. Stephen.
  The complete book of Bible promises / J. Stephen Lang.
    p. cm.
  Includes index.
  ISBN 0-8423-4701-1 (softcover)
  1. Bible—Indexes. 2. God—Promises. I. Title.
BS432.L34 1997
220.5′20836—dc21   97-2382

Printed in the United States of America

04   03   02   01   00   99   98   97
9   8   7   6   5   4   3   2   1

You have done many good things for me, LORD, just as you promised.

PSALM 119:65

CONTENTS

PREFACE

"Give your burdens to the LORD, and he will take care of you" (Psalm 55:22). A lovely promise, isn't it? This verse does not even specify that we bring life-threatening or major burdens to the Lord. We can bring *any* of them, great or small, physical or emotional or spiritual. The Bible promises God's faithful people that he watches over them constantly. The Bible promises people who lack faith that they may *have* faith if they desire it. In short, there is no human difficulty and no human being who is excluded from the promises of the Bible.

This is good news, considering that many people promise us things, then let us down. Politicians, advertisers, self-help gurus, and a thousand self-appointed "experts" surround us, promising us a better life—*if* we give them our vote, money, time, etc. We know all too well what those promises usually lead to: frustration, disappointment, cynicism. We wonder, *Does anyone keep promises anymore?*

Even people close to us will let us down. How often have we heard a relative or close friend say, "I'm sorry, I'll do better"? We are human beings, and our intentions may be good, but our promises are not always trustworthy. Welcome to the real world, where human promises are temporary, fragile, and often just downright meaningless. But this is also God's world. Our bad experiences with human disappointment can make us even more appreciative of the steadfast Lord, who never fails his people.

The book you are holding is a comprehensive attempt to gather together the Bible's promises on every possible concern. The chapters are titled according to their topics ("Anger," "Heaven,"

"Marriage," "Self-Esteem," etc.) and arranged alphabetically. If you are searching for a particular topic ("Drugs," for example) and don't find it in the alphabetical table of contents, look for it in the topical index. The index, also arranged alphabetically, will refer you to a related chapter. (In the index, you will find "Drugs," referring you to the chapter on "Alcohol and Other Substance Abuse.") You will also find, at the end of each chapter, referrals to related topics.

It is hoped this book will lead you to a richer understanding and appreciation for the God who keeps his promises.

Adultery

One book about extramarital affairs is titled *The Myth of the Greener Grass*. The title is fitting, since for many people, even Christians, the grass seems greener somewhere away from one's own spouse. The world used to take adultery seriously, but how things have changed! The tabloids and TV chat shows send the message that adultery is—well, normal. "Everybody's doing it" has become a moral guideline, pushing aside that rather blunt statement from the Ten Commandments:

Do not commit adultery. EXODUS 20:14

Ah, but the attractions of the "greener grass" are strong. God's Word takes a painfully realistic view of the lure of adultery—and of its consequences as well.

The lips of an immoral woman are as sweet as honey, and her mouth is smoother than oil. But the result is as bitter as poison, sharp as a double-edged sword. PROVERBS 5:3-4

A prostitute will bring you to poverty, and sleeping with another man's wife may cost you your very life. Can a man scoop fire into his lap and not be burned? Can he walk on hot coals and not blister his feet? So it is with the man who sleeps with another man's wife. He who embraces her will not go unpunished. . . . But the man who commits adultery is an utter fool, for he destroys his own soul. PROVERBS 6:26-32

> Destruction of the soul is not something a person thinks about in the heat of passion. The more likely thought is "No one will ever know" or "No one will care." But we have God's promise that, indeed, someone *does* know.

Why be captivated, my son, with an immoral woman, or embrace the breasts of an adulterous woman?

For the LORD sees clearly what a man does, examining every path he takes. An evil man is held captive by his own sins; they are ropes that catch and hold him. He will die for lack of self-control; he will be lost because of his incredible folly.
PROVERBS 5:20-23

The adulterer waits for the twilight, for he says, "No one will see me then." He masks his face so no one will know him. . . . They are not acquainted with the light. The black night is their morning. They ally themselves with the terrors of the darkness.

But they disappear from the earth as quickly as foam is swept down a river. Everything they own is cursed, so that no one enters their vineyard. Death consumes sinners just as drought and heat consume snow. JOB 24:15-19

Give honor to marriage, and remain faithful to one another in marriage. God will surely judge people who are immoral and those who commit adultery. HEBREWS 13:4

We don't like to think of God as a judge, do we? It goes against the modern grain, for we are expected to be "tolerant" and "nonjudgmental." But the Bible pulls no punches: God is a merciful Father—and also our final Judge. The prohibition of adultery isn't just an arbitrary rule designed to kill our pleasure. It's a moral guide to being the type of person whom God wants for his eternal Kingdom.

The apostle Paul, confronted with the many sexual sins of the church of Corinth, made this clear:

Run away from sexual sin! No other sin so clearly affects the body as this one does. For sexual immorality is a sin against your own body. 1 CORINTHIANS 6:18

Don't you know that those who do wrong will have no share in the Kingdom of God? Don't fool yourselves. Those who indulge in sexual sin, who are idol worshipers, adulterers, male prostitutes, homosexuals, thieves, greedy people, drunkards, abusers, and swindlers—none of these will have a share in the Kingdom of God. 1 CORINTHIANS 6:9-10

Harsh words, aren't they? Lumping adulterers together with thieves, swindlers, and drunkards. In spite of the world's indifference toward adultery, the Christian standard is higher.

Jesus took the "no adultery" standard one step further:

You have heard that the law of Moses says, "Do not commit adultery." But I say, anyone who even looks at a woman with lust in his eye has already committed adultery with her in his heart. MATTHEW 5:27-28

Did Jesus mean that every wayward glance was as wicked as the act itself? More likely he was saying something we all know too well: Our hearts and imaginations can be sinful even when we're unwilling to commit the actual sin. While there are many adulterers in the world, there are even more people who fantasize—who are unfaithful *inside* while remaining faithful *outside*. Jesus' message to people who want to be part of God's Kingdom was this: Keep your body *and* your mind from being unfaithful. God beholds not only our actions but our thoughts as well. Jesus made this clear enough. Addressing people who placed high value on right behavior, Jesus claimed that the inner person is where sins like adultery begin:

From the heart come evil thoughts, murder, adultery, all other sexual immorality, theft, lying, and slander. These are what defile you. MATTHEW 15:19-20

But isn't God a forgiving God, a God of mercy? Of course. He is a God of new beginnings, even for adulterers. There is no more beautiful passage in the Bible than this story from John's Gospel:

As he was speaking, the teachers of religious law and Pharisees brought a woman they had caught in the act of adultery. They put her in front of the crowd.

"Teacher," they said to Jesus, "this woman was caught in the very act of adultery. The law of Moses says to stone her. What do you say?"

They were trying to trap him into saying something they could use against him, but Jesus stooped down and wrote in the dust with his finger. They kept demanding an answer, so he stood up again and said, "All right, stone her. But let those who have never sinned throw the first stones!" Then he stooped down again and wrote in the dust.

When the accusers heard this, they slipped away one by one, beginning with the oldest, until only Jesus was left in the middle of the crowd with the woman. Then Jesus stood up again and said to her, "Where are your accusers? Didn't even one of them condemn you?"

"No, Lord," she said.

And Jesus said, "Neither do I. Go and sin no more."
JOHN 8:3-11

This person, caught in the very act of adultery, was told by Jesus she was *not* condemned. This declaration of divine mercy was followed by words that are too often forgotten: "Go and sin no more."

God is the one who judges sin, *and* he is the God of mercy.

See also Marriage, Sexuality, Temptation.

Aging

Who wants to grow old? Comedian George Burns, who lived past the age of one hundred, quipped, "It's better than the alternative." But is it? For the person who is faithful, the alternative to living on in this world is heaven. God's Word has a lot to say about heaven, but it also has a lot to say about aging. We can be thankful that the Lord has a more gracious attitude toward aging than our youth-obsessed society does.

Gray hair is a crown of glory; it is gained by living a godly life.
PROVERBS 16:31

The glory of the young is their strength; the gray hair of experience is the splendor of the old. PROVERBS 20:29

What an unfashionable idea! Gray hair as a "crown of glory," a sign of "experience." The Almighty's values are a far cry from our own. Instead of being considered disposable seniors, the elderly are promised God's continuing esteem and concern.

I will be your God throughout your lifetime—until your hair is white with age. I made you, and I will care for you. I will carry you along and save you.   ISAIAH 46:4

Grandchildren are the crowning glory of the aged.
PROVERBS 17:6

Show your fear of God by standing up in the presence of elderly people and showing respect for the aged. I am the LORD.
LEVITICUS 19:32

The godly will flourish like palm trees and grow strong like the cedars of Lebanon. For they are transplanted into the LORD's own house. They flourish in the courts of our God. Even in old age they will still produce fruit; they will remain vital and green.
PSALM 92:12-14

> Is this a rosy, unrealistic view of old age? Not in a spiritual sense, for a godly person really can produce fruit, even in old age. But the Bible, being always rooted in reality, is clear that aging has its unpleasant side.

Lord, through all the generations you have been our home! Before the mountains were created, before you made the earth and the world, you are God, without beginning or end.
   You turn people back to dust, saying, "Return to dust!" For you, a thousand years are as yesterday! They are like a few hours! You sweep people away like dreams that disappear or like grass that springs up in the morning. In the morning it blooms and flourishes, but by evening it is dry and withered.
   Seventy years are given to us! Some may even reach eighty. But even the best of these years are filled with pain and trouble; soon they disappear, and we are gone. Who can comprehend the power of your anger? Your wrath is as awesome as the fear you

deserve. Teach us to make the most of our time, so that we may grow in wisdom. PSALM 90:1-6, 10-12

> What is the message of this passage? Grow old and despair? Hardly. The last verse is a message to anyone, whatever their age: Make the most of the time you do have. Our life in this world does not continue, but the spiritual heritage we leave *does* endure. Consider the following passages:

Praise the LORD! Happy are those who fear the LORD. Yes, happy are those who delight in doing what he commands. Their children will be successful everywhere; an entire generation of godly people will be blessed. PSALM 112:1-2

In the last days, God said, I will pour out my Spirit upon all people. Your sons and daughters will prophesy, your young men will see visions, and your old men will dream dreams. In those days I will pour out my Spirit upon all my servants, men and women alike, and they will prophesy. ACTS 2:17-18

> Paul, that great apostle, left us the following promise, perhaps the most comforting of all promises to seniors and a great comfort to faithful believers whatever their age.

I am sure that God, who began the good work within you, will continue his work until it is finally finished on that day when Christ Jesus comes back again. PHILIPPIANS 1:6

See also Hope, Personal Growth.

Alcohol and Other Substance Abuse

In recent years people have become more conscious of alcohol and other substance abuse. In spite of our growing awareness of the personal and social harm that is done, we seem to be losing the drug war, and alcoholism is on the rise.

What does the Bible say about such practices? Well, you will search in vain for a verse that says, "Don't drink alcohol, period." And the Bible says nothing whatsoever about illegal drugs, since they weren't available in Bible times. The Bible does have much to say about any substance that makes us less than human. Happily, it also has much to say about the alternatives to a chemical high. In the Bible's view, being "filled with the Spirit" is far superior to any kick that a drink or drug can give us.

Wine produces mockers; liquor leads to brawls. Whoever is led astray by drink cannot be wise. PROVERBS 20:1

Those who love pleasure become poor; wine and luxury are not the way to riches. PROVERBS 21:17

Do not carouse with drunkards and gluttons, for they are on their way to poverty. Too much sleep clothes a person with rags.

Who has anguish? Who has sorrow? Who is always fighting? Who is always complaining? Who has unnecessary bruises? Who has bloodshot eyes? It is the one who spends long hours in the taverns, trying out new drinks. Don't let the sparkle and smooth taste of wine deceive you. For in the end it bites like a poisonous serpent; it stings like a viper. You will see hallucinations, and you will say crazy things. You will stagger like a sailor tossed at sea, clinging to a swaying mast. And you will say, "They hit me, but I didn't feel it. I didn't even know it when they beat me up. When will I wake up so I can have another drink?"
PROVERBS 23:20-21, 29-35

Destruction is certain for you who get up early to begin long drinking bouts that last late into the night. . . . Destruction is certain for those who are heroes when it comes to drinking, who boast about all the liquor they can hold. They take bribes to pervert justice. They let the wicked go free while punishing the innocent.

Therefore, they will all disappear like burning straw. Their roots will rot and their flowers wither, for they have rejected the law of the LORD Almighty. They have despised the word of the Holy One of Israel. ISAIAH 5:11, 22-24

Alcohol and prostitution have robbed my people of their brains.
HOSEA 4:11

Watch out! Don't let me find you living in careless ease and drunkenness, and filled with the worries of this life. Don't let that day catch you unaware, as in a trap. For that day will come upon everyone living on the earth. LUKE 21:34-35

> The New Testament gives an ideal to strive for: the Kingdom of God. Our lives in this world should show that we have already placed

our entire lives under God's sovereignty. There is no place in the
Kingdom for those who prefer a chemical substance to a fulfilling
life with God.

We should be decent and true in everything we do, so that
everyone can approve of our behavior. Don't participate in wild
parties and getting drunk, or in adultery and immoral living, or in
fighting and jealousy.   ROMANS 13:13

Don't be drunk with wine, because that will ruin your life. Instead,
let the Holy Spirit fill and control you.   EPHESIANS 5:18

You have had enough in the past of the evil things that godless
people enjoy—their immorality and lust, their feasting and
drunkenness and wild parties, and their terrible worship of idols.
   Of course, your former friends are very surprised when you no
longer join them in the wicked things they do, and they say evil
things about you. But just remember that they will have to face
God, who will judge everyone, both the living and the dead.
1 PETER 4:3-5

See also Bad Company, The Body, Sickness, Temptation.

Ambition

Is anything wrong with ambition—having high hopes of success, pursuing goals? Not at all. People who have made the world a more livable place were often very driven, ambitious people. Ambition is not a vice and neither is success. God finds no fault with human energy.

But what about when the goal in life becomes something besides loving God and our fellow human beings? Ambition would be wonderful if it didn't so often crowd out love and kindness. In the life of faith, the greatest ambition must be to please God—and in the Bible's view, everything else is secondary to that.

Those who are wise must finally die, just like the foolish and senseless, leaving all their wealth behind. The grave is their eternal home, where they will stay forever. They may name their estates after themselves, but they leave their wealth to others. They will not last long despite their riches—they will die like the animals. PSALM 49:10-12

You can make many plans, but the LORD's purpose will prevail. PROVERBS 19:21

If you are bitterly jealous and there is selfish ambition in your hearts, don't brag about being wise. That is the worst kind of lie. For jealousy and selfishness are not God's kind of wisdom. Such things are earthly, unspiritual, and motivated by the Devil. For wherever there is jealousy and selfish ambition, there you will find disorder and every kind of evil.

But the wisdom that comes from heaven is first of all pure. It is also peace loving, gentle at all times, and willing to yield to others. JAMES 3:14-17

The world offers only the lust for physical pleasure, the lust for everything we see, and pride in our possessions. These are not from the Father. They are from this evil world. 1 JOHN 2:16

> Jesus understood the human hunger of ambition. Yet he promised his followers that the values of God's Kingdom are radically different from the values of this world. Power and control and prestige are the goals of human ambition, but Jesus promised that his Kingdom is very, very different.

Jesus told them, "In this world the kings and great men order their people around, and yet they are called 'friends of the people.' But among you, those who are the greatest should take the lowest rank, and the leader should be like a servant. Normally the master sits at the table and is served by his servants. But not here! For I am your servant." LUKE 22:25-27

Jesus said to the disciples, "If any of you wants to be my follower, you must put aside your selfish ambition, shoulder your cross, and follow me. If you try to keep your life for yourself, you will lose it. But if you give up your life for me, you will find true life. And how do you benefit if you gain the whole world but lose your own soul in the process? Is anything worth more than your soul?" MATTHEW 16:24-26

Those who exalt themselves will be humbled, and those who humble themselves will be exalted. MATTHEW 23:12

No wonder you can't believe! For you gladly honor each other, but you don't care about the honor that comes from God alone. JOHN 5:44

> Ambition is as human as . . . well, as being human. The authors of the New Testament had some sensible advice about dealing with ambition. They perceived that one key to dealing with it was to give some thought to others' happiness, not just their own. And of course, the best way to squelch ungodly ambition is to have a nobler ambition found in living for God.

Don't be selfish; don't live to make a good impression on others. Be humble, thinking of others as better than yourself. Don't think only about your own affairs, but be interested in others, too, and what they are doing. PHILIPPIANS 2:3-4

This should be your ambition: to live a quiet life, minding your own business and working with your hands, just as we commanded you before. As a result, people who are not Christians will respect the way you live. 1 THESSALONIANS 4:11-12

See also Self-Esteem, Success.

Angels

Throughout history people have shown a considerable curiosity about angels. The most recent revival of this topic was at the end of the twentieth century. The Bible says a lot about angels, most of it a great comfort to God's people. But, this fascination with angels is not always healthy. With a vague interest in spiritual matters, many simply show an interest in angels as just one form of supernatural beings. But they do not always bear a resemblance to the angels in the Bible.

Angels *are* supernatural beings, of course. They are God's messengers, invisible except when they assume a shape to appear before human beings. We don't know what they look like, except they appear as grand, awe-inspiring beings—not the chubby, sweet-faced infants in classical art. Biblical accounts and other Christian literature speak of angels as magnificent beings who inspire awe but also bring solace.

Angels appear in many places in the Bible, but the most familiar passages remind us of their roles as *protectors* and *comforters* of God's people.

The angel of the LORD guards all who fear him, and he rescues them.

Taste and see that the LORD is good. Oh, the joys of those who trust in him! PSALM 34:7-8

If you make the LORD your refuge, if you make the Most High your shelter, no evil will conquer you; no plague will come near your dwelling. For he orders his angels to protect you wherever you go. They will hold you with their hands to keep you from striking your foot on a stone. PSALM 91:9-12

The high priest and his friends, who were Sadducees, reacted with violent jealousy. They arrested the apostles and put them in the jail. But an angel of the Lord came at night, opened the gates of the jail, and brought them out. ACTS 5:17-19

The night before Peter was to be placed on trial, he was asleep, chained between two soldiers, with others standing guard at the prison gate. Suddenly, there was a bright light in the cell, and an angel of the Lord stood before Peter. The angel tapped him on the side to awaken him and said, "Quick! Get up!" And the chains fell off his wrists. Then the angel told him, "Get dressed and put on your sandals." And he did. "Now put on your coat and follow me," the angel ordered.

So Peter left the cell, following the angel. But all the time he thought it was a vision. He didn't realize it was really happening. They passed the first and second guard posts and came to the iron gate to the street, and this opened to them all by itself. So they passed through and started walking down the street, and then the angel suddenly left him.

Peter finally realized what had happened. "It's really true!" he said to himself. "The Lord has sent his angel and saved me from Herod and from what the Jews were hoping to do to me!"
ACTS 12:6-11

Beware that you don't despise a single one of these little ones. For I tell you that in heaven their angels are always in the presence of my heavenly Father. MATTHEW 18:10

I assure you of this: If anyone acknowledges me publicly here on earth, I, the Son of Man, will openly acknowledge that person in the presence of God's angels. But if anyone denies me here on earth, I will deny that person before God's angels. LUKE 12:8-9

There is joy in the presence of God's angels when even one sinner repents. LUKE 15:10

> Jesus and the apostle Paul promised that angels would play a key role in the second coming of the Lord. The angels are reapers, gathering in the harvest of God's faithful people. They are also heralds, announcing Jesus' glorious arrival on earth.

I, the Son of Man, will send my angels, and they will remove from my Kingdom everything that causes sin and all who do evil, and they will throw them into the furnace and burn them. There will be weeping and gnashing of teeth. Then the godly will shine like the sun in their Father's Kingdom. Anyone who is willing to hear should listen and understand! MATTHEW 13:41-43

And then at last, the sign of the coming of the Son of Man will appear in the heavens, and there will be deep mourning among all the nations of the earth. And they will see the Son of Man arrive on the clouds of heaven, with power and great glory. And he will send forth his angels with the sound of a mighty trumpet blast, and they will gather together his chosen ones from the farthest ends of the earth and heaven. MATTHEW 24:30-31

The Lord himself will come down from heaven with a commanding shout, with the call of the archangel, and with the trumpet call of God. First, all the Christians who have died will

rise from their graves. Then, together with them, we who are still alive and remain on the earth will be caught up in the clouds to meet the Lord in the air and remain with him forever. So comfort and encourage each other with these words.
1 THESSALONIANS 4:16-18

In New Testament times, people were actually *worshiping* angels since they are supernatural beings. This danger has reappeared from time to time since then as some people show more interest in angels and other celestial beings than in God himself. The letter to the Hebrews warned against this, stating that angels are only servants of God:

Angels are only servants. They are spirits sent from God to care for those who will receive salvation. HEBREWS 1:14

You have come to Mount Zion, to the city of the living God, the heavenly Jerusalem, and to thousands of angels in joyful assembly. HEBREWS 12:22

The apostle Paul warned Christians that every supernatural being isn't an angel and does not necessarily have benevolent intentions. In fact, the New Testament reminds us that what is good can sometimes become evil. Satan and his demons were originally angels.

Satan can disguise himself as an angel of light. So it is no wonder his servants can also do it by pretending to be godly ministers. In the end they will get every bit of punishment their wicked deeds deserve. 2 CORINTHIANS 11:14-15

God did not spare even the angels when they sinned; he threw them into hell, in gloomy caves and darkness until the judgment day. 2 PETER 2:4

I remind you of the angels who did not stay within the limits of authority God gave them but left the place where they belonged. God has kept them chained in prisons of darkness, waiting for the day of judgment. JUDE 6

See also The Devil.

Anger

The Bible doesn't say to never be angry. In fact, it tells how Jesus, God's perfect Son, drove the greedy money changers out of the Temple (John 2:14-16). Jesus' example illustrates the kind of anger Christians should feel—at oppression, at the injustice in the world, at blatant cruelty. In other words, we should be angry at *sin*.

But this isn't the kind of anger most of us feel. Don't we usually feel anger—sometimes boiling rage—at being slighted, ignored, or insulted? Don't pride and ego lead to most of our anger? This is the kind of anger the Bible warns against. It promises sad consequences if we persist in it.

Dear friends, be quick to listen, slow to speak, and slow to get angry. Your anger can never make things right in God's sight.
JAMES 1:19-20

Don't be quick-tempered, for anger is the friend of fools.
ECCLESIASTES 7:9

Stop your anger! Turn from your rage! Do not envy others—it only leads to harm. PSALM 37:8

Surely resentment destroys the fool, and jealousy kills the simple. JOB 5:2

Stay away from fools, for you won't find knowledge there.
PROVERBS 14:7

It is better to be patient than powerful; it is better to have self-control than to conquer a city. PROVERBS 16:32

A hot-tempered person starts fights and gets into all kinds of sin.
PROVERBS 29:22

I say, if you are angry with someone, you are subject to judgment! If you say to your friend, "You idiot," you are in danger of being brought before the court. And if you curse someone, you are in danger of the fires of hell. MATTHEW 5:22

> We can control our anger, for God promises to help us. In doing so, however, we go against the usual wisdom the world offers: "Let your feelings out. Don't hold back." Why not? Do we really feel better about ourselves for having lashed out at another human being? Or are we just more inclined to act that way again, ignoring its effects on other people and the higher wisdom that says, "Let this pass"?

Dear friends, never avenge yourselves. Leave that to God. For it is written, "I will take vengeance; I will repay those who deserve it," says the Lord. Instead, do what the Scriptures say: "If your enemies are hungry, feed them. If they are thirsty, give them something to drink, and they will be ashamed of what they have done to you." Don't let evil get the best of you, but conquer evil by doing good. ROMANS 12:19-21

A gentle answer turns away wrath, but harsh words stir up anger. PROVERBS 15:1

A fool is quick-tempered, but a wise person stays calm when insulted. PROVERBS 12:16

A hothead starts fights; a cool-tempered person tries to stop them. PROVERBS 15:18

Beginning a quarrel is like opening a floodgate, so drop the matter before a dispute breaks out. PROVERBS 17:14

People with good sense restrain their anger; they earn esteem by overlooking wrongs. PROVERBS 19:11

Mockers can get a whole town agitated, but those who are wise will calm anger. PROVERBS 29:8

"Don't sin by letting anger gain control over you." Don't let the sun go down while you are still angry. EPHESIANS 4:26

Get rid of all bitterness, rage, anger, harsh words, and slander, as well as all types of malicious behavior. Instead, be kind to each other, tenderhearted, forgiving one another, just as God through Christ has forgiven you. EPHESIANS 4:31-32

> Proverbs, that extremely practical book of the Old Testament, probably has more to say about anger than any other part of the Bible. Some things never change—like human nature, obviously— and Proverbs gives some timeless wisdom about a timeless problem.

Short-tempered people must pay their own penalty. If you rescue them once, you will have to do it again. PROVERBS 19:19

Keep away from angry, short-tempered people, or you will learn to be like them and endanger your soul. PROVERBS 22:24-25

The New Testament gives new insight into controlling anger: Christians are the body of Christ, and as fellow members of that body, we have a special obligation to care for each other. Anger will arise, even among the most faithful of people. But it should be gotten rid of as soon as possible.

Now is the time to get rid of anger, rage, malicious behavior, slander, and dirty language. Don't lie to each other, for you have stripped off your old evil nature and all its wicked deeds. In its place you have clothed yourselves with a brand-new nature that is continually being renewed as you learn more and more about Christ, who created this new nature within you.

COLOSSIANS 3:8-10

See also Hate; Meekness, Humility, Gentleness; Pride and Conceit, Self-Control and Self-Denial.

Bad Company

The famous line "It is better to be alone than in bad company" was, believe it or not, first uttered by George Washington. But the thought goes back much further than the first president. It occurs again and again in the Bible. But according to the Bible, we never are completely alone. Even when in bad company, we *can* commune with God.

Don't copy the behavior and customs of this world, but let God transform you into a new person by changing the way you think. Then you will know what God wants you to do, and you will know how good and pleasing and perfect his will really is.
ROMANS 12:2

Do not join a crowd that intends to do evil. When you are on the witness stand, do not be swayed in your testimony by the opinion of the majority.   EXODUS 23:2

Oh, the joys of those who do not follow the advice of the wicked, or stand around with sinners, or join in with scoffers. But they delight in doing everything the LORD wants; day and night they think about his law. They are like trees planted along the riverbank, bearing fruit each season without fail. Their leaves never wither, and in all they do, they prosper.

But this is not true of the wicked. They are like worthless chaff, scattered by the wind. They will be condemned at the time of judgment. Sinners will have no place among the godly.

For the LORD watches over the path of the godly, but the path of the wicked leads to destruction. PSALM 1

Wise planning will watch over you. Understanding will keep you safe.

Wisdom will save you from evil people, from those whose speech is corrupt. PROVERBS 2:11-12

The godly give good advice to their friends; the wicked lead them astray. PROVERBS 12:26

Whoever walks with the wise will become wise; whoever walks with fools will suffer harm. PROVERBS 13:20

Violent people deceive their companions, leading them down a harmful path. PROVERBS 16:29

Young people who obey the law are wise; those who seek out worthless companions bring shame to their parents.
PROVERBS 28:7

Don't be fooled by those who say such things, for "bad company corrupts good character." 1 CORINTHIANS 15:33

> Folks in New Testatment times faced a problem common to many Christians today. They were people who had turned from immoral lives to the life of faith but still lived among unbelieving friends and neighbors. How easy it was (and still is) to slip back into old ways. But the apostles reminded them that they had a new loyalty to God.

> They couldn't return to their old life, even if that meant putting up with slights and insults from their former companions.

If you are willing to suffer for Christ, you have decided to stop sinning. And you won't spend the rest of your life chasing after evil desires, but you will be anxious to do the will of God. You have had enough in the past of the evil things that godless people enjoy—their immorality and lust, their feasting and drunkenness and wild parties, and their terrible worship of idols.

Of course, your former friends are very surprised when you no longer join them in the wicked things they do, and they say evil things about you. But just remember that they will have to face God, who will judge everyone, both the living and the dead.
1 PETER 4:1-5

Don't be fooled by those who try to excuse these sins, for the terrible anger of God comes upon all those who disobey him. Don't participate in the things these people do. For though your hearts were once full of darkness, now you are full of light from the Lord, and your behavior should show it! For this light within you produces only what is good and right and true.
EPHESIANS 5:6-9

See also Fellowship with Other Believers, Friends, Temptation, Witnessing.

Baptism of the Spirit and Gifts of the Spirit

Baptism is done with water, but the Bible talks about another baptism, much more important that the water ritual. This is the baptism of the Spirit, a teaching that was neglected for many years but has been given a renewed emphasis in many churches. This fresh interest in the Spirit is something to rejoice over. Christians of past times knew that without the Spirit there is only the lifeless, mechanical performance of religious duties. For centuries, Christians have said the words "I believe in the Holy Spirit" as part of their statements of faith—often without having much knowledge of just who the Spirit is. That situation has, thankfully, changed.

The Old Testament prophets looked forward to the outpouring of the Spirit. In the New, the prophecy was fulfilled. This was not merely a onetime historical event. The Spirit was, is, and will be given to all God's children.

I will give you abundant water to quench your thirst and to moisten your parched fields. And I will pour out my Spirit and my blessings on your children. ISAIAH 44:3

Then after I have poured out my rains again, I will pour out my Spirit upon all people. Your sons and daughters will prophesy. Your old men will dream dreams. Your young men will see visions. In those days, I will pour out my Spirit even on servants, men and women alike. JOEL 2:28-29

[John the Baptist:] "I baptize with water those who turn from their sins and turn to God. But someone is coming soon who is far greater than I am—so much greater that I am not even worthy to be his slave. He will baptize you with the Holy Spirit and with fire." MATTHEW 3:11

Jesus replied, "The truth is, no one can enter the Kingdom of God without being born of water and the Spirit." JOHN 3:5

Some of us are Jews, some are Gentiles, some are slaves, and some are free. But we have all been baptized into Christ's body by one Spirit, and we have all received the same Spirit.
1 CORINTHIANS 12:13

He saved us, not because of the good things we did, but because of his mercy. He washed away our sins and gave us a new life through the Holy Spirit. TITUS 3:5

> You cannot talk about the Spirit without speaking of spiritual gifts. While the Spirit himself is *the* gift to all Christians, the Bible also promises that each of us is given a special gift through the Spirit. Through our collective and individual use of these gifts, we become the church—not a building, but a living fellowship.

God verified the message by signs and wonders and various miracles and by giving gifts of the Holy Spirit whenever he chose to do so. HEBREWS 2:4

I can never stop thanking God for all the generous gifts he has given you, now that you belong to Christ Jesus. He has enriched your church with the gifts of eloquence and every kind of knowledge. This shows that what I told you about Christ is true. Now you have every spiritual gift you need as you eagerly wait for the return of our Lord Jesus Christ. 1 CORINTHIANS 1:4-7

> The Bible's key passage on gifts of the Spirit is chapter twelve of Paul's first letter to the Corinthians. Paul knew how the Corinthian Christians were inclined to bicker and dispute about who had the most status in the fellowship. But Paul promised them—and us—that each of us has a place in the fellowship. Each of us has a gift, and we fool ourselves in thinking we can do without each other. This great passage not only promises a gift for each of us but also gives a needed push in the direction of humility. It reminds us that "my gift" is important, but so are "our gifts." Happily, the Spirit is generous.

Now there are different kinds of spiritual gifts, but it is the same Holy Spirit who is the source of them all. There are different kinds of service in the church, but it is the same Lord we are serving. There are different ways God works in our lives, but it is the same God who does the work through all of us. A spiritual gift is given to each of us as a means of helping the entire church.

To one person the Spirit gives the ability to give wise advice; to another he gives the gift of special knowledge. The Spirit gives special faith to another, and to someone else he gives the power to heal the sick. He gives one person the power to perform miracles, and to another the ability to prophesy. He gives someone else the ability to know whether it is really the Spirit of God or another spirit that is speaking. Still another person is given the ability to speak in unknown languages, and another is given the ability to interpret what is being said. It is the one and only Holy Spirit who distributes these gifts. He alone decides which gift each person should have.

The human body has many parts, but the many parts make up only one body. So it is with the body of Christ. Some of us are Jews, some are Gentiles, some are slaves, and some are free. But we have all been baptized into Christ's body by one Spirit, and we have all received the same Spirit.

Yes, the body has many different parts, not just one part. If the foot says, "I am not a part of the body because I am not a hand," that does not make it any less a part of the body. And if the ear says, "I am not part of the body because I am only an ear and not an eye," would that make it any less a part of the body? Suppose the whole body were an eye—then how would you hear? Or if your whole body were just one big ear, how could you smell anything?

But God made our bodies with many parts, and he has put each part just where he wants it. What a strange thing a body would be if it had only one part! Yes, there are many parts, but only one body. The eye can never say to the hand, "I don't need you." The head can't say to the feet, "I don't need you."

In fact, some of the parts that seem weakest and least important are really the most necessary. And the parts we regard as less honorable are those we clothe with the greatest care. So we carefully protect from the eyes of others those parts that should not be seen, while other parts do not require this special care. So God has put the body together in such a way that extra honor and care are given to those parts that have less dignity. This makes for harmony among the members, so that all the members care for each other equally. If one part suffers, all the parts suffer with it, and if one part is honored, all the parts are glad.

Now all of you together are Christ's body, and each one of you is a separate and necessary part of it. Here is a list of some of the members that God has placed in the body of Christ: first are apostles, second are prophets, third are teachers, then those who do miracles, those who have the gift of healing, those who can help others, those who can get others to work together, those who speak in unknown languages. Is everyone an apostle? Of course not. Is everyone a prophet? No. Are all teachers? Does everyone have the power to do miracles? Does everyone have the gift of healing? Of course not. Does God give all of us the ability to speak in unknown languages? Can everyone interpret unknown languages? No! And in any event, you should desire the most helpful gifts. 1 CORINTHIANS 12:4-31

See also The Holy Spirit.

The Bible

I s the Bible just one religious book among many? Or does it have divine authority? Can the Bible, in fact, be proven to be true? People still debate these questions. One thing that can be said of the Bible that does not apply to texts of other religions is that it is consistent. It does not contradict itself or basic logic. While scientists and scholars confirm that many historical facts in the Bible are definitely true, the answer ultimately comes down to faith. One has to either accept the Bible as the genuine Word of God or reject it. The best witnesses to the Bible's authority and inspiration are people. Lives have been changed—and still are being changed—because as people have read the Bible, they have encountered God, revealing himself as Savior and Lord.

I am not ashamed of this Good News about Christ. It is the power of God at work, saving everyone who believes. ROMANS 1:16

Faith comes from listening to this message of good news—the Good News about Christ. ROMANS 10:17

Just as your car and home appliances come with an owner's manual, so does the life of the believer. God's manual for his people is the Bible. Believers throughout history have sung the praises of the Great Manual, which is more inspiring and life-changing than any manual for a home appliance.

You must understand that no prophecy in Scripture ever came from the prophets themselves or because they wanted to prophesy. It was the Holy Spirit who moved the prophets to speak from God. 2 PETER 1:20-21

Your word is a lamp for my feet and a light for my path.
As your words are taught, they give light; even the simple can understand them. PSALM 119:105, 130

These commands and this teaching are a lamp to light the way ahead of you. The correction of discipline is the way to life. PROVERBS 6:23

You have been taught the holy Scriptures from childhood, and they have given you the wisdom to receive the salvation that comes by trusting in Christ Jesus. All Scripture is inspired by God and is useful to teach us what is true and to make us realize what is wrong in our lives. It straightens us out and teaches us to do what is right. It is God's way of preparing us in every way, fully equipped for every good thing God wants us to do. 2 TIMOTHY 3:15-17

Things were written in the Scriptures long ago to teach us. They give us hope and encouragement as we wait patiently for God's promises. ROMANS 15:4

The word of God is full of living power. It is sharper than the sharpest knife, cutting deep into our innermost thoughts and desires. It exposes us for what we really are. Nothing in all creation can hide from him. Everything is naked and exposed before his eyes. This is the God to whom we must explain all that we have done. HEBREWS 4:12-13

> Even people who have read the Bible for years admit that it isn't always easy to understand. Why should it be? Our own human mind-set makes us slow to grasp ideas like personal responsibility, sin, and a God who sees our every move. Some people find the following passage consoling, as Peter admits that, indeed, some of Scripture is not easy to grasp.

Our beloved brother Paul wrote to you with the wisdom God gave him—speaking of these things in all of his letters. Some of his comments are hard to understand, and those who are ignorant and unstable have twisted his letters around to mean something quite different from what he meant, just as they do the other parts of Scripture—and the result is disaster for them. 2 PETER 3:15-16

> Peter's wise observations about Scripture remind us of something important: The Bible is not something we should use to support peculiar ideas and lifestyle choices. History is full of sad tales of people who twisted parts of the Bible to advance their own ungodly agendas. Many offbeat cults and sects—and even revolutionary movements—have begun when some unwise leader took part of the Bible out of context.
>
> Does this mean we are likely to make wrong assumptions as we strive to interpret the Bible for our own life? It can happen, yes, and part of the life of faith is maturing in our understanding of God's Word—making some mistakes and learning from them. Happily, God gives us not only the Bible but an aid—or perhaps Aide would be more accurate—to help us. Perhaps the most consoling promise concerning the Bible is the following, in which Jesus promises that we are given divine aid in understanding God's will:

When the Father sends the Counselor as my representative—and by the Counselor I mean the Holy Spirit—he will teach you everything and will remind you of everything I myself have told you. JOHN 14:26

> If you're ever touring an art gallery or historic church, you may see a picture or statue of the great apostle Paul. He is often shown holding a sword, which puzzles some people, since Paul wasn't a violent man. Artists show him with a sword for a reason: He wrote about the most powerful sword in all the world. That sword is part of the spiritual weaponry that every believer carries.

Put on salvation as your helmet, and take the sword of the Spirit, which is the Word of God. EPHESIANS 6:17

The Body

If you've ever seen some of the ancient Greek statues, you can't help but be impressed with their beauty. Artists throughout the centuries remind us that the human body is a beautiful thing. Some of the great artists have been able to make average or even ugly people look appealing.

But the reality of the video camera doesn't allow this. The bodies in advertising and films have been "adjusted" by makeup artists and the camera itself. The world is full of average and ugly people, who too often compare themselves with these perfect bodies captured by the camera. No wonder business is booming for health spas and weight-loss centers. We want to be like those perfectly formed people in the ads. Considering the time, sweat, and money we spend, it appears that we worship the body—or at least an ideal version of it.

The Bible is *not* anti-body. (You can prove this by reading the Bible's Song of Solomon.) The Bible is pro-God, and that means worshiping him alone.

The LORD doesn't make decisions the way you do! People judge by outward appearance, but the LORD looks at a person's thoughts and intentions. 1 SAMUEL 16:7

Dear Christian friends, I plead with you to give your bodies to God. Let them be a living and holy sacrifice—the kind he will accept. When you think of what he has done for you, is this too much to ask? Don't copy the behavior and customs of this world, but let God transform you into a new person by changing the way you think. Then you will know what God wants you to do, and you will know how good and pleasing and perfect his will really is. ROMANS 12:1-2

Don't you know that your body is the temple of the Holy Spirit, who lives in you and was given to you by God? You do not belong to yourself, for God bought you with a high price. So you must honor God with your body. 1 CORINTHIANS 6:19-20

Don't be concerned about the outward beauty that depends on fancy hairstyles, expensive jewelry, or beautiful clothes. You should be known for the beauty that comes from within, the unfading beauty of a gentle and quiet spirit, which is so precious to God. 1 PETER 3:3-4

The most important piece of clothing you must wear is love. Love is what binds us all together in perfect harmony. COLOSSIANS 3:14

Because we have these promises, dear friends, let us cleanse ourselves from everything that can defile our body or spirit. And let us work toward complete purity because we fear God. 2 CORINTHIANS 7:1

> Does God mind if we take care of ourselves, trying to stay fit and healthy? Not at all. The Bible tells Christians that their bodies are "temples of the Holy Spirit," something to be cared for and not abused. But making an idol of the body means we are worshiping something besides God. This has no place in the Christian life, and neither does using the body—or someone else's—as a sexual plaything. Neither does neglecting our spiritual life.

Turning to his disciples, Jesus said, "So I tell you, don't worry about everyday life—whether you have enough food to eat or clothes to wear. For life consists of far more than food and clothing. Look at the ravens. They don't need to plant or harvest or put food in barns because God feeds them. And you are far more valuable to him than any birds! Can all your worries add a single moment to your life? Of course not! And if worry can't do little things like that, what's the use of worrying over bigger things?" LUKE 12:22-26

> Some people have the idea that Christianity is an anti-body religion. It isn't so. But the Bible takes a painfully realistic look at the harm that can be done by using the body in ways God didn't intend. The world of the Bible wasn't so different from today in terms of the harm done by sexual sinning. Far from being antisex, the Bible celebrates the body but makes it clear that sex should not be a god that we worship.

Keep alert and pray. Otherwise temptation will overpower you. For though the spirit is willing enough, the body is weak! MATTHEW 26:41

If your eye—even if it is your good eye—causes you to lust, gouge it out and throw it away. It is better for you to lose one part of your body than for your whole body to be thrown into hell. MATTHEW 5:29

The world offers only the lust for physical pleasure, the lust for everything we see, and pride in our possessions. These are not from the Father. They are from this evil world. And this world is fading away, along with everything it craves. But if you do the will of God, you will live forever. 1 JOHN 2:16-17

Do not let sin control the way you live; do not give in to its lustful desires. Do not let any part of your body become a tool of

wickedness, to be used for sinning. Instead, give yourselves
completely to God since you have been given new life. And use
your whole body as a tool to do what is right for the glory of God.
Sin is no longer your master, for you are no longer subject to the
law, which enslaves you to sin. Instead, you are free by God's
grace. ROMANS 6:12-14

Don't you know that those who do wrong will have no share in
the Kingdom of God? Don't fool yourselves. Those who indulge
in sexual sin, who are idol worshipers, adulterers, male
prostitutes, homosexuals, thieves, greedy people, drunkards,
abusers, and swindlers—none of these will have a share in the
Kingdom of God. There was a time when some of you were just
like that, but now your sins have been washed away, and you
have been set apart for God. You have been made right with God
because of what the Lord Jesus Christ and the Spirit of our God
have done for you.
   You may say, "I am allowed to do anything." But I reply, "Not
everything is good for you." And even though "I am allowed to
do anything," I must not become a slave to anything. You say,
"Food is for the stomach, and the stomach is for food." This is
true, though someday God will do away with both of them. But
our bodies were not made for sexual immorality. They were made
for the Lord, and the Lord cares about our bodies. And God will
raise our bodies from the dead by his marvelous power, just as he
raised our Lord from the dead. 1 CORINTHIANS 6:9-14

Those who belong to Christ Jesus have nailed the passions and
desires of their sinful nature to his cross and crucified them there.
GALATIANS 5:24

I advise you to live according to your new life in the Holy Spirit.
Then you won't be doing what your sinful nature craves. The old
sinful nature loves to do evil, which is just opposite from what the
Holy Spirit wants. And the Spirit gives us desires that are

opposite from what the sinful nature desires. These two forces are constantly fighting each other, and your choices are never free from this conflict. But when you are directed by the Holy Spirit, you are no longer subject to the law. GALATIANS 5:16-18

God wants you to be holy, so you should keep clear of all sexual sin. Then each of you will control your body and live in holiness and honor—not in lustful passion as the pagans do, in their ignorance of God and his ways.
  Never cheat another Christian in this matter by taking his wife, for the Lord avenges all such sins, as we have solemnly warned you before. God has called us to be holy, not to live impure lives.
1 THESSALONIANS 4:3-7

If you keep yourself pure, you will be a utensil God can use for his purpose. Your life will be clean, and you will be ready for the Master to use you for every good work.
  Run from anything that stimulates youthful lust. Follow anything that makes you want to do right. Pursue faith and love and peace, and enjoy the companionship of those who call on the Lord with pure hearts. 2 TIMOTHY 2:21-22

The grace of God has been revealed, bringing salvation to all people. And we are instructed to turn from godless living and sinful pleasures. We should live in this evil world with self-control, right conduct, and devotion to God, while we look forward to that wonderful event when the glory of our great God and Savior, Jesus Christ, will be revealed. TITUS 2:11-13

Temptation comes from the lure of our own evil desires. These evil desires lead to evil actions, and evil actions lead to death.
JAMES 1:14-15

Run away from sexual sin! No other sin so clearly affects the body as this one does. For sexual immorality is a sin against your own body. 1 CORINTHIANS 6:18

> The apostle Paul wrote to the Christians in Corinth, a city noted for its sexual immorality. The Christians there seemed to be in constant danger of lapsing into sexual sin. Paul reminded them that their present bodies, which could be abused through sexual sin, were not their final state. In the Kingdom of Heaven, we will have a new body, different from the present one and better.

We know that when this earthly tent we live in is taken down—when we die and leave these bodies—we will have a home in heaven, an eternal body made for us by God himself and not by human hands. We grow weary in our present bodies, and we long for the day when we will put on our heavenly bodies like new clothing. For we will not be spirits without bodies, but we will put on new heavenly bodies. Our dying bodies make us groan and sigh, but it's not that we want to die and have no bodies at all. We want to slip into our new bodies so that these dying bodies will be swallowed up by everlasting life.
2 CORINTHIANS 5:1-4

Though our bodies are dying, our spirits are being renewed every day. 2 CORINTHIANS 4:16

See also Alcohol and Other Substance Abuse, Food, Pride and Conceit, Self-Esteem, Sexuality, Temptation.

Children

Every family—whether healthy, broken, or dysfunctional—has its ups and downs. Aside from husband-wife difficulties, naturally there are parent-child problems. These are nothing new. The people of Bible times did not have round-the-clock TV, radio, and video to contend with, but they did have some universal problems, such as unruly children, parents too weak or doting to use discipline, and parents who were too harsh. Some things never change.

You will find many promises in the Bible concerning children. They are a blessing, especially if reared with discipline and kindness. Hymn writer John Bowring claimed that "a happy family is an earlier heaven."

Some promises are not as hopeful: Children who go astray are a terrible burden to bear. Whether the family turns out good or bad is, of course, partly the parents' own responsibility.

Children are a gift from the LORD; they are a reward from him. Children born to a young man are like sharp arrows in a warrior's hands. How happy is the man whose quiver is full of them! He will not be put to shame when he confronts his accusers at the city gates. PSALM 127:3-5

Grandchildren are the crowning glory of the aged; parents are the pride of their children. PROVERBS 17:6

> What happens to weak-willed parents who can't—or won't—insist on discipline in the home? The Bible gives a painfully realistic answer:

If you refuse to discipline your children, it proves you don't love them; if you love your children, you will be prompt to discipline them. PROVERBS 13:24

Discipline your children while there is hope. If you don't, you will ruin their lives. PROVERBS 19:18

A youngster's heart is filled with foolishness, but discipline will drive it away. PROVERBS 22:15

To discipline and reprimand a child produces wisdom, but a mother is disgraced by an undisciplined child. PROVERBS 29:15

Teach your children to choose the right path, and when they are older, they will remain upon it. PROVERBS 22:6

Don't fail to correct your children. They won't die if you spank them. Physical discipline may well save them from death.
PROVERBS 23:13-14

> Parenting is much, much more than mere discipline, however. Godly parents also have a duty to pass on their own beliefs to their children:

You must commit yourselves wholeheartedly to these commands I am giving you today. Repeat them again and again to your children. Talk about them when you are at home and when you are away on a journey, when you are lying down and when you are getting up again. Tie them to your hands as a reminder, and wear them on your forehead. Write them on the doorposts of your house and on your gates. DEUTERONOMY 6:6-9

> Not all the Bible's promises are for parents alone. Children, too, have some words from the Lord addressed to them. Just as the Bible promises good to people who are thankful toward God, so it promises blessing to those who are grateful to their parents.

Children, obey your parents because you belong to the Lord, for this is the right thing to do. "Honor your father and mother." This is the first of the Ten Commandments that ends with a promise. And this is the promise: If you honor your father and mother, "you will live a long life, full of blessing." EPHESIANS 6:1-3

My son, obey your father's commands, and don't neglect your mother's teaching. Keep their words always in your heart. Tie them around your neck. Wherever you walk, their counsel can lead you. When you sleep, they will protect you. When you wake up in the morning, they will advise you. For these commands and this teaching are a lamp to light the way ahead of you. The correction of discipline is the way to life. PROVERBS 6:20-23

Listen to your father, who gave you life, and don't despise your mother's experience when she is old. PROVERBS 23:22

A wise child accepts a parent's discipline; a young mocker refuses to listen. PROVERBS 13:1

A wise child brings joy to a father; a foolish child brings grief to a mother. PROVERBS 10:1

Only a fool despises a parent's discipline; whoever learns from correction is wise. PROVERBS 15:5

Even children are known by the way they act, whether their conduct is pure and right. PROVERBS 20:11

The father of godly children has cause for joy. What a pleasure it is to have wise children. So give your parents joy! May she who gave you birth be happy. O my son, give me your heart. May your eyes delight in my ways of wisdom. PROVERBS 23:24-26

Young people who obey the law are wise; those who seek out worthless companions bring shame to their parents.
PROVERBS 28:7

> One of the most beautiful scenes in the Gospels is the one of Jesus blessing the children. Not only does this show how he loved children, but it also shows that he admired their innocence and trust, two traits that almost everyone admires in children. He commended these qualities to adults. In fact, those qualities are essential for anyone who wants to be a child of God.

One day some parents brought their children to Jesus so he could touch them and bless them, but the disciples told them not to bother him. But when Jesus saw what was happening, he was very displeased with his disciples. He said to them, "Let the children come to me. Don't stop them! For the Kingdom of God belongs to such as these. I assure you, anyone who doesn't have their kind of faith will never get into the Kingdom of God."
MARK 10:13-15

See also Marriage, Parents.

Citizenship

The Bible shows no reason people of faith cannot also be good citizens. In fact, they are encouraged to be both. But Jesus predicted that he and his followers would suffer hardship, some of it at the hands of government officials. The New Testament never condones a Christian showing disrespect or violence toward these people. Still, there is a tension in the Christian life: Our first loyalty is to God, not to the state. God promises us inner peace—not necessarily peaceful coexistence with government.

The captain went with his Temple guards and arrested them [the apostles], but without violence, for they were afraid the people would kill them if they treated the apostles roughly. Then they brought the apostles in before the council. "Didn't we tell you never again to teach in this man's name?" the high priest demanded. "Instead, you have filled all Jerusalem with your teaching about Jesus, and you intend to blame us for his death!"
But Peter and the apostles replied, "We must obey God rather than human authority." ACTS 5:26-29

The Pharisees met together to think of a way to trap Jesus into saying something for which they could accuse him. They decided to send some of their disciples, along with the supporters of Herod, to ask him this question: "Teacher, we know how honest you are. You teach about the way of God regardless of the consequences. You are impartial and don't play favorites. Now tell us what you think about this: Is it right to pay taxes to the Roman government or not?"

But Jesus knew their evil motives. "You hypocrites!" he said. "Whom are you trying to fool with your trick questions? Here, show me the Roman coin used for the tax." When they handed him the coin, he asked, "Whose picture and title are stamped on it?"

"Caesar's," they replied.

"Well, then," he said, "give to Caesar what belongs to him. But everything that belongs to God must be given to God."
MATTHEW 22:15-21

After Jesus' arrest he faced Pilate, the Roman governor. Pilate assumed he had a political agitator on his hands, but Jesus assured him that the revolution he was staging was in human hearts, not in the area of politics:

Then Pilate went back inside and called for Jesus to be brought to him. "Are you the King of the Jews?" he asked him. . . .

Then Jesus answered, "I am not an earthly king. If I were, my followers would have fought when I was arrested by the Jewish leaders. But my Kingdom is not of this world."

Pilate replied, "You are a king then?"

"You say that I am a king, and you are right," Jesus said. "I was born for that purpose. And I came to bring truth to the world. All who love the truth recognize that what I say is true."
JOHN 18:33-37

In the New Testament period, the government was often hostile to God's people. Is history repeating itself? The anti-Christian bias in our culture becomes more and more blatant, and sometimes believers feel that the government is downright antagonistic. Should this make us cynical about government or make us openly oppose it? Not according to Jesus' followers.

Obey the government, for God is the one who put it there. All governments have been placed in power by God. So those who refuse to obey the laws of the land are refusing to obey God, and punishment will follow. For the authorities do not frighten people who are doing right, but they frighten those who do wrong. So do what they say, and you will get along well. The authorities are sent by God to help you. But if you are doing something wrong, of course you should be afraid, for you will be punished. The authorities are established by God for that very purpose, to punish those who do wrong. So you must obey the government for two reasons: to keep from being punished and to keep a clear conscience.

Pay your taxes, too, for these same reasons. For government workers need to be paid so they can keep on doing the work God intended them to do. Give to everyone what you owe them: Pay your taxes and import duties, and give respect and honor to all to whom it is due. ROMANS 13:1-7

Pray this way for kings and all others who are in authority, so that we can live in peace and quietness, in godliness and dignity. This is good and pleases God our Savior, for he wants everyone to be saved and to understand the truth. 1 TIMOTHY 2:2-4

Remind your people to submit to the government and its officers. They should be obedient, always ready to do what is good. TITUS 3:1

For the Lord's sake, accept all authority—the king as head of state, and the officials he has appointed. For the king has sent them to punish all who do wrong and to honor those who do right.

It is God's will that your good lives should silence those who make foolish accusations against you. . . . Show respect for everyone. Love your Christian brothers and sisters. Fear God. Show respect for the king.   1 PETER 2:13-17

> The New Testament never loses sight of heaven. Christians did actually transform the world by transforming individual human beings. But they never tried to shake up the political order, and they had no desire to. As the following passages promise, there is something better and more enduring than our current home.

All these faithful ones died without receiving what God had promised them, but they saw it all from a distance and welcomed the promises of God. They agreed that they were no more than foreigners and nomads here on earth. And obviously people who talk like that are looking forward to a country they can call their own. If they had meant the country they came from, they would have found a way to go back. But they were looking for a better place, a heavenly homeland. That is why God is not ashamed to be called their God, for he has prepared a heavenly city for them.

For this world is not our home; we are looking forward to our city in heaven, which is yet to come.   HEBREWS 11:13-16; 13:14

You are citizens along with all of God's holy people. You are members of God's family. We are his house, built on the foundation of the apostles and the prophets. And the cornerstone is Christ Jesus himself.   EPHESIANS 2:19-20

We are citizens of heaven, where the Lord Jesus Christ lives. And we are eagerly waiting for him to return as our Savior. He will take these weak mortal bodies of ours and change them into glorious bodies like his own, using the same mighty power that he will use to conquer everything, everywhere.   PHILIPPIANS 3:20-21

See also Politics and Government.

Comfort in Times of Trouble

N o one likes to suffer—this is a fact we can all accept. If Christianity promised and delivered release from all troubles in this life, everyone would be a Christian. In fact, our faith *does* promise this—but it doesn't deliver us *in this life.* The end of all our troubles is heaven. Most people aren't willing to wait that long.

In the meantime, what does God promise his people? Relief from all troubles in the next world, relief from *some* troubles in this life. Faithful people throughout the centuries are witness to dramatic deliverances from sickness, from financial woes, from all manner of troubles. Flesh-and-blood human beings have testified—and still testify—to miracles. They do happen.

But not always. Sometimes we aren't relieved by God. Sometimes we merely *endure.* This isn't such a bad thing. We are never nearer to God than when we are troubled. In times of comfort and ease we forget him. In the worst of times, we suddenly remember, What if I asked God for help? Sometimes the answer is the help we pray for. Sometimes the answer is "Lean on me, and you will survive and thrive."

Whom have I in heaven but you? I desire you more than anything on earth. My health may fail, and my spirit may grow weak, but God remains the strength of my heart; he is mine forever.

How good it is to be near God! I have made the Sovereign LORD my shelter. PSALM 73:25-26, 28

God will not reject a person of integrity, nor will he make evildoers prosper. He will yet fill your mouth with laughter and your lips with shouts of joy. JOB 8:20-21

Remember your promise to me, for it is my only hope. Your promise revives me; it comforts me in all my troubles. PSALM 119:49-50

The LORD is a shelter for the oppressed, a refuge in times of trouble. PSALM 9:9

The LORD is my shepherd; I have everything I need. He lets me rest in green meadows; he leads me beside peaceful streams. He renews my strength. He guides me along right paths, bringing honor to his name.

Even when I walk through the dark valley of death, I will not be afraid, for you are close beside me. Your rod and your staff protect and comfort me. PSALM 23:1-4

The LORD is my rock, my fortress, and my savior; my God is my rock, in whom I find protection. He is my shield, the strength of my salvation, and my stronghold. PSALM 18:2

Weeping may go on all night, but joy comes with the morning. PSALM 30:5

I am overcome with joy because of your unfailing love, for you have seen my troubles, and you care about the anguish of my soul. PSALM 31:7

I prayed to the LORD, and he answered me, freeing me from all my fears. PSALM 34:4

God is our refuge and strength, always ready to help in times of trouble. So we will not fear, even if earthquakes come and the mountains crumble into the sea. PSALM 46:1-2

Trust me in your times of trouble, and I will rescue you, and you will give me glory. PSALM 50:15

Give your burdens to the LORD, and he will take care of you. PSALM 55:22

You have allowed me to suffer much hardship, but you will restore me to life again and lift me up from the depths of the earth. PSALM 71:20

He orders his angels to protect you wherever you go. PSALM 91:11

The LORD is like a father to his children, tender and compassionate to those who fear him. PSALM 103:13

Those who plant in tears will harvest with shouts of joy. They weep as they go to plant their seed, but they sing as they return with the harvest. PSALM 126:5-6

He heals the brokenhearted, binding up their wounds. PSALM 147:3

Fearing people is a dangerous trap, but to trust the LORD means safety. PROVERBS 29:25

Don't be afraid, for I am with you. Do not be dismayed, for I am your God. I will strengthen you. I will help you. I will uphold you with my victorious right hand. ISAIAH 41:10

The LORD saves the godly; he is their fortress in times of trouble. The LORD helps them, rescuing them from the wicked. He saves them, and they find shelter in him. PSALM 37:39-40

When you go through deep waters and great trouble, I will be with you. When you go through rivers of difficulty, you will not drown! When you walk through the fire of oppression, you will not be burned up; the flames will not consume you. For I am the LORD, your God, the Holy One of Israel, your Savior. ISAIAH 43:2-3

God blesses those who mourn, for they will be comforted.
    God blesses those who are persecuted because they live for God, for the Kingdom of Heaven is theirs.
    God blesses you when you are mocked and persecuted and lied about because you are my followers. Be happy about it! Be very glad! For a great reward awaits you in heaven. And remember, the ancient prophets were persecuted, too. MATTHEW 5:4, 10-12

"I know the plans I have for you," says the LORD. "They are plans for good and not for disaster, to give you a future and a hope. In those days when you pray, I will listen. If you look for me in earnest, you will find me when you seek me." JEREMIAH 29:11-13

The Lord does not abandon anyone forever. Though he brings grief, he also shows compassion according to the greatness of his unfailing love. For he does not enjoy hurting people or causing them sorrow. LAMENTATIONS 3:31-33

Jesus, in the famous prayer in the garden of Gethsemane, prayed for deliverance. We know what followed:

He took Peter, James, and John with him, and he began to be filled with horror and deep distress. He told them, "My soul is crushed with grief to the point of death. Stay here and watch with me."

He went on a little farther and fell face down on the ground. He prayed that, if it were possible, the awful hour awaiting him might pass him by. "Abba, Father," he said, "everything is possible for you. Please take this cup of suffering away from me. Yet I want your will, not mine." MARK 14:33-36

> Jesus was constantly aware of God as his Father. Perhaps our rebellious nature makes us resist the idea that some almighty Father is watching our every move. Yet Jesus reminded us of the positive side of this: God is watching over us, not to squelch our pleasure, but to keep us from harm and to comfort us when we do experience hurt.

Not even a sparrow, worth only half a penny, can fall to the ground without your Father knowing it. And the very hairs on your head are all numbered. So don't be afraid; you are more valuable to him than a whole flock of sparrows. MATTHEW 10:29-31

Jesus said, "Come to me, all of you who are weary and carry heavy burdens, and I will give you rest. Take my yoke upon you. Let me teach you, because I am humble and gentle, and you will find rest for your souls. For my yoke fits perfectly, and the burden I give you is light." MATTHEW 11:28-30

> Does the Bible promise Christians freedom from sorrow? No, indeed not. Just as Jesus himself endured persecution, so do his followers, then and now. Yet we are promised peace of mind and the strength to endure anything.

I am leaving you with a gift—peace of mind and heart. And the peace I give isn't like the peace the world gives. So don't be troubled or afraid. JOHN 14:27

I have told you all this so that you may have peace in me. Here on earth you will have many trials and sorrows. But take heart, because I have overcome the world.   JOHN 16:33

We know that God causes everything to work together for the good of those who love God and are called according to his purpose for them.
   Can anything ever separate us from Christ's love? Does it mean he no longer loves us if we have trouble or calamity, or are persecuted, or are hungry or cold or in danger or threatened with death?   ROMANS 8:28, 35

All praise to the God and Father of our Lord Jesus Christ. He is the source of every mercy and the God who comforts us. He comforts us in all our troubles so that we can comfort others. When others are troubled, we will be able to give them the same comfort God has given us. You can be sure that the more we suffer for Christ, the more God will shower us with his comfort through Christ. So when we are weighed down with troubles, it is for your benefit and salvation! For when God comforts us, it is so that we, in turn, can be an encouragement to you. Then you can patiently endure the same things we suffer. We are confident that as you share in suffering, you will also share God's comfort.
2 CORINTHIANS 1:3-7

We are pressed on every side by troubles, but we are not crushed and broken. We are perplexed, but we don't give up and quit.
   That is why we never give up. Though our bodies are dying, our spirits are being renewed every day. For our present troubles are quite small and won't last very long. Yet they produce for us an immeasurably great glory that will last forever!   2 CORINTHIANS 4:8, 16-17

I have received wonderful revelations from God. But to keep me from getting puffed up, I was given a thorn in my flesh, a messenger from Satan to torment me and keep me from getting proud.

Three different times I begged the Lord to take it away. Each time he said, "My gracious favor is all you need. My power works best in your weakness." So now I am glad to boast about my weaknesses, so that the power of Christ may work through me. Since I know it is all for Christ's good, I am quite content with my weaknesses and with insults, hardships, persecutions, and calamities. For when I am weak, then I am strong.
2 CORINTHIANS 12:7-10

Because God's children are human beings—made of flesh and blood—Jesus also became flesh and blood by being born in human form.

This High Priest of ours understands our weaknesses, for he faced all of the same temptations we do, yet he did not sin.
HEBREWS 2:14; 4:15

God blesses the people who patiently endure testing. Afterward they will receive the crown of life that God has promised to those who love him. JAMES 1:12

Dear friends, don't be surprised at the fiery trials you are going through, as if something strange were happening to you. Instead, be very glad—because these trials will make you partners with Christ in his suffering, and afterward you will have the wonderful joy of sharing his glory when it is displayed to all the world.

Be happy if you are insulted for being a Christian, for then the glorious Spirit of God will come upon you. 1 PETER 4:12-14

Just as the Bible begins with the creation of the world, it ends with the creation of the new world. While the old world—our world—is filled with troubles too numerous to count, this will not be so in the next world. For everyone who suffers in body or in mind, this must be one of the most comforting promises in the Bible.

Then I saw a new heaven and a new earth, for the old heaven and the old earth had disappeared. And the sea was also gone. And I saw the holy city, the new Jerusalem, coming down from God out of heaven like a beautiful bride prepared for her husband.

I heard a loud shout from the throne, saying, "Look, the home of God is now among his people! He will live with them, and they will be his people. God himself will be with them. He will remove all of their sorrows, and there will be no more death or sorrow or crying or pain. For the old world and its evils are gone forever."

And the one sitting on the throne said, "Look, I am making all things new!" REVELATION 21:1-5

See also Patience, Peace, Perseverance, Sickness, Trusting God, Worldly Cares, Worry and Anxiety.

Confessing Sin

C onfession is good for the soul"—so says the old
cliché. And, like many clichés, it has the virtue of being true.

For the Christian, confession is not a choice. We sin, and through
confession our life with God goes on. It cannot be otherwise.
Augustine, the great Christian teacher, noted that "the confession of
evil works is the first beginning of good works."

People who cover over their sins will not prosper. But if they
confess and forsake them, they will receive mercy.
PROVERBS 28:13

Oh, what joy for those whose rebellion is forgiven, whose sin is
put out of sight! Yes, what joy for those whose record the LORD
has cleared of sin, whose lives are lived in complete honesty!

When I refused to confess my sin, I was weak and miserable,
and I groaned all day long. Day and night your hand of discipline
was heavy on me. My strength evaporated like water in the
summer heat.

Finally, I confessed all my sins to you and stopped trying to hide
them. I said to myself, "I will confess my rebellion to the LORD."

And you forgave me! All my guilt is gone.

Therefore, let all the godly confess their rebellion to you while there is time, that they may not drown in the floodwaters of judgment. PSALM 32:1-6

> The great "sin song" of the Bible, Psalm 51, was supposedly written by King David at the time when he felt guilt over his adultery. The most beautiful thing about the psalm is David's full confidence that God would accept his repentant heart and restore again his spiritual health.

Have mercy on me, O God, because of your unfailing love. Because of your great compassion, blot out the stain of my sins. Wash me clean from my guilt. Purify me from my sin.

For I recognize my shameful deeds—they haunt me day and night. Against you, and you alone, have I sinned; I have done what is evil in your sight. You will be proved right in what you say, and your judgment against me is just.

For I was born a sinner—yes, from the moment my mother conceived me. But you desire honesty from the heart, so you can teach me to be wise in my inmost being.

Purify me from my sins, and I will be clean; wash me, and I will be whiter than snow. Oh, give me back my joy again; you have broken me—now let me rejoice. Don't keep looking at my sins. Remove the stain of my guilt. Create in me a clean heart, O God. Renew a right spirit within me. PSALM 51:1-10

I will sprinkle clean water on you, and you will be clean. Your filth will be washed away, and you will no longer worship idols. And I will give you a new heart with new and right desires, and I will put a new spirit in you. I will take out your stony heart of sin and give you a new, obedient heart. And I will put my Spirit in you so you will obey my laws and do whatever I command. . . . You will be my people, and I will be your God. EZEKIEL 36:25-28

The Scriptures say, "'As surely as I live,' says the Lord, 'every knee will bow to me and every tongue will confess allegiance to God.'" Yes, each of us will have to give a personal account to God. ROMANS 14:11-12

You were dead because of your sins and because your sinful nature was not yet cut away. Then God made you alive with Christ. He forgave all our sins. He canceled the record that contained the charges against us. He took it and destroyed it by nailing it to Christ's cross. COLOSSIANS 2:13-14

If we confess our sins to him, he is faithful and just to forgive us and to cleanse us from every wrong. 1 JOHN 1:9

> Paul introduced a new idea into the life of faith: confessing sins to each other as well as to God. This makes perfect sense, for not only are we accountable to God but also to fellow members of Christ's body. It is unfortunate that this practice has fallen into disuse or, conversely, that Christians sometimes use another's confession to judge harshly. Perhaps the modern attitude of MYOB ("mind your own business") needs replacing with a healthy concern for each other's moral and spiritual welfare.

Confess your sins to each other and pray for each other so that you may be healed. The earnest prayer of a righteous person has great power and wonderful results. JAMES 5:16

See also Guilt, Repentance, Sin and Redemption.

Conflict

Part of the human condition is that people do quarrel. Wherever there are at least two human beings, fighting is practically inevitable. Some of the bitterest fights are between people who are closest—husband and wife, parent and child, siblings, longtime friends, and even fellow Christians.

The Bible has a lot to say about the source of conflicts and how to squelch them.

Hatred stirs up quarrels, but love covers all offenses.
PROVERBS 10:12

Pride leads to arguments; those who take advice are wise.
PROVERBS 13:10

A hothead starts fights; a cool-tempered person tries to stop them.   PROVERBS 15:18

A gentle answer turns away wrath, but harsh words stir up anger.   PROVERBS 15:1

A troublemaker plants seeds of strife; gossip separates the best of friends. PROVERBS 16:28

Anyone who loves to quarrel loves sin; anyone who speaks boastfully invites disaster. PROVERBS 17:19

Avoiding a fight is a mark of honor; only fools insist on quarreling. PROVERBS 20:3

Throw out the mocker, and fighting, quarrels, and insults will disappear. PROVERBS 22:10

Greed causes fighting; trusting the LORD leads to prosperity.
PROVERBS 28:25

A hot-tempered person starts fights and gets into all kinds of sin.
PROVERBS 29:22

You are still controlled by your own sinful desires. You are jealous of one another and quarrel with each other. Doesn't that prove you are controlled by your own desires? You are acting like people who don't belong to the Lord. 1 CORINTHIANS 3:3

What is causing the quarrels and fights among you? Isn't it the whole army of evil desires at war within you? You want what you don't have, so you scheme and kill to get it. You are jealous for what others have, and you can't possess it, so you fight and quarrel to take it away from them. And yet the reason you don't have what you want is that you don't ask God for it. And even when you do ask, you don't get it because your whole motive is wrong—you want only what will give you pleasure.

You adulterers! Don't you realize that friendship with this world makes you an enemy of God? I say it again, that if your aim is to enjoy this world, you can't be a friend of God. What do you think the Scriptures mean when they say that the Holy Spirit, whom

God has placed within us, jealously longs for us to be faithful? He gives us more and more strength to stand against such evil desires. JAMES 4:1-6

> Paul's letters to Timothy and Titus are called the "Pastoral Letters," since they are filled with advice on how to be good Christian pastors. Paul reminded Timothy of something every church member knows: Christians do quarrel, often over very trivial matters, but such petty feuds have no place in the family of God.

Remind everyone of these things, and command them in God's name to stop fighting over words. Such arguments are useless, and they can ruin those who hear them.

Avoid godless, foolish discussions that lead to more and more ungodliness. 2 TIMOTHY 2:14, 16

Don't get involved in foolish, ignorant arguments that only start fights. The Lord's servants must not quarrel but must be kind to everyone. They must be able to teach effectively and be patient with difficult people. They should gently teach those who oppose the truth. Perhaps God will change those people's hearts, and they will believe the truth. 2 TIMOTHY 2:23-25

> Paul, writing to the Christians in the city of Corinth, was shocked at how immoral and quarrelsome they were. He was especially appalled that Christians—people who belong to the family of God—were suing one another. Paul assured them that they could solve these "family feuds" without resorting to the courtroom:

When you have something against another Christian, why do you file a lawsuit and ask a secular court to decide the matter, instead of taking it to other Christians to decide who is right? Don't you know that someday we Christians are going to judge the world? And since you are going to judge the world, can't you decide these little things among yourselves? Don't you realize that we

Christians will judge angels? So you should surely be able to resolve ordinary disagreements here on earth. If you have legal disputes about such matters, why do you go to outside judges who are not respected by the church? I am saying this to shame you. Isn't there anyone in all the church who is wise enough to decide these arguments? 1 CORINTHIANS 6:1-5

See also Fellowship with Other Believers, Hate, Peace.

Contentment

The comic Will Rogers described advertising as "making people want what they don't need and pay for it with money they don't have." He understood a basic principle of advertising: Make the person feel discontent and that their life would be better if they had product X. "My life would be fine if only I had . . ." What? A better job? a new car? more vacation time? bigger muscles? a new hair color?

Our striving isn't limited just to material matters. Our "if only" list can also include a different home, different spouse, a relocation, whatever. Everywhere around us are suggestions that life would be fine if only some particular part of our life would change. This feeling didn't begin with the age of advertising. It's as old as humanity. The Bible writers were familiar with it. They also knew this ageless truth: Nothing brings contentment except living within God's will. Until we experience *that* satisfaction, the grass will always be greener in someone else's yard.

A relaxed attitude lengthens life; jealousy rots it away.
PROVERBS 14:30

For the happy heart, life is a continual feast. PROVERBS 15:15

It is better to be poor and godly than rich and dishonest.
PROVERBS 16:8

A dry crust eaten in peace is better than a great feast with strife.
PROVERBS 17:1

A cheerful heart is good medicine, but a broken spirit saps a
person's strength. PROVERBS 17:22

Don't envy sinners, but always continue to fear the LORD. For
surely you have a future ahead of you; your hope will not be
disappointed. PROVERBS 23:17-18

I decided there is nothing better than to enjoy food and drink and
to find satisfaction in work. Then I realized that this pleasure is
from the hand of God. ECCLESIASTES 2:24

People who work hard sleep well, whether they eat little or much.
But the rich are always worrying and seldom get a good night's
sleep. ECCLESIASTES 5:12

Enjoy what you have rather than desiring what you don't have.
Just dreaming about nice things is meaningless; it is like chasing
the wind. ECCLESIASTES 6:9

Stay away from the love of money; be satisfied with what you
have. For God has said, "I will never fail you. I will never forsake
you." HEBREWS 13:5

Perhaps the Bible's expert on contentment was the apostle Paul.
Having been beaten, imprisoned, shipwrecked, slandered, and
persecuted, he had learned that life's outward circumstances don't

have to dictate our inner peace. The two following passages are just a sampling.

I have learned how to get along happily whether I have much or little. I know how to live on almost nothing or with everything. I have learned the secret of living in every situation, whether it is with a full stomach or empty, with plenty or little. For I can do everything with the help of Christ who gives me the strength I need. PHILIPPIANS 4:11-13

True religion with contentment is great wealth. After all, we didn't bring anything with us when we came into the world, and we certainly cannot carry anything with us when we die. So if we have enough food and clothing, let us be content. 1 TIMOTHY 6:6-8

See also Ambition, Envy, Peace, Worldly Cares, Worry and Anxiety.

Death

We could respond to death in three ways: ignore it, fear it, or desire it. Most people choose the first option—ignoring it. But this is hard to do if someone close to you has died or may soon die. And it is hard to do if you yourself have been diagnosed with a serious illness. So in these situations, when it can't be ignored, we can fear it—or desire it.

Desire death? Does that mean flirting with suicide? No, indeed not. It means that many people—including the apostle Paul—have indicated that they would not mind going to be with the Lord in the next life. Some people, especially those with long and lingering illnesses, have welcomed death, certain that their next life would be vastly better.

But most of us fear death, don't we? We may *say* we believe in eternal life, in a heaven that is a life of bliss, a life much better than this world. But we *act* as if we fear death, and our actions speak louder than our words. We don't act much different from people who claim to have no belief at all in heaven and hell. How long has it been since you've heard someone speak of a friend or relative as being "with the Lord"? Unfortunately, this phrase is not as common as once it was. It appears sometimes that believers don't believe too strongly that life really endures—and even improves—beyond the grave. Isn't it amazing that, centuries ago, Christians sometimes celebrated a believer's funeral as his "birthday," the person's entry day into heaven? They celebrated because they really believed it was so.

We need to go back to the Bible. It reminds us many times that nothing, not even death, can snatch God's people from him. It reminds us that, whether our life in this world is delightful or dreadful, it will end. We have one lifetime—whatever length it may be—to prepare us. In that lifetime we have either chosen God as the center of our universe—or ourselves as the center. Those who have chosen God will continue with God.

Even when I walk through the dark valley of death, I will not be afraid, for you are close beside me. PSALM 23:4

As for me, God will redeem my life. He will snatch me from the power of death. PSALM 49:15

Do you think, asks the Sovereign LORD, that I like to see wicked people die? Of course not! I only want them to turn from their wicked ways and live. EZEKIEL 18:23

My health may fail, and my spirit may grow weak, but God remains the strength of my heart; he is mine forever. PSALM 73:26

He will swallow up death forever! The Sovereign LORD will wipe away all tears. ISAIAH 25:8

As to whether there will be a resurrection of the dead—haven't you ever read about this in the Scriptures? Long after Abraham, Isaac, and Jacob had died, God said, "I am the God of Abraham, the God of Isaac, and the God of Jacob." So he is the God of the living, not the dead. MATTHEW 22:31-32

None of this means that we can't grieve and mourn over someone we've lost. Jesus did. Jesus also promised comfort to those who mourn.

The LORD's loved ones are precious to him; it grieves him when they die. PSALM 116:15

God blesses those who mourn, for they will be comforted. MATTHEW 5:4

One of the most touching scenes in the Bible is Jesus at the tomb of his dear friend Lazarus. Jesus raised Lazarus from the dead, but before doing so he did a very human and normal thing: he wept over the death of a friend.

When Jesus saw her weeping and saw the other people wailing with her, he was moved with indignation and was deeply troubled. "Where have you put him?" he asked them.
   They told him, "Lord, come and see." Then Jesus wept. The people who were standing nearby said, "See how much he loved him." JOHN 11:33-36

Jesus' weeping reflects a basic idea in the Bible: Death is *not natural*. It was not part of God's original plan for human beings. It entered human existence because man disobeyed God, as told in Genesis 3. Sin and death are connected. The New Testament is concerned with how Jesus as Savior removed the penalty of sin. We still have to die, but there is another life, thanks to God.

We are not our own masters when we live or when we die. ROMANS 14:7

Humans can reproduce only human life, but the Holy Spirit gives new life from heaven. JOHN 3:6

All who believe in God's Son have eternal life. Those who don't obey the Son will never experience eternal life, but the wrath of God remains upon them. JOHN 3:36

I assure you, those who listen to my message and believe in God who sent me have eternal life. They will never be condemned for their sins, but they have already passed from death into life. JOHN 5:24

> One of the key beliefs of Christianity is Jesus' resurrection. This is not an additive or afterthought; rather, it is at the very heart of belief. The New Testament repeats this again and again: Jesus, the Son of God and a perfect human being, died and came back from the dead. Just as God raised him to a new life, so God will someday raise all believers to a new life.

Many of those whose bodies lie dead and buried will rise up, some to everlasting life and some to shame and everlasting contempt. Those who are wise will shine as bright as the sky, and those who turn many to righteousness will shine like stars forever. DANIEL 12:2-3

Jesus told her, "I am the resurrection and the life. Those who believe in me, even though they die like everyone else, will live again." JOHN 11:25

Can anything ever separate us from Christ's love? Does it mean he no longer loves us if we have trouble or calamity, or are persecuted, or are hungry or cold or in danger or threatened with death? . . . No, despite all these things, overwhelming victory is ours through Christ, who loved us.

And I am convinced that nothing can ever separate us from his love. Death can't, and life can't. The angels can't, and the demons can't. Our fears for today, our worries about tomorrow, and even the powers of hell can't keep God's love away. ROMANS 8:35-38

Let me tell you a wonderful secret God has revealed to us. Not all of us will die, but we will all be transformed. It will happen in a moment, in the blinking of an eye, when the last trumpet is blown. For when the trumpet sounds, the Christians who have died will be raised with transformed bodies. And then we who are living will be transformed so that we will never die. For our perishable earthly bodies must be transformed into heavenly bodies that will never die.

When this happens—when our perishable earthly bodies have been transformed into heavenly bodies that will never die—then at last the Scriptures will come true: "Death is swallowed up in victory. O death, where is your victory? O death, where is your sting?" 1 CORINTHIANS 15:51-55

We know that when this earthly tent we live in is taken down—when we die and leave these bodies—we will have a home in heaven, an eternal body made for us by God himself and not by human hands.

We want to slip into our new bodies so that these dying bodies will be swallowed up by everlasting life.

So we are always confident, even though we know that as long as we live in these bodies we are not at home with the Lord.
2 CORINTHIANS 5:1, 4, 6

To me, living is for Christ, and dying is even better. Yet if I live, that means fruitful service for Christ. I really don't know which is better. I'm torn between two desires: Sometimes I want to live, and sometimes I long to go and be with Christ. PHILIPPIANS 1:21-23

Because God's children are human beings—made of flesh and blood—Jesus also became flesh and blood by being born in human form. For only as a human being could he die, and only by dying could he break the power of the Devil, who had the power of death. Only in this way could he deliver those who have lived all their lives as slaves to the fear of dying. HEBREWS 2:14-15

I heard a voice from heaven saying, "Write this down: Blessed are
those who die in the Lord from now on. Yes, says the Spirit, they
are blessed indeed, for they will rest from all their toils and trials;
for their good deeds follow them!" REVELATION 14:13

I saw a great white throne, and I saw the one who was sitting on
it. . . . I saw the dead, both great and small, standing before God's
throne. And the books were opened, including the Book of Life.
And the dead were judged according to the things written in the
books, according to what they had done. The sea gave up the
dead in it, and death and the grave gave up the dead in them.
They were all judged according to their deeds. And death and the
grave were thrown into the lake of fire. This is the second
death—the lake of fire. And anyone whose name was not found
recorded in the Book of Life was thrown into the lake of fire.
REVELATION 20:11-15

I saw the holy city, the new Jerusalem, coming down from God
out of heaven like a beautiful bride prepared for her husband.
   I heard a loud shout from the throne, saying, "Look, the home of
God is now among his people! He will live with them, and they
will be his people. God himself will be with them. He will remove
all of their sorrows, and there will be no more death or sorrow or
crying or pain. For the old world and its evils are gone forever."
REVELATION 21:2-4

See also Eternal Life, Heaven, Hell, Hope, Jesus' Second Coming.

The Devil

Can people in our day and age really believe in Satan, an actual *devil?* Why not? With so many people believing in reincarnation, astral projection, and other unbiblical beliefs, why not a devil? Unlike those other beliefs, belief in Satan is clearly taught in the Bible and has been an article of faith for Christians for two thousand years.

Maybe we've outgrown the old pictures of the devil with horns, a pitchfork, and a pointy tail. That's fine. The Bible shows no concern about the devil's looks. The Bible *is* concerned with a spiritual being who acts in direct opposition to a loving, merciful God.

What effect does this belief have on our life? In the first place, if there really is a supernatural being dedicated to our harm, we should know about him. In the second place, we need to know if there is a way of escaping his power—and there is. Jesus made it plain in his days on earth that the Kingdom of God involves actively tearing down the kingdom of the devil.

If I am casting out demons by the Spirit of God, then the Kingdom of God has arrived among you. MATTHEW 12:28

When the seventy-two disciples returned, they joyfully reported to him, "Lord, even the demons obey us when we use your name!"

"Yes," he told them, "I saw Satan falling from heaven as a flash of lightning! And I have given you authority over all the power of the enemy, and you can walk among snakes and scorpions and crush them. Nothing will injure you. But don't rejoice just because evil spirits obey you; rejoice because your names are registered as citizens of heaven." LUKE 10:17-20

The time of judgment for the world has come, when the prince of this world will be cast out. JOHN 12:31

You know what happened all through Judea, beginning in Galilee after John the Baptist began preaching. And no doubt you know that God anointed Jesus of Nazareth with the Holy Spirit and with power. Then Jesus went around doing good and healing all who were oppressed by the Devil, for God was with him. ACTS 10:37-38

When Jesus appeared to Paul on the Damascus road, he specifically mentioned tearing down the works of the devil:

I am going to send you to the Gentiles, to open their eyes so they may turn from darkness to light, and from the power of Satan to God. Then they will receive forgiveness for their sins and be given a place among God's people, who are set apart by faith in me. ACTS 26:17-18

The apostle Paul, like Jesus, understood the incredible power of Satan. He understood even better that God is much stronger and ultimately triumphs.

The God of peace will soon crush Satan under your feet. ROMANS 16:20

Satan can disguise himself as an angel of light. So it is no wonder his servants can also do it by pretending to be godly ministers. In the end they will get every bit of punishment their wicked deeds deserve. 2 CORINTHIANS 11:14-15

And "don't sin by letting anger gain control over you." Don't let the sun go down while you are still angry, for anger gives a mighty foothold to the Devil. EPHESIANS 4:26-27

> The Bible's classic passage about our safety from Satan is Paul's letter to the Ephesians. It, as well as other parts of the Bible, reminds us that, frail though we are, we have a divine "armor" to protect us against the powers of darkness.

Put on all of God's armor so that you will be able to stand firm against all strategies and tricks of the Devil. For we are not fighting against people made of flesh and blood, but against the evil rulers and authorities of the unseen world, against those mighty powers of darkness who rule this world, and against wicked spirits in the heavenly realms.

Use every piece of God's armor to resist the enemy in the time of evil, so that after the battle you will still be standing firm. Stand your ground, putting on the sturdy belt of truth and the body armor of God's righteousness. For shoes, put on the peace that comes from the Good News, so that you will be fully prepared. In every battle you will need faith as your shield to stop the fiery arrows aimed at you by Satan. Put on salvation as your helmet, and take the sword of the Spirit, which is the Word of God. EPHESIANS 6:11-17

Because God's children are human beings—made of flesh and blood—Jesus also became flesh and blood by being born in human form. For only as a human being could he die, and only by dying could he break the power of the Devil, who had the power of death. HEBREWS 2:14

Jealousy and selfishness are not God's kind of wisdom. Such things are earthly, unspiritual, and motivated by the Devil. For wherever there is jealousy and selfish ambition, there you will find disorder and every kind of evil. JAMES 3:15-16

Humble yourselves before God. Resist the Devil, and he will flee from you. Draw close to God, and God will draw close to you. JAMES 4:7-8

> The New Testament letters from Peter and John mention something we often forget: Satan takes pleasure in persecuting God's people. But the God we serve is stronger than any persecutor.

Be careful! Watch out for attacks from the Devil, your great enemy. He prowls around like a roaring lion, looking for some victim to devour. Take a firm stand against him, and be strong in your faith. Remember that Christians all over the world are going through the same kind of suffering you are. 1 PETER 5:8-9

When people keep on sinning, it shows they belong to the Devil, who has been sinning since the beginning. But the Son of God came to destroy these works of the Devil. Those who have been born into God's family do not sin, because God's life is in them. So they can't keep on sinning, because they have been born of God. So now we can tell who are children of God and who are children of the Devil. Anyone who does not obey God's commands and does not love other Christians does not belong to God. 1 JOHN 3:8-10

> In recent years it has become more commonly accepted for people to dabble in the occult, sometimes worshiping or conjuring up demons and evil spirits. This development has surprised and alarmed many Christians, but, strangely, it was clearly predicted in the Bible.

The Holy Spirit tells us clearly that in the last times some will turn away from what we believe; they will follow lying spirits and teachings that come from demons. These teachers are hypocrites and liars. They pretend to be religious, but their consciences are dead. 1 TIMOTHY 4:1-2

> The Bible's last book, Revelation, paints a vivid picture of the present world's end, the "wrapping up" of everything. Part of that dramatic picture is the final triumph over the Devil and those who serve him.

Then the Devil, who betrayed them, was thrown into the lake of fire that burns with sulfur, joining the beast and the false prophet. There they will be tormented day and night forever and ever.
REVELATION 20:10

See also Angels, Hell, Spiritual Power, Temptation.

Discipline and Correction

Being nonjudgmental is considered a virtue these days. Odd, isn't it, since people hire personal fitness trainers to critique and give advice. Physical trainers know that the people they critique ask for help because they desire to be fit and improve their abilities. "Tell me what I'm doing wrong. I want to do better." We say this so easily to a sports trainer but don't like the idea of a "morality pro" disciplining us and correcting our mistakes. And, we resist the idea of a God who acts in this way.

But that is exactly the kind of God revealed in the Bible. He wants us to do better, to improve, to show more love to him and to other people. God is one who loves, and genuine love involves discipline. His people should expect—even welcome—this. And his people should show the same loving concern for each other's spiritual welfare.

Just as a parent disciplines a child, the LORD your God disciplines you to help you.

So obey the commands of the LORD your God by walking in his ways and fearing him. DEUTERONOMY 8:5-6

Consider the joy of those corrected by God! Do not despise the chastening of the Almighty when you sin. For though he wounds, he also bandages. He strikes, but his hands also heal. JOB 5:17-18

He knows everything—doesn't he also know what you are doing? The LORD knows people's thoughts, that they are worthless!
   Happy are those whom you discipline, LORD, and those whom you teach from your law. PSALM 94:10-12

Fear of the LORD is the beginning of knowledge. Only fools despise wisdom and discipline. PROVERBS 1:7

The LORD corrects those he loves, just as a father corrects a child in whom he delights. PROVERBS 3:12

These commands and this teaching are a lamp to light the way ahead of you. The correction of discipline is the way to life.
PROVERBS 6:23

To learn, you must love discipline; it is stupid to hate correction.
PROVERBS 12:1

Only a fool despises a parent's discipline; whoever learns from correction is wise. PROVERBS 15:5

If you listen to constructive criticism, you will be at home among the wise. PROVERBS 15:31

A single rebuke does more for a person of understanding than a hundred lashes on the back of a fool. PROVERBS 17:10

Valid criticism is as treasured by the one who heeds it as jewelry made from finest gold. PROVERBS 25:12

An open rebuke is better than hidden love!
  Wounds from a friend are better than many kisses from an
enemy. PROVERBS 27:5-6

It is better to be criticized by a wise person than to be praised by a
fool! ECCLESIASTES 7:5

When we are judged and disciplined by the Lord, we will not be
condemned with the world. 1 CORINTHIANS 11:32

Our present troubles are quite small and won't last very long. Yet
they produce for us an immeasurably great glory that will last
forever! So we don't look at the troubles we can see right now;
rather, we look forward to what we have not yet seen. For the
troubles we see will soon be over, but the joys to come will last
forever. 2 CORINTHIANS 4:17-18

All Scripture is inspired by God and is useful to teach us what is
true and to make us realize what is wrong in our lives. It
straightens us out and teaches us to do what is right. It is God's
way of preparing us in every way, fully equipped for every good
thing God wants us to do. 2 TIMOTHY 3:16-17

> The great "discipline chapter" in the Bible is Hebrews 12. The
> author held out a wonderful promise to Christians: God's fatherly
> discipline has the purpose of making us fit to live with him forever.

Have you entirely forgotten the encouraging words God spoke to
you, his children? He said, "My child, don't ignore it when the
Lord disciplines you, and don't be discouraged when he corrects
you. For the Lord disciplines those he loves, and he punishes
those he accepts as his children." As you endure this divine
discipline, remember that God is treating you as his own children.
Whoever heard of a child who was never disciplined? If God
doesn't discipline you as he does all of his children, it means that

you are illegitimate and are not really his children after all. Since we respect our earthly fathers who disciplined us, should we not all the more cheerfully submit to the discipline of our heavenly Father and live forever?

For our earthly fathers disciplined us for a few years, doing the best they knew how. But God's discipline is always right and good for us because it means we will share in his holiness. No discipline is enjoyable while it is happening—it is painful! But afterward there will be a quiet harvest of right living for those who are trained in this way. HEBREWS 12:5-11

> In the Bible's view, we are accountable not only to God but also to each other. This doesn't mean we should be busybodies. It means that if we want to lead a loving, godly life, we ought to appreciate the guidance of other loving, godly people. God is our Father, but some of his wisdom comes from the discipline given by our earthly brothers and sisters.

Let the godly strike me! It will be a kindness! If they reprove me, it is soothing medicine. Don't let me refuse it.

But I am in constant prayer against the wicked and their deeds. PSALM 141:5

Don't bother rebuking mockers; they will only hate you. But the wise, when rebuked, will love you all the more. PROVERBS 9:8

Anyone who sins should be rebuked in front of the whole church so that others will have a proper fear of God. 1 TIMOTHY 5:20

You must warn each other every day, as long as it is called "today," so that none of you will be deceived by sin and hardened against God. HEBREWS 3:13

> Revelation, the last book of the Bible, looks at the end of this present world and the coming of a new world. It is appropriate that

in the closing chapters of the Bible Jesus gives both a promise and a warning:

I am the one who corrects and disciplines everyone I love. Be diligent and turn from your indifference.   REVELATION 3:19

See also Fellowship with God, Patience, Perseverance, Personal Growth.

Duty to the Poor

The poor get a lot of attention, mostly through requests for more government aid. "If only the government would provide more . . ." But the Bible has a message much more personal and individual: Each person of faith ought to help the poor. While the debates about welfare and government dependence rage on, there are still genuinely poor people in the world, some of them very close to us.

Bear in mind that *poor* doesn't just refer to financial status. In the Bible, the *poor* person is, like Jesus himself, humble, more dependent on God than on his own resources. The *rich* person isn't just a person with money, but someone who relies on himself instead of God. In the Bible's view, a person with few possessions could be as materialistic, selfish, and forgetful of God as a person with great wealth. The flip side is that a wealthy person could be a good, loving, God-centered person. Such people are rare, but they exist. Someone who is truly centered on God will show concern to those who have less.

The Bible is very bold in its promises: If you are a person of faith, give to the poor and God will be pleased. If you do nothing to aid the poor, you are not living the life of faith, and you cannot expect God's blessing.

Oh, the joys of those who are kind to the poor. The LORD rescues them in times of trouble. The LORD protects them and keeps them alive. He gives them prosperity and rescues them from their enemies. The LORD nurses them when they are sick and eases their pain and discomfort. PSALM 41:1-3

When darkness overtakes the godly, light will come bursting in. They are generous, compassionate, and righteous. All goes well for those who are generous, who lend freely and conduct their business fairly. Such people will not be overcome by evil circumstances. Those who are righteous will be long remembered.
   They give generously to those in need. Their good deeds will never be forgotten. They will have influence and honor.
PSALM 112:4-6, 9

Whoever gives to the poor will lack nothing. But a curse will come upon those who close their eyes to poverty. PROVERBS 28:27

The godly know the rights of the poor; the wicked don't care to know. PROVERBS 29:7

"When you put on a luncheon or a dinner," [Jesus] said, "don't invite your friends, brothers, relatives, and rich neighbors. For they will repay you by inviting you back. Instead, invite the poor, the crippled, the lame, and the blind. Then at the resurrection of the godly, God will reward you for inviting those who could not repay you." LUKE 14:12-14

On more than one occasion, Jesus encountered a wealthy person who was spiritually lacking. His words to them were blunt: If you want eternal life, *give*. This giving is not our way of buying God's favor. Plainly stated, it can't be bought. Generous, heartfelt giving is

a natural response to a generous God. It's a way of saying thank you
to him by showing generosity toward those who have little.
Stinginess shows that we're willing to accept gifts from God without
sharing ourselves. This has no place in the life of love and faith.
Jesus had some warnings about people who are morally good but
who lack a generous spirit.

Once a religious leader asked Jesus this question: "Good teacher,
what should I do to get eternal life?"

"Why do you call me good?" Jesus asked him. "Only God is
truly good. But as for your question, you know the
commandments: 'Do not commit adultery. Do not murder. Do not
steal. Do not testify falsely. Honor your father and mother.'"

The man replied, "I've obeyed all these commandments since I
was a child."

"There is still one thing you lack," Jesus said. "Sell all you have
and give the money to the poor, and you will have treasure in
heaven. Then come, follow me." But when the man heard this, he
became sad because he was very rich.

Jesus watched him go and then said to his disciples, "How hard
it is for rich people to get into the Kingdom of God! It is easier for
a camel to go through the eye of a needle than for a rich person to
enter the Kingdom of God!" LUKE 18:18-25

You must each make up your own mind as to how much you
should give. Don't give reluctantly or in response to pressure. For
God loves the person who gives cheerfully. And God will
generously provide all you need. Then you will always have
everything you need and plenty left over to share with others.
2 CORINTHIANS 9:7-8

Pure and lasting religion in the sight of God our Father means that
we must care for orphans and widows in their troubles, and
refuse to let the world corrupt us. JAMES 1:27

Sell what you have and give to those in need. This will store up treasure for you in heaven! And the purses of heaven have no holes in them. Your treasure will be safe—no thief can steal it and no moth can destroy it. Wherever your treasure is, there your heart and thoughts will also be. L U K E 12:33-34

> The New Testament speaks of a problem that was—and is—too common among Christians: neglecting other Christians. While the Bible tells us to be concerned for *all* poor people, we are expected to show a special concern for our own brothers and sisters in the faith. After all, aren't we family?

If one of you has enough money to live well, and sees a brother or sister in need and refuses to help—how can God's love be in that person?

Dear children, let us stop just saying we love each other; let us really show it by our actions. It is by our actions that we know we are living in the truth, so we will be confident when we stand before the Lord, even if our hearts condemn us. For God is greater than our hearts, and he knows everything. 1 JOHN 3:17-20

My dear brothers and sisters, how can you claim that you have faith in our glorious Lord Jesus Christ if you favor some people more than others?

For instance, suppose someone comes into your meeting dressed in fancy clothes and expensive jewelry, and another comes in who is poor and dressed in shabby clothes. If you give special attention and a good seat to the rich person, but you say to the poor one, "You can stand over there, or else sit on the floor"—well, doesn't this discrimination show that you are guided by wrong motives?

Listen to me, dear brothers and sisters. Hasn't God chosen the poor in this world to be rich in faith? Aren't they the ones who will inherit the kingdom God promised to those who love him?
JAMES 2:1-5

Curiously, Paul, who taught the necessity of caring for the poor, also promised that there is no worth in our generosity unless our motives are right.

If I gave everything I have to the poor and even sacrificed my body, I could boast about it; but if I didn't love others, I would be of no value whatsoever. 1 CORINTHIANS 13:3

See also Generosity, God's Concern for the Poor, Kindness, Money.

The Earth and Nature

T here is not one color, not one blade of grass, that was not created to make man rejoice." So said John Calvin. He understood that God created the earth and all nature. Thus, it demands our reverence. It is *good,* as the first chapter of Genesis makes clear. And as several of the Psalms indicate, nature is a pointer to God. For those with ears, nature shouts the message: "Someone—the great Someone—made all of this!"

But nature itself is never divine. This is one way that religion in the Bible differs radically from nature religions of yesterday and today. The bumper stickers that say, "Love Your Mother" (referring to the earth) would have shocked the authors of the Bible. They respected and valued nature as God's handiwork. But it is not divine itself, and worshiping it (and anything else besides the Maker himself) is a sin. Christians can support care for the environment—but only to a point. We cannot go along with the idea that nature is *sacred.*

God looked over all he had made, and he saw that it was excellent in every way. GENESIS 1:31

By wisdom the LORD founded the earth; by understanding he established the heavens. By his knowledge the deep fountains of the earth burst forth, and the clouds poured down rain.
PROVERBS 3:19-20

When I look at the night sky and see the work of your fingers— the moon and the stars you have set in place—what are mortals that you should think of us, mere humans that you should care for us? For you made us only a little lower than God, and you crowned us with glory and honor. You put us in charge of everything you made, giving us authority over all things—the sheep and the cattle and all the wild animals, the birds in the sky, the fish in the sea, and everything that swims the ocean currents.

O LORD, our Lord, the majesty of your name fills the earth!
PSALM 8:3-9

The heavens tell of the glory of God. The skies display his marvelous craftsmanship. Day after day they continue to speak; night after night they make him known. They speak without a sound or a word; their voice is silent in the skies; yet their message has gone out to all the earth, and their words to all the world.

The sun lives in the heavens where God placed it.   PSALM 19:1-4

O LORD God Almighty! Where is there anyone as mighty as you, LORD? Faithfulness is your very character.

You are the one who rules the oceans. When their waves rise in fearful storms, you subdue them. . . . The heavens are yours, and the earth is yours; everything in the world is yours—you created it all.   PSALM 89:8-11

> Jesus himself appreciated the beauties of nature. It is touching to remember when we admire the delicacy of a flower that Jesus, who was human as we are, did the same.

Look at the lilies and how they grow. They don't work or make their clothing, yet Solomon in all his glory was not dressed as beautifully as they are. LUKE 12:27

> The Bible reminds us that we are not an intrusion on nature. God made us in his image, and he gave us power over creation, although not ultimate power like his own. Following the great Flood in Genesis, God told Noah and his family that the things of earth were a gift from him—not to be abused, but to be treated well and used for human good.

God blessed Noah and his sons and told them, "Multiply and fill the earth. All the wild animals, large and small, and all the birds and fish will be afraid of you. I have placed them in your power. I have given them to you for food, just as I have given you grain and vegetables." GENESIS 9:1-3

The heavens belong to the LORD, but he has given the earth to all humanity. PSALM 115:16

> One of the Ten Commandments specifically forbids idols—setting up something to worship besides God. Israel, the chosen people in the Old Testament, was surrounded by nature-worshiping nations. These pagan religions often infiltrated Israel's worship, and the prophets had to constantly preach against the worship of God the Creator being mingled with worship of some part of his creation. The commandment in Exodus not only refers to bowing down to physical idols but also to worshiping nature itself or any part of it.

Do not make idols of any kind, whether in the shape of birds or animals or fish. You must never worship or bow down to them, for I, the LORD your God, am a jealous God who will not share your affection with any other god! EXODUS 20:4-5

The earth seems so solid and secure. Yet because of pollution and the way we abuse the earth, environmentalists have predicted catastrophes—and there is no shortage of prophets of doom. In this they agree with the Bible: This present earth will not last. The Bible gives no hint, however, as to what will bring about the destruction. Throughout history men have predicted dates for the end of the world and so far have been incorrect. But the Bible promises this *will* occur—when God wills it. This is not something we can forget, for God's Word encourages us to enjoy the earth but to fix our mind on heaven. The earth is a way station, not the destination. After all, as the New Testament promises us, it isn't meant to last forever. History will reach its climax, not in a worshiped and unpolluted earth, but in a new creation—the ultimate home of those who love God.

In ages past you laid the foundation of the earth, and the heavens are the work of your hands. Even they will perish, but you remain forever; they will wear out like old clothing. You will change them like a garment, and they will fade away. But you are always the same; your years never end. PSALM 102:25-27

Look up to the skies above, and gaze down on the earth beneath. For the skies will disappear like smoke, and the earth will wear out like a piece of clothing. The people of the earth will die like flies, but my salvation lasts forever. My righteous rule will never end! ISAIAH 51:6

Immediately after those horrible days end, the sun will be darkened, the moon will not give light, the stars will fall from the sky, and the powers of heaven will be shaken. And then at last, the sign of the coming of the Son of Man will appear in the heavens, and there will be deep mourning among all the nations of the earth. And they will see the Son of Man arrive on the clouds of heaven with power and great glory.

Heaven and earth will disappear, but my words will remain forever. MATTHEW 24:29-30, 35

God has also commanded that the heavens and the earth will be consumed by fire on the day of judgment, when ungodly people will perish.

The day of the Lord will come as unexpectedly as a thief. Then the heavens will pass away with a terrible noise, and everything in them will disappear in fire, and the earth and everything on it will be exposed to judgment.

Since everything around us is going to melt away, what holy, godly lives you should be living! 2 PETER 3:7, 10-11

I saw a new heaven and a new earth, for the old heaven and the old earth had disappeared. And the sea was also gone. And I saw the holy city, the new Jerusalem, coming down from God out of heaven like a beautiful bride prepared for her husband.

I heard a loud shout from the throne, saying, "Look, the home of God is now among his people! He will live with them, and they will be his people. God himself will be with them."
REVELATION 21:1-3

Stop loving this evil world and all that it offers you, for when you love the world, you show that you do not have the love of the Father in you. For the world offers only the lust for physical pleasure, the lust for everything we see, and pride in our possessions. These are not from the Father. They are from this evil world. And this world is fading away, along with everything it craves. But if you do the will of God, you will live forever.
1 JOHN 2:15-17

See also Heaven.

Enemies

The Bible doesn't promise that you will never have enemies. In fact, the Bible makes it plain that people of faith will have enemies and will endure persecution.

But the Bible does promise us that God is greater than any foe we will ever face. We may be small and weak compared with those who oppose us, but our enemies are small and weak compared with God. Even if justice is not done in this life, God guarantees that there is a final justice.

The LORD is for me, so I will not be afraid. What can mere mortals do to me? Yes, the LORD is for me; he will help me. I will look in triumph at those who hate me. It is better to trust the LORD than to put confidence in people. It is better to trust the LORD than to put confidence in princes. PSALM 118:6-9

He will save you from death in time of famine, from the power of the sword in time of war. JOB 5:20

He will conceal me there when troubles come; he will hide me in his sanctuary. He will place me out of reach on a high rock. Then I

will hold my head high, above my enemies who surround me.
PSALM 27:5-6

The LORD saves the godly; he is their fortress in times of trouble.
The LORD helps them, rescuing them from the wicked. He saves
them, and they find shelter in him. PSALM 37:39-40

With God's help we will do mighty things, for he will trample
down our foes. PSALM 60:12

You who love the LORD, hate evil! He protects the lives of his
godly people and rescues them from the power of the wicked.
PSALM 97:10

When the ways of people please the LORD, he makes even their
enemies live at peace with them. PROVERBS 16:7

Fearing people is a dangerous trap, but to trust the LORD means
safety. PROVERBS 29:25

See, all your angry enemies lie there, confused and ashamed.
Anyone who opposes you will die. You will look for them in vain.
They will all be gone! I am holding you by your right hand—I, the
LORD your God. And I say to you, "Do not be afraid. I am here to
help you." ISAIAH 41:11-13

I will rescue you from those you fear so much. Because you
trusted me, I will preserve your life and keep you safe. I, the
LORD, have spoken! JEREMIAH 39:17-18

Don't you think God will surely give justice to his chosen people
who plead with him day and night? Will he keep putting them
off? I tell you, he will grant justice to them quickly! LUKE 18:7-8

I have told you all this so that you may have peace in me. Here on earth you will have many trials and sorrows. But take heart, because I have overcome the world. JOHN 16:33

> Since God is a God of mercy, his people are expected to be merciful also. Contrary to normal inclinations, we are told to not hate our enemies. In fact, we are to do just the opposite and love them. This is a sign that we really love God and are doing his will.

If people persecute you because you are a Christian, don't curse them; pray that God will bless them.

Instead, do what the Scriptures say: "If your enemies are hungry, feed them. If they are thirsty, give them something to drink, and they will be ashamed of what they have done to you."
ROMANS 12:14, 20

You have heard that the law of Moses says, "Love your neighbor" and hate your enemy. But I say, love your enemies! Pray for those who persecute you! In that way, you will be acting as true children of your Father in heaven. For he gives his sunlight to both the evil and the good, and he sends rain on the just and on the unjust, too. If you love only those who love you, what good is that? Even corrupt tax collectors do that much. If you are kind only to your friends, how are you different from anyone else? Even pagans do that. But you are to be perfect, even as your Father in heaven is perfect. MATTHEW 5:43-48

Do not rejoice when your enemies fall into trouble. Don't be happy when they stumble. For the LORD will be displeased with you and will turn his anger away from them. PROVERBS 24:17-18

See also Forgiving Others, Mercy.

Envy

Envy is one of those "invisible" sins. Unlike adultery, drunkenness, or even greed, no one can know that another person is envious. We may give ourselves away by the things we say, but, in fact, envy is easily hidden. Being easily concealed, it's also rarely admitted to.

Is that so bad? Isn't it human, and normal, to admire another person's looks, clothing, car, house, social position? Of course it's normal. What the Bible condemns is not admiration but *coveting*—making an idol of what we don't have. A key element of envy is the feeling of injustice: *Donna shouldn't really have that beautiful house; I deserve that more than she does. Bill doesn't deserve that high-paying job, but I certainly do.*

How easily we forget that this "invisible" sin is so serious that it is forbidden in the Ten Commandments.

Do not covet your neighbor's house. Do not covet your neighbor's wife, male or female servant, ox or donkey, or anything else your neighbor owns. EXODUS 20:17

One of the saddest things about envy is that we usually envy bad people, not good ones. (How often have you envied someone who gave away things to charity?) How much energy do we waste mulling over what some greedy, materialistic person has?

Be still in the presence of the LORD, and wait patiently for him to act. Don't worry about evil people who prosper or fret about their wicked schemes.

Stop your anger! Turn from your rage! Do not envy others—it only leads to harm. For the wicked will be destroyed, but those who trust in the LORD will possess the land. PSALM 37:7-9

Do not envy violent people; don't copy their ways. Such wicked people are an abomination to the LORD, but he offers his friendship to the godly. PROVERBS 3:31-32

Don't envy sinners, but always continue to fear the LORD. For surely you have a future ahead of you; your hope will not be disappointed. PROVERBS 23:17-18

Don't envy evil people; don't desire their company. For they spend their days plotting violence, and their words are always stirring up trouble. PROVERBS 24:1-2

Most people are motivated to success by their envy of their neighbors. But this, too, is meaningless, like chasing the wind. ECCLESIASTES 4:4

Anger is cruel, and wrath is like a flood, but who can survive the destructiveness of jealousy? PROVERBS 27:4

Do we normally think of jealousy as *destructive?* If it causes us to waste valuable spiritual energy, then, yes, it's horribly destructive. God's Word urges us to contentment. What can discontent do except lead to that much dreaded word *stress?*

A relaxed attitude lengthens life; jealousy rots it away.
PROVERBS 14:30

> Christians often forget how often envy is condemned in God's
> Word. Perhaps, since it is an invisible sin, we take it less seriously
> than others. But the New Testament writers made it plain that envy,
> destructive as it is, mars the Christian's relationship with God and
> with other people.

We should be decent and true in everything we do, so that
everyone can approve of our behavior. Don't participate in wild
parties and getting drunk, or in adultery and immoral living, or in
fighting and jealousy. But let the Lord Jesus Christ take control of
you, and don't think of ways to indulge your evil desires.
ROMANS 13:13-14

You are still controlled by your own sinful desires. You are jealous
of one another and quarrel with each other. Doesn't that prove
you are controlled by your own desires? You are acting like people
who don't belong to the Lord. 1 CORINTHIANS 3:3

Jealousy and selfishness are not God's kind of wisdom. Such
things are earthly, unspiritual, and motivated by the Devil.
JAMES 3:15

Get rid of all malicious behavior and deceit. Don't just pretend to
be good! Be done with hypocrisy and jealousy and backstabbing.
1 PETER 2:1

When you follow the desires of your sinful nature, your lives will
produce these evil results . . . envy, drunkenness, wild parties, and
other kinds of sin. Let me tell you again, as I have before, that
anyone living that sort of life will not inherit the Kingdom of God.
  But when the Holy Spirit controls our lives, he will produce this
kind of fruit in us: love, joy, peace, patience, kindness, goodness,

faithfulness, gentleness, and self-control. Here there is no conflict with the law.

Those who belong to Christ Jesus have nailed the passions and desires of their sinful nature to his cross and crucified them there. If we are living now by the Holy Spirit, let us follow the Holy Spirit's leading in every part of our lives. Let us not become conceited, or irritate one another, or be jealous of one another. GALATIANS 5:19-26

> When talking about *conversion* and *new birth,* often the focus is on giving up bad habits like cursing, drinking, adultery—all visible sins. But the New Testament indicates that envy is a key part of the sinful life—one that should be thrown aside by the converted person.

Once we, too, were foolish and disobedient. We were misled by others and became slaves to many wicked desires and evil pleasures. Our lives were full of evil and envy. We hated others, and they hated us.

But then God our Savior showed us his kindness and love. He saved us, not because of the good things we did, but because of his mercy. He washed away our sins and gave us a new life through the Holy Spirit. TITUS 3:3-5

> If we have committed our life to the Lord and now have new life in the Spirit, we have the one thing that can rid our lives of jealousy and every other sin: love.

Love is patient and kind. Love is not jealous or boastful or proud or rude. Love does not demand its own way. Love is not irritable, and it keeps no record of when it has been wronged. 1 CORINTHIANS 13:4-5

See also Contentment, Hate.

Eternal Life

Loving and obeying God will not, alas, necessarily make us rich, handsome, or successful—not by this world's standards, anyway. In fact, the Bible actually promises that we will have to endure some scorn for holding fast to God. How could it be otherwise? The world hates nonconformists, so they can't help but sneer at people who believe that the next life is so good that the present life can't begin to compare with it.

Too bad we neglect this belief. The Bible certainly doesn't. It gives so much attention to eternal life that we wonder if our life in this world matters. It does. But our present circumstances, whether pleasant or painful, can't compare with the good that lies ahead.

You will not leave my soul among the dead or allow your godly one to rot in the grave. You will show me the way of life, granting me the joy of your presence and the pleasures of living with you forever. PSALM 16:10-11

We have this assurance: Those who belong to God will live; their bodies will rise again! Those who sleep in the earth will rise up and sing for joy! For God's light of life will fall like dew on his people in the place of the dead! ISAIAH 26:19

I know that my Redeemer lives, and that he will stand upon the earth at last. And after my body has decayed, yet in my body I will see God! I will see him for myself. Yes, I will see him with my own eyes. I am overwhelmed at the thought! JOB 19:25-27

Many of those whose bodies lie dead and buried will rise up, some to everlasting life and some to shame and everlasting contempt. Those who are wise will shine as bright as the sky, and those who turn many to righteousness will shine like stars forever. DANIEL 12:2-3

> The Old Testament has little to say about eternal life. The four preceding passages are rarities, being some of the few Old Testament sections that promise an afterlife of joy. This changed dramatically in the New Testament. Jesus preached the Kingdom of God as a reality that begins in this life and continues on forever. He made no bones about eternity: It is real, it is life with the Father, and it is gained by having faith in Christ himself.

As to whether the dead will be raised—even Moses proved this when he wrote about the burning bush. Long after Abraham, Isaac, and Jacob had died, he referred to the Lord as "the God of Abraham, the God of Isaac, and the God of Jacob." So he is the God of the living, not the dead. They are all alive to him. LUKE 20:37-38

Humans can reproduce only human life, but the Holy Spirit gives new life from heaven.

All who believe in God's Son have eternal life. Those who don't obey the Son will never experience eternal life, but the wrath of God remains upon them. JOHN 3:6, 36

This is the will of God, that I should not lose even one of all those he has given me, but that I should raise them to eternal life at the last day. For it is my Father's will that all who see his Son and believe in him should have eternal life—that I should raise them at the last day. JOHN 6:39-40

I assure you, anyone who obeys my teaching will never die!
JOHN 8:51

Jesus told her, "I am the resurrection and the life. Those who believe in me, even though they die like everyone else, will live again. They are given eternal life for believing in me and will never perish." JOHN 11:25-26

There are many rooms in my Father's home, and I am going to prepare a place for you. If this were not so, I would tell you plainly. When everything is ready, I will come and get you, so that you will always be with me where I am. JOHN 14:2-3

> Eternity is never put on the back burner in the New Testament. Paul especially had plenty to say about eternal life. His letters are full of promises about heaven. Anyone who thinks of Christianity as a legalistic religion of don'ts has never read the Bible carefully.

If we have hope in Christ only for this life, we are the most miserable people in the world.

But the fact is that Christ has been raised from the dead. He has become the first of a great harvest of those who will be raised to life again.

So you see, just as death came into the world through a man, Adam, now the resurrection from the dead has begun through another man, Christ. Everyone dies because all of us are related to Adam, the first man. But all who are related to Christ, the other man, will be given new life. 1 CORINTHIANS 15:19-22

Our earthly bodies, which die and decay, will be different when they are resurrected, for they will never die. Our bodies now disappoint us, but when they are raised, they will be full of glory. They are weak now, but when they are raised, they will be full of power. They are natural human bodies now, but when they are raised, they will be spiritual bodies. For just as there are natural bodies, so also there are spiritual bodies.

The Scriptures tell us, "The first man, Adam, became a living person." But the last Adam—that is, Christ—is a life-giving Spirit. What came first was the natural body, then the spiritual body comes later. Adam, the first man, was made from the dust of the earth, while Christ, the second man, came from heaven. Every human being has an earthly body just like Adam's, but our heavenly bodies will be just like Christ's. Just as we are now like Adam, the man of the earth, so we will someday be like Christ, the man from heaven.

What I am saying, dear brothers and sisters, is that flesh and blood cannot inherit the Kingdom of God. These perishable bodies of ours are not able to live forever. 1 CORINTHIANS 15:42-50

The wages of sin is death, but the free gift of God is eternal life through Christ Jesus our Lord. ROMANS 6:23

The Spirit of God, who raised Jesus from the dead, lives in you. And just as he raised Christ from the dead, he will give life to your mortal body by this same Spirit living within you. ROMANS 8:11

Let me tell you a wonderful secret God has revealed to us. Not all of us will die, but we will all be transformed. It will happen in a moment, in the blinking of an eye, when the last trumpet is blown. For when the trumpet sounds, the Christians who have died will be raised with transformed bodies. And then we who are living will be transformed so that we will never die. For our perishable earthly bodies must be transformed into heavenly bodies that will never die.

When this happens—when our perishable earthly bodies have been transformed into heavenly bodies that will never die—then at last the Scriptures will come true: "Death is swallowed up in victory. O death, where is your victory? O death, where is your sting?" 1 CORINTHIANS 15:51-54

Though our bodies are dying, our spirits are being renewed every day. For our present troubles are quite small and won't last very long. Yet they produce for us an immeasurably great glory that will last forever! So we don't look at the troubles we can see right now; rather, we look forward to what we have not yet seen. For the troubles we see will soon be over, but the joys to come will last forever.

For we know that when this earthly tent we live in is taken down—when we die and leave these bodies—we will have a home in heaven, an eternal body made for us by God himself and not by human hands. We grow weary in our present bodies, and we long for the day when we will put on our heavenly bodies like new clothing. For we will not be spirits without bodies, but we will put on new heavenly bodies.

So we are always confident, even though we know that as long as we live in these bodies we are not at home with the Lord.
2 CORINTHIANS 4:16–5:3, 6

Those who live only to satisfy their own sinful desires will harvest the consequences of decay and death. But those who live to please the Spirit will harvest everlasting life from the Spirit.
GALATIANS 6:8

In his kindness God called you to his eternal glory by means of Jesus Christ. After you have suffered a little while, he will restore, support, and strengthen you, and he will place you on a firm foundation. All power is his forever and ever. Amen.
1 PETER 5:10-11

Dear friends, work hard to prove that you really are among those God has called and chosen. Doing this, you will never stumble or fall away. And God will open wide the gates of heaven for you to enter into the eternal Kingdom of our Lord and Savior Jesus Christ. 2 PETER 1:10-11

Do we miss out on life's pleasures if we focus our mind on heaven? Not according to the Bible:

The world offers only the lust for physical pleasure, the lust for everything we see, and pride in our possessions. These are not from the Father. They are from this evil world. And this world is fading away, along with everything it craves. But if you do the will of God, you will live forever. 1 JOHN 2:16-17

Yes, dear friends, we are already God's children, and we can't even imagine what we will be like when Christ returns. But we do know that when he comes we will be like him, for we will see him as he really is. 1 JOHN 3:2

This is what God has testified: He has given us eternal life, and this life is in his Son. So whoever has God's Son has life; whoever does not have his Son does not have life.
I write this to you who believe in the Son of God, so that you may know you have eternal life. 1 JOHN 5:11-13

The book of Revelation was written to people who were suffering for their faith. In the era that the book was written, a Christian could hardly be comfortable in this world, knowing that he or his fellow believers could be persecuted and perhaps even put to death. For such a person, the promise of heaven must have been comforting. The world has not changed since that time as much as we might think. Across the globe God's people are still being persecuted and martyred. Christians need to remember our solidarity and the promise of fellowship in heaven with these courageous people:

I saw a vast crowd, too great to count, from every nation and tribe and people and language, standing in front of the throne and before the Lamb. They were clothed in white and held palm branches in their hands. And they were shouting with a mighty shout, "Salvation comes from our God on the throne and from the Lamb!"

And all the angels were standing around the throne and around the elders and the four living beings. And they fell face down before the throne and worshiped God. They said, "Amen! Blessing and glory and wisdom and thanksgiving and honor and power and strength belong to our God forever and forever. Amen!"

Then one of the twenty-four elders asked me, "Who are these who are clothed in white? Where do they come from?"

And I said to him, "Sir, you are the one who knows."

Then he said to me, "These are the ones coming out of the great tribulation. They washed their robes in the blood of the Lamb and made them white. That is why they are standing in front of the throne of God, serving him day and night in his Temple. And he who sits on the throne will live among them and shelter them. They will never again be hungry or thirsty, and they will be fully protected from the scorching noontime heat. For the Lamb who stands in front of the throne will be their Shepherd. He will lead them to the springs of life-giving water. And God will wipe away all their tears." REVELATION 7:9-17

I heard a loud shout from the throne, saying, "Look, the home of God is now among his people! He will live with them, and they will be his people. God himself will be with them. He will remove all of their sorrows, and there will be no more death or sorrow or crying or pain. For the old world and its evils are gone forever."

And the one sitting on the throne said, "Look, I am making all things new!" REVELATION 21:3-5

See also Heaven, Hell, Jesus' Second Coming, Worldly Cares.

Faith

Martin Luther defined faith as "a living, daring confidence in God's grace." It is such an important element in the good life that we refer to our relationship with God as "the life of faith," and we refer to our beliefs as "the faith." Faith goes well beyond mental beliefs and ideas. After all, as Luther said, it is "living, daring." More than a "head thing," it is a "heart thing" and a "will thing."

One of the greatest promises made in the Bible is Jesus' assurance that we do not need to be giants of the faith to please God. Even a little faith is a good thing—and powerful, too. Small faith can always grow:

I assure you, even if you had faith as small as a mustard seed you could say to this mountain, "Move from here to there," and it would move. Nothing would be impossible. MATTHEW 17:20

The truth is, anyone who believes in me will do the same works I have done, and even greater works, because I am going to be with the Father. You can ask for anything in my name, and I will do it, because the work of the Son brings glory to the Father. Yes, ask anything in my name, and I will do it! JOHN 14:12-14

Accept Christians who are weak in faith, and don't argue with them about what they think is right or wrong. ROMANS 14:1

There are three things that will endure—faith, hope, and love.
1 CORINTHIANS 13:13

We live by believing and not by seeing. 2 CORINTHIANS 5:7

I myself no longer live, but Christ lives in me. So I live my life in this earthly body by trusting in the Son of God, who loved me and gave himself for me. GALATIANS 2:20

I pray that Christ will be more and more at home in your hearts as you trust in him. May your roots go down deep into the soil of God's marvelous love. And may you have the power to understand, as all God's people should, how wide, how long, how high, and how deep his love really is. May you experience the love of Christ, though it is so great you will never fully understand it. Then you will be filled with the fullness of life and power that comes from God. EPHESIANS 3:17-19

Just as you accepted Christ Jesus as your Lord, you must continue to live in obedience to him. Let your roots grow down into him and draw up nourishment from him, so you will grow in faith, strong and vigorous in the truth you were taught. Let your lives overflow with thanksgiving for all he has done.
COLOSSIANS 2:6-7

Every child of God defeats this evil world by trusting Christ to give the victory. And the ones who win this battle against the world are the ones who believe that Jesus is the Son of God.
1 JOHN 5:4-5

Dear brothers and sisters, whenever trouble comes your way, let it be an opportunity for joy. For when your faith is tested, your endurance has a chance to grow. So let it grow, for when your endurance is fully developed, you will be strong in character and ready for anything. JAMES 1:2-4

> Paul, the author of much of the New Testament, had much to say about faith. For him, faith was the keystone of a person's salvation. The important thing is believing that Christ has brought us into a right relationship with a loving, forgiving Father.

We are made right in God's sight when we trust in Jesus Christ to take away our sins. And we all can be saved in this same way, no matter who we are or what we have done. ROMANS 3:22

Since we have been made right in God's sight by faith, we have peace with God because of what Jesus Christ our Lord has done for us. Because of our faith, Christ has brought us into this place of highest privilege where we now stand, and we confidently and joyfully look forward to sharing God's glory.

We can rejoice, too, when we run into problems and trials, for we know that they are good for us—they help us learn to endure. ROMANS 5:1-3

You are all children of God through faith in Christ Jesus. And all who have been united with Christ in baptism have been made like him. GALATIANS 3:26-27

God saved you by his special favor when you believed. And you can't take credit for this; it is a gift from God. Salvation is not a reward for the good things we have done, so none of us can boast about it. For we are God's masterpiece. He has created us anew in Christ Jesus, so that we can do the good things he planned for us long ago. EPHESIANS 2:8-10

The Letter of James has been called the "faith that works" letter. James made it plain that faith that is all talk and no walk is no faith at all. If a person truly has faith, his deeds will show it. There is no such thing as a completely inward faith. Every believer must also be a deed-doer.

Dear brothers and sisters, what's the use of saying you have faith if you don't prove it by your actions? That kind of faith can't save anyone. Suppose you see a brother or sister who needs food or clothing, and you say, "Well, good-bye and God bless you; stay warm and eat well"—but then you don't give that person any food or clothing. What good does that do?

So you see, it isn't enough just to have faith. Faith that doesn't show itself by good deeds is no faith at all—it is dead and useless.

Now someone may argue, "Some people have faith; others have good deeds." I say, "I can't see your faith if you don't have good deeds, but I will show you my faith through my good deeds."

Fool! When will you ever learn that faith that does not result in good deeds is useless? JAMES 2:14-18, 20

The Letter to the Hebrews has the best-known faith chapter in the Bible: "The Faith Hall of Fame." In it the author defines faith and then describes people who were great examples of faith. It is more than a history lesson. It is a promise that we, like the great heroes of the Bible, can be people of faith also.

What is faith? It is the confident assurance that what we hope for is going to happen. It is the evidence of things we cannot yet see. God gave his approval to people in days of old because of their faith. . . .

You see, it is impossible to please God without faith. Anyone who wants to come to him must believe that there is a God and that he rewards those who sincerely seek him. . . .

All these faithful ones died without receiving what God had promised them, but they saw it all from a distance and welcomed the promises of God. They agreed that they were no more than foreigners and nomads here on earth. And obviously people who talk like that are looking forward to a country they can call their own. If they had meant the country they came from, they would have found a way to go back. But they were looking for a better place, a heavenly homeland. That is why God is not ashamed to be called their God, for he has prepared a heavenly city for them. . . .

By faith these people overthrew kingdoms, ruled with justice, and received what God had promised them. They shut the mouths of lions, quenched the flames of fire, and escaped death by the edge of the sword. Their weakness was turned to strength. They became strong in battle and put whole armies to flight. . . .

But others trusted God and were tortured, preferring to die rather than turn from God and be free. They placed their hope in the resurrection to a better life. Some were mocked, and their backs were cut open with whips. Others were chained in dungeons. Some died by stoning, and some were sawed in half; others were killed with the sword. Some went about in skins of sheep and goats, hungry and oppressed and mistreated. They were too good for this world. They wandered over deserts and mountains, hiding in caves and holes in the ground.

All of these people we have mentioned received God's approval because of their faith, yet none of them received all that God had promised. For God had far better things in mind for us that would also benefit them, for they can't receive the prize at the end of the race until we finish the race.

Therefore, since we are surrounded by such a huge crowd of witnesses to the life of faith, let us strip off every weight that slows us down, especially the sin that so easily hinders our progress. And let us run with endurance the race that God has set before us. We do this by keeping our eyes on Jesus, on whom our faith depends from start to finish. HEBREWS 11:1–12:2

See also God's Guidance, Hope, Trusting God.

False Teachings

It doesn't matter what you believe, so long as you're sincere"—so said Linus in the comic strip "Peanuts." Linus was defending his belief in the Great Pumpkin, but his sentiment is shared by many people, including many who consider themselves Christians.

Linus, along with many Christians, might point to the famous passage in Luke's Gospel, which speaks of the two greatest commandments:

"You must love the Lord your God with all your heart, all your soul, all your strength, and all your mind." And, "Love your neighbor as yourself." LUKE 10:27

Love is understandable—warm and fuzzy. Doctrine and teaching sound cold, difficult, demanding. But note that the commandment says we are to love God with all our mind as well. So sound beliefs are more important than just spiritual sincerity.

The Bible, the New Testament especially, says a lot about teaching. It promises good to those who follow right belief (in addition to loving God and their neighbor, of course). It promises judgment for people who willingly lead others into wrong beliefs.

If you break the smallest commandment and teach others to do the same, you will be the least in the Kingdom of Heaven. But anyone who obeys God's laws and teaches them will be great in the Kingdom of Heaven. MATTHEW 5:19

You hypocrites! Isaiah was prophesying about you when he said, "These people honor me with their lips, but their hearts are far away. Their worship is a farce, for they replace God's commands with their own man-made teachings." MATTHEW 15:7-9

Not all people who sound religious are really godly. They may refer to me as "Lord," but they still won't enter the Kingdom of Heaven. The decisive issue is whether they obey my Father in heaven. MATTHEW 7:21

If anyone causes one of these little ones who trusts in me to lose faith, it would be better for that person to be thrown into the sea with a large millstone tied around the neck. MARK 9:42

> Jesus promised his followers that popularity itself was no measure of truth. In fact, popularity can sometimes be a sign of false teaching:

What sorrows await you who are praised by the crowds, for their ancestors also praised false prophets. LUKE 6:26

Jesus told them, "I'm not teaching my own ideas, but those of God who sent me. Anyone who wants to do the will of God will know whether my teaching is from God or is merely my own. Those who present their own ideas are looking for praise for themselves, but those who seek to honor the one who sent them are good and genuine." JOHN 7:16-18

Right belief was something Paul stressed over and over. Happily, he didn't tell Christians they had to be brilliant scholars or professional theologians. In fact, he was aware that too much so-called wisdom could lead people away from the basic truths of the gospel.

Watch out for people who cause divisions and upset people's faith by teaching things that are contrary to what you have been taught. Stay away from them. Such people are not serving Christ our Lord; they are serving their own personal interests. By smooth talk and glowing words they deceive innocent people. ROMANS 16:17-18

No one can lay any other foundation than the one we already have—Jesus Christ. 1 CORINTHIANS 3:11

Just as you accepted Christ Jesus as your Lord, you must continue to live in obedience to him.
   Don't let anyone lead you astray with empty philosophy and high-sounding nonsense that come from human thinking and from the evil powers of this world, and not from Christ. COLOSSIANS 2:6, 8

You have died with Christ, and he has set you free from the evil powers of this world. So why do you keep on following rules of the world, such as, "Don't handle, don't eat, don't touch." Such rules are mere human teaching about things that are gone as soon as we use them. These rules may seem wise because they require strong devotion, humility, and severe bodily discipline. But they have no effect when it comes to conquering a person's evil thoughts and desires. COLOSSIANS 2:20-23

Do not be attracted by strange, new ideas. Your spiritual strength comes from God's special favor, not from ceremonial rules about food, which don't help those who follow them. HEBREWS 13:9

These people are false apostles. They have fooled you by disguising themselves as apostles of Christ. But I am not surprised! Even Satan can disguise himself as an angel of light. So it is no wonder his servants can also do it by pretending to be godly ministers. In the end they will get every bit of punishment their wicked deeds deserve. 2 CORINTHIANS 11:13-15

Now the Holy Spirit tells us clearly that in the last times some will turn away from what we believe; they will follow lying spirits and teachings that come from demons. These teachers are hypocrites and liars. They pretend to be religious, but their consciences are dead.

They will say it is wrong to be married and wrong to eat certain foods. But God created those foods to be eaten with thanksgiving by people who know and believe the truth. 1 TIMOTHY 4:1-3

Some false teachers may deny these things, but these are the sound, wholesome teachings of the Lord Jesus Christ, and they are the foundation for a godly life. Anyone who teaches anything different is both conceited and ignorant. Such a person has an unhealthy desire to quibble over the meaning of words. This stirs up arguments ending in jealousy, fighting, slander, and evil suspicions. These people always cause trouble. Their minds are corrupt, and they don't tell the truth. 1 TIMOTHY 6:3-5

Evil people and impostors will flourish. They will go on deceiving others, and they themselves will be deceived. 2 TIMOTHY 3:13

A time is coming when people will no longer listen to right teaching. They will follow their own desires and will look for teachers who will tell them whatever they want to hear. They will reject the truth and follow strange myths.

But you should keep a clear mind in every situation. Don't be afraid of suffering for the Lord. Work at bringing others to Christ. Complete the ministry God has given you. 2 TIMOTHY 4:3-5

Some of the harshest words concerning false teachers are found in Peter's second letter. Here he condemned so-called "Christian teachers" who were leading people astray, not just in beliefs, but also in moral behavior. Then, as today, leaders calling themselves "Christians" were tossing morality out the window and taking pride in what they did.

There were also false prophets in Israel, just as there will be false teachers among you. They will cleverly teach their destructive heresies about God and even turn against their Master who bought them. Theirs will be a swift and terrible end. Many will follow their evil teaching and shameful immorality. And because of them, Christ and his true way will be slandered. . . . But God condemned them long ago, and their destruction is on the way.

For God did not spare even the angels when they sinned; he threw them into hell, in gloomy caves and darkness until the judgment day. . . .

So you see, the Lord knows how to rescue godly people from their trials, even while punishing the wicked right up until the day of judgment. He is especially hard on those who follow their own evil, lustful desires and who despise authority. These people are proud and arrogant, daring even to scoff at the glorious ones without so much as trembling. . . .

These false teachers are like unthinking animals, creatures of instinct, who are born to be caught and killed. They laugh at the terrifying powers they know so little about, and they will be destroyed along with them. Their destruction is their reward for the harm they have done. They love to indulge in evil pleasures in broad daylight. They are a disgrace and a stain among you. They revel in deceitfulness while they feast with you. They commit adultery with their eyes, and their lust is never satisfied. They make a game of luring unstable people into sin. . . .

These people are as useless as dried-up springs of water or as clouds blown away by the wind—promising much and delivering nothing. They are doomed to blackest darkness. They

brag about themselves with empty, foolish boasting. With lustful
desire as their bait, they lure back into sin those who have just
escaped from such wicked living. They promise freedom, but
they themselves are slaves to sin and corruption. For you are a
slave to whatever controls you. 2 PETER 2:1-19

You, my dear friends, must remember what the apostles of our
Lord Jesus Christ told you, that in the last times there would be
scoffers whose purpose in life is to enjoy themselves in every evil
way imaginable. Now they are here, and they are the ones who
are creating divisions among you. They live by natural instinct
because they do not have God's Spirit living in them. JUDE 17-19

> Is quarreling over beliefs always bad? Not at all. Paul recognized
> that a family feud within the Christian fellowship might serve a good
> purpose: bring false beliefs into the open so people could judge
> them. He knew that a united church is no good at all if it is united
> behind falsehood.

I hear that there are divisions among you when you meet as a
church, and to some extent I believe it. But, of course, there must
be divisions among you so that those of you who are right will be
recognized! 1 CORINTHIANS 11:18-19

> Jesus gave the world the memorable phrase about "wolves in
> sheep's clothing." It is a striking image of how deceptive false
> teachers can be. Yet Jesus assured his followers that false teachers
> do not have to go undetected. In fact, it is usually quite easy for the
> eye of faith to see false teaching for what it is.

Beware of false prophets who come disguised as harmless sheep,
but are really wolves that will tear you apart. You can detect them
by the way they act, just as you can identify a tree by its fruit. You
don't pick grapes from thornbushes, or figs from thistles. A
healthy tree produces good fruit, and an unhealthy tree produces

bad fruit. A good tree can't produce bad fruit, and a bad tree can't produce good fruit. So every tree that does not produce good fruit is chopped down and thrown into the fire. Yes, the way to identify a tree or a person is by the kind of fruit that is produced.
MATTHEW 7:15-20

Dear friends, do not believe everyone who claims to speak by the Spirit. You must test them to see if the spirit they have comes from God. For there are many false prophets in the world. . . . If a prophet does not acknowledge Jesus, that person is not from God. Such a person has the spirit of the Antichrist. You have heard that he is going to come into the world, and he is already here.

But you belong to God, my dear children. You have already won your fight with these false prophets, because the Spirit who lives in you is greater than the spirit who lives in the world. These people belong to this world, so they speak from the world's viewpoint, and the world listens to them. But we belong to God; that is why those who know God listen to us. If they do not belong to God, they do not listen to us. That is how we know if someone has the Spirit of truth or the spirit of deception. 1 JOHN 4:1-6

See also Wisdom and Discernment.

Fear

Franklin Roosevelt assured people that "we have nothing to fear but fear itself." The Bible makes an even bolder promise: We have *nothing* to fear, period.

This doesn't mean our life will be trouble-free—far from it. But the message of God's Word is that fear—of enemies, of the future, of failure, whatever—need not dominate our life and paralyze us. The reason we can be at peace is simple: God's presence with us.

Even when I walk through the dark valley of death, I will not be afraid, for you are close beside me. Your rod and your staff protect and comfort me.

You prepare a feast for me in the presence of my enemies. You welcome me as a guest, anointing my head with oil. My cup overflows with blessings. PSALM 23:4-5

The LORD is my light and my salvation—so why should I be afraid? The LORD protects me from danger—so why should I tremble?

When evil people come to destroy me, when my enemies and foes attack me, they will stumble and fall. Though a mighty army surrounds me, my heart will know no fear. Even if they attack me, I remain confident. PSALM 27:1-3

God is our refuge and strength, always ready to help in times of trouble. So we will not fear, even if earthquakes come and the mountains crumble into the sea. Let the oceans roar and foam. Let the mountains tremble as the waters surge!

A river brings joy to the city of our God, the sacred home of the Most High. God himself lives in that city; it cannot be destroyed. PSALM 46:1-5

He will shield you with his wings. He will shelter you with his feathers. His faithful promises are your armor and protection. Do not be afraid of the terrors of the night, nor fear the dangers of the day, nor dread the plague that stalks in darkness, nor the disaster that strikes at midday. PSALM 91:4-6

My child, don't lose sight of good planning and insight. Hang on to them, for they fill you with life and bring you honor and respect. They keep you safe on your way and keep your feet from stumbling. You can lie down without fear and enjoy pleasant dreams. You need not be afraid of disaster or the destruction that comes upon the wicked, for the LORD is your security. He will keep your foot from being caught in a trap. PROVERBS 3:21-26

Fearing people is a dangerous trap, but to trust the LORD means safety. PROVERBS 29:25

Don't be afraid, for I am with you. Do not be dismayed, for I am your God. I will strengthen you. I will help you. I will uphold you with my victorious right hand.

See, all your angry enemies lie there, confused and ashamed. Anyone who opposes you will die. You will look for them in vain. They will all be gone! I am holding you by your right hand—I, the

LORD your God. And I say to you, "Do not be afraid. I am here to help you." ISAIAH 41:10-13

The LORD who created you says: "Do not be afraid, for I have ransomed you. I have called you by name; you are mine. When you go through deep waters and great trouble, I will be with you. When you go through rivers of difficulty, you will not drown! When you walk through the fire of oppression, you will not be burned up; the flames will not consume you. For I am the LORD, your God, the Holy One of Israel, your Savior." ISAIAH 43:1-3

Sorrow and mourning will disappear, and they will be overcome with joy and gladness. I, even I, am the one who comforts you. So why are you afraid of mere humans, who wither like the grass and disappear? ISAIAH 51:11-12

Don't be afraid of those who want to kill you. They can only kill your body; they cannot touch your soul. Fear only God, who can destroy both soul and body in hell. MATTHEW 10:28

Don't worry about food—what to eat and drink. Don't worry whether God will provide it for you. These things dominate the thoughts of most people, but your Father already knows your needs. He will give you all you need from day to day if you make the Kingdom of God your primary concern.

So don't be afraid, little flock. For it gives your Father great happiness to give you the Kingdom. LUKE 12:29-32

I am leaving you with a gift—peace of mind and heart. And the peace I give isn't like the peace the world gives. So don't be troubled or afraid. JOHN 14:27

No, despite all these things, overwhelming victory is ours through Christ, who loved us.

And I am convinced that nothing can ever separate us from his love. Death can't, and life can't. The angels can't, and the demons can't. Our fears for today, our worries about tomorrow, and even the powers of hell can't keep God's love away. Whether we are high above the sky or in the deepest ocean, nothing in all creation will ever be able to separate us from the love of God that is revealed in Christ Jesus our Lord. ROMANS 8:37-39

Don't be afraid of what you are about to suffer. The Devil will throw some of you into prison and put you to the test. . . . Remain faithful even when facing death, and I will give you the crown of life. REVELATION 2:10

This is why I remind you to fan into flames the spiritual gift God gave you when I laid my hands on you. For God has not given us a spirit of fear and timidity, but of power, love, and self-discipline. 2 TIMOTHY 1:6-7

> The New Testament authors wrote about a great fear that can wreck the spiritual life: fear of God himself. The apostles' promise is plain enough: If we are truly born again, part of God's family, we need have no fear of him abandoning us or changing his mind.

All who are led by the Spirit of God are children of God.
So you should not be like cowering, fearful slaves. You should behave instead like God's very own children, adopted into his family—calling him "Father, dear Father." For his Holy Spirit speaks to us deep in our hearts and tells us that we are God's children. And since we are his children, we will share his treasures—for everything God gives to his Son, Christ, is ours, too. ROMANS 8:14-17

Because of Christ and our faith in him, we can now come fearlessly into God's presence, assured of his glad welcome.
EPHESIANS 3:12

As we live in God, our love grows more perfect. So we will not be afraid on the day of judgment, but we can face him with confidence because we are like Christ here in this world.

Such love has no fear because perfect love expels all fear. If we are afraid, it is for fear of judgment, and this shows that his love has not been perfected in us. 1 JOHN 4:17-18

See also Contentment, Hope, Worry and Anxiety.

Fellowship with God

The Bible reminds us again and again that God is a *personal* God—not some faraway, distant idea, but the Supreme Person, who actually enjoys the fellowship of his people. Unlike some of the cold, unapproachable gods of some religions, our God is approachable. He wants to be near us, and he wants our devotion and love.

The good news is, we don't have to wait for death to enjoy this. Fellowship with God begins now, and it continues forever and ever without end.

I will live among you, and I will not despise you. I will walk among you; I will be your God, and you will be my people.
LEVITICUS 26:11-12

We are telling you about what we ourselves have actually seen and heard, so that you may have fellowship with us. And our fellowship is with the Father and with his Son, Jesus Christ.

This is the message he has given us to announce to you: God is light and there is no darkness in him at all. So we are lying if we say we have fellowship with God but go on living in spiritual darkness. We are not living in the truth. But if we are living in the light of God's presence, just as Christ is, then we have fellowship with each other, and the blood of Jesus, his Son, cleanses us from every sin. 1 JOHN 1:3, 5-7

Where two or three gather together because they are mine, I am there among them. MATTHEW 18:20

Remain in me, and I will remain in you. For a branch cannot produce fruit if it is severed from the vine, and you cannot be fruitful apart from me.

Yes, I am the vine; you are the branches. Those who remain in me, and I in them, will produce much fruit. For apart from me you can do nothing.

But if you stay joined to me and my words remain in you, you may ask any request you like, and it will be granted! JOHN 15:4-5, 7

My prayer for all of them is that they will be one, just as you and I are one, Father—that just as you are in me and I am in you, so they will be in us, and the world will believe you sent me.

I have given them the glory you gave me, so that they may be one, as we are—I in them and you in me, all being perfected into one. Then the world will know that you sent me and will understand that you love them as much as you love me. Father, I want these whom you've given me to be with me, so they can see my glory. You gave me the glory because you loved me even before the world began!

O righteous Father, the world doesn't know you, but I do; and these disciples know you sent me. And I have revealed you to them and will keep on revealing you. I will do this so that your love for me may be in them and I in them. JOHN 17:21-26

Since Christ lives within you, even though your body will die because of sin, your spirit is alive because you have been made right with God.

And since we are his children, we will share his treasures—for everything God gives to his Son, Christ, is ours, too. But if we are to share his glory, we must also share his suffering.
ROMANS 8:10, 17

> The best kind of fellowship, far better than any human companionship, is fellowship with the one who made us and loves us. But the Bible doesn't portray God as some cosmic softy who doesn't care how we live our life. Like any good friend, and like the Father he is, he wants us to do right. We may not like the idea of obedience, but it's something that the Bible refuses to separate from the idea of fellowship. To love God and accept him as Father means being willing to accept his authority. It's that simple.

Jesus replied, "All those who love me will do what I say. My Father will love them, and we will come to them and live with them." JOHN 14:23

Those who obey God's commandments live in fellowship with him, and he with them. And we know he lives in us because the Holy Spirit lives in us. 1 JOHN 3:24

If you wander beyond the teaching of Christ, you will not have fellowship with God. But if you continue in the teaching of Christ, you will have fellowship with both the Father and the Son.
2 JOHN 1:9

> The word *heaven* conjures up images of harp playing and white robes—and boredom. People overlook the fact that fellowship with God is the great attraction of heaven. Just as one of life's greatest pleasures is pleasant company, so the next life will provide the greatest of company—God himself.

I heard a loud shout from the throne, saying, "Look, the home of God is now among his people! He will live with them, and they

will be his people. God himself will be with them. He will remove all of their sorrows, and there will be no more death or sorrow or crying or pain. For the old world and its evils are gone forever."
REVELATION 21:3-4

> The last book of the Bible, Revelation, contains one of the most stunning promises in the whole Bible. Jesus promises us that we will fellowship with him forever—not as his groveling slaves, but as friends.

Look! Here I stand at the door and knock. If you hear me calling and open the door, I will come in, and we will share a meal as friends. REVELATION 3:20

See also Eternal Life, Heaven, Loneliness, Prayer.

Fellowship with Other Believers

This chapter could have been titled "The Church." But the word *church* doesn't sound quite as alive or as dynamic as *fellowship*. A *church* can be a building or an institution. But a *fellowship* is a group of alive human beings, bonded together for some common purpose and enjoying each other's company.

There are no solitary Christians—the Bible makes it clear. We may *feel* alone without faith sometimes, but across the globe and across the centuries we are part of the living body of Christ. Part of the joy we are promised as believers is not just fellowship with God but also fellowship with other believers in our spiritual family.

When we bless the cup at the Lord's Table, aren't we sharing in the benefits of the blood of Christ? And when we break the loaf of bread, aren't we sharing in the benefits of the body of Christ? And we all eat from one loaf, showing that we are one body.

1 CORINTHIANS 10:16-17

Anyone who says, "I am in the light" but rejects another Christian is still in darkness. But anyone who loves other Christians is walking in the light and does not cause anyone to stumble. Those who reject other Christians are wandering in spiritual darkness and don't know where they are going, for the darkness has made them blind. 1 JOHN 2:9-11

If we love other Christians, it proves that we have passed from death to eternal life. But a person who doesn't love them is still dead. 1 JOHN 3:14

Let us not neglect our meeting together, as some people do, but encourage and warn each other, especially now that the day of his coming back again is drawing near. HEBREWS 10:25

We are telling you about what we ourselves have actually seen and heard, so that you may have fellowship with us. And our fellowship is with the Father and with his Son, Jesus Christ. 1 JOHN 1:3

Whenever we have the opportunity, we should do good to everyone, especially to our Christian brothers and sisters. GALATIANS 6:10

Show respect for everyone. Love your Christian brothers and sisters. 1 PETER 2:17

Why do you condemn another Christian? Why do you look down on another Christian? Remember, each of us will stand personally before the judgment seat of God. For the Scriptures say, "'As surely as I live,' says the Lord, 'every knee will bow to me and every tongue will confess allegiance to God.'" Yes, each of us will have to give a personal account to God. So don't condemn each other anymore. Decide instead to live in such a way that you will not put an obstacle in another Christian's path. ROMANS 14:10-13

So many social groups, including churches, gather together because it meets a basic human need: togetherness, the "warm fuzzy" feeling we all enjoy. But fellowship with believers goes beyond a temporary feel-good session together. It is easy to *say* that our group is a loving fellowship. But the Bible insists on putting all that love talk into practice. Fellowship with people we love often involves rolling up our sleeves to work.

All the believers met together constantly and shared everything they had. They sold their possessions and shared the proceeds with those in need. They worshiped together at the Temple each day, met in homes for the Lord's Supper, and shared their meals with great joy and generosity—all the while praising God and enjoying the goodwill of all the people. And each day the Lord added to their group those who were being saved. ACTS 2:44-47

Don't just pretend that you love others. Really love them. Hate what is wrong. Stand on the side of the good. Love each other with genuine affection, and take delight in honoring each other.

When God's children are in need, be the one to help them out. And get into the habit of inviting guests home for dinner or, if they need lodging, for the night.

When others are happy, be happy with them. If they are sad, share their sorrow. Live in harmony with each other. Don't try to act important, but enjoy the company of ordinary people. And don't think you know it all! ROMANS 12:9-10, 13, 15-16

All the believers were of one heart and mind, and they felt that what they owned was not their own; they shared everything they had. And the apostles gave powerful witness to the resurrection of the Lord Jesus, and God's great favor was upon them all. There was no poverty among them, because people who owned land or houses sold them and brought the money to the apostles to give to others in need. ACTS 4:32-35

Dear brothers and sisters, what's the use of saying you have faith if you don't prove it by your actions? That kind of faith can't save anyone. Suppose you see a brother or sister who needs food or clothing, and you say, "Well, good-bye and God bless you; stay warm and eat well"—but then you don't give that person any food or clothing. What good does that do?

So you see, it isn't enough just to have faith. Faith that doesn't show itself by good deeds is no faith at all—it is dead and useless. JAMES 2:14-17

Dear friends, if a Christian is overcome by some sin, you who are godly should gently and humbly help that person back onto the right path. And be careful not to fall into the same temptation yourself. Share each other's troubles and problems, and in this way obey the law of Christ. If you think you are too important to help someone in need, you are only fooling yourself. You are really a nobody. GALATIANS 6:1-3

Just as our bodies have many parts and each part has a special function, so it is with Christ's body. We are all parts of his one body, and each of us has different work to do. And since we are all one body in Christ, we belong to each other, and each of us needs all the others.

God has given each of us the ability to do certain things well. So if God has given you the ability to prophesy, speak out when you have faith that God is speaking through you. If your gift is that of serving others, serve them well. If you are a teacher, do a good job of teaching. If your gift is to encourage others, do it! If you have money, share it generously. If God has given you leadership ability, take the responsibility seriously. And if you have a gift for showing kindness to others, do it gladly. ROMANS 12:4-8

Quarrels were and are a familiar part of church life. Are they always bad? Paul didn't think so. In the important matter of separating false teaching from true, a dispute served a useful purpose:

I hear that there are divisions among you when you meet as a church, and to some extent I believe it. But, of course, there must be divisions among you so that those of you who are right will be recognized! 1 CORINTHIANS 11:18-19

> Still, most quarrels among believers (just like quarrels within families) are pointless. In fact, the family of God, like all human families, is at its best when each member stops his selfish whining and looks at how all the other members make a contribution. Paul, who understood how believers function (and sometimes *dys*function) as a family, also compared the fellowship of believers to something else: the human body.

We have all been baptized into Christ's body by one Spirit, and we have all received the same Spirit.

Yes, the body has many different parts, not just one part. If the foot says, "I am not a part of the body because I am not a hand," that does not make it any less a part of the body. And if the ear says, "I am not part of the body because I am only an ear and not an eye," would that make it any less a part of the body? Suppose the whole body were an eye—then how would you hear? Or if your whole body were just one big ear, how could you smell anything?

But God made our bodies with many parts, and he has put each part just where he wants it. What a strange thing a body would be if it had only one part! Yes, there are many parts, but only one body.

If one part suffers, all the parts suffer with it, and if one part is honored, all the parts are glad.

Now all of you together are Christ's body, and each one of you is a separate and necessary part of it. Here is a list of some of the members that God has placed in the body of Christ: first are apostles, second are prophets, third are teachers, then those who do miracles, those who have the gift of healing, those who can help others, those who can get others to work together, those who speak in unknown languages. Is everyone an apostle? Of course not. Is everyone a prophet? No. Are all teachers? Does everyone have the power to do miracles? Does everyone have the gift of healing? Of course not. Does God give all of us the ability to speak in unknown languages? Can everyone interpret unknown languages? No! And in any event, you should desire the most helpful gifts. 1 CORINTHIANS 12:13-20, 26-31

See also Bad Company, Fellowship with God, Friends, Loneliness, Temptation.

Food

Does this seem like an odd topic for a book like this? It shouldn't. Think of how food dominates people's thoughts. It seems half the conversations today revolve around calories, cholesterol, fat, and nutrition. Many claim to feel guilt over eating chocolate or donuts. Restaurants advertise rich desserts as "decadent" and "sinfully rich." Have we devised a new morality based on food consumption?

The book of Proverbs, so full of practical advice, gives a blunt commandment regarding people in love with food:

If you are a big eater, put a knife to your throat. PROVERBS 23:2

In fact, this pretty much summarizes the Bible's view. The Bible isn't literally recommending that people who love food should slit their throats. It is saying that they have a serious problem that needs attention. They are trying to find satisfaction in food, and for the believer, our ultimate satisfaction is in God.

Still, it is a consolation that the Bible gives us a lot of leeway in regard to food. We aren't supposed to make it our god, but we are free to enjoy it. If you've been beating yourself about what you eat and drink, you will be happy to find that the Bible's attitude toward food is radically different from our society's. While gluttony and drunkenness are condemned, the attitude toward food in general is: Eat, and enjoy the good gifts of God.

I know and am perfectly sure on the authority of the Lord Jesus that no food, in and of itself, is wrong to eat.

For the Kingdom of God is not a matter of what we eat or drink, but of living a life of goodness and peace and joy in the Holy Spirit. ROMANS 14:14, 17

Don't let anyone condemn you for what you eat or drink. . . . Don't let anyone condemn you by insisting on self-denial. . . . These people claim to be so humble, but their sinful minds have made them proud. But they are not connected to Christ, the head of the body. For we are joined together in his body by his strong sinews, and we grow only as we get our nourishment and strength from God.

You have died with Christ, and he has set you free from the evil powers of this world. So why do you keep on following rules of the world, such as, "Don't handle, don't eat, don't touch." Such rules are mere human teaching about things that are gone as soon as we use them. These rules may seem wise because they require strong devotion, humility, and severe bodily discipline. But they have no effect when it comes to conquering a person's evil thoughts and desires. COLOSSIANS 2:16-23

Now the Holy Spirit tells us clearly that in the last times some will turn away from what we believe; they will follow lying spirits and teachings that come from demons.

They will say it is wrong to be married and wrong to eat certain foods. But God created those foods to be eaten with thanksgiving by people who know and believe the truth. Since everything God created is good, we should not reject any of it. We may receive it gladly, with thankful hearts. For we know it is made holy by the word of God and prayer. 1 TIMOTHY 4:1, 3-5

Everything is pure to those whose hearts are pure. But nothing is pure to those who are corrupt and unbelieving, because their minds and consciences are defiled. TITUS 1:15

Eat your food and drink your wine with a happy heart, for God approves of this! ECCLESIASTES 9:7

If I can thank God for the food and enjoy it, why should I be condemned for eating it? Whatever you eat or drink or whatever you do, you must do all for the glory of God.
1 CORINTHIANS 10:30-31

See also The Body, Worldly Cares, Worry and Anxiety.

Forgiving Others

An often-quoted line of poetry is Alexander Pope's "To err is human, to forgive divine." Pope caught the essence of the Bible's message. God forgives us, and if we are his people, his children, we must be forgiving also. There is no way around this. Grudges have no place in the Christian life. Just as we desperately need God's forgiveness of our failings, so we desperately need to forgive those who fail us.

People with good sense restrain their anger; they earn esteem by overlooking wrongs. PROVERBS 19:11

Don't say, "I will get even for this wrong." Wait for the LORD to handle the matter. PROVERBS 20:22

God blesses those who are merciful, for they will be shown mercy. Don't resist an evil person! If you are slapped on the right cheek, turn the other, too. If you are ordered to court and your shirt is taken from you, give your coat, too. If a soldier demands that you carry his gear for a mile, carry it two miles. Give to those who ask, and don't turn away from those who want to borrow.

You have heard that the law of Moses says, "Love your neighbor" and hate your enemy. But I say, love your enemies! Pray for those who persecute you! In that way, you will be acting as true children of your Father in heaven. For he gives his sunlight to both the evil and the good, and he sends rain on the just and on the unjust, too. If you love only those who love you, what good is that? Even corrupt tax collectors do that much. If you are kind only to your friends, how are you different from anyone else? Even pagans do that. MATTHEW 5:7, 39-47

If you forgive those who sin against you, your heavenly Father will forgive you. But if you refuse to forgive others, your Father will not forgive your sins. MATTHEW 6:14-15

Listen to me! You can pray for anything, and if you believe, you will have it. But when you are praying, first forgive anyone you are holding a grudge against, so that your Father in heaven will forgive your sins, too.

But if you do not forgive, neither will your Father who is in heaven forgive your sins. MARK 11:24-26

Love your enemies! Do good to them! Lend to them! And don't be concerned that they might not repay. Then your reward from heaven will be very great, and you will truly be acting as children of the Most High, for he is kind to the unthankful and to those who are wicked. You must be compassionate, just as your Father is compassionate.

Stop judging others, and you will not be judged. Stop criticizing others, or it will all come back on you. If you forgive others, you will be forgiven. LUKE 6:35-37

If people persecute you because you are a Christian, don't curse them; pray that God will bless them. . . . Never pay back evil for evil to anyone. Do things in such a way that everyone can see you are honorable. . . .

Dear friends, never avenge yourselves. Leave that to God. For it is written, "I will take vengeance; I will repay those who deserve it," says the Lord. Instead, do what the Scriptures say: "If your enemies are hungry, feed them. If they are thirsty, give them something to drink, and they will be ashamed of what they have done to you." Don't let evil get the best of you, but conquer evil by doing good. ROMANS 12:14, 17, 19-21

You must make allowance for each other's faults and forgive the person who offends you. Remember, the Lord forgave you, so you must forgive others. COLOSSIANS 3:13

> Forgiveness is something we owe everyone—but especially the people we call our brothers and sisters in the faith. They should be shown special kindness, and grudges and ongoing fights have no place in the church.

I am warning you! If another believer sins, rebuke him; then if he repents, forgive him. Even if he wrongs you seven times a day and each time turns again and asks forgiveness, forgive him. LUKE 17:3-4

Get rid of all bitterness, rage, anger, harsh words, and slander, as well as all types of malicious behavior. Instead, be kind to each other, tenderhearted, forgiving one another, just as God through Christ has forgiven you. EPHESIANS 4:31-32

See also Anger, Enemies, Mercy, Revenge.

Freedom

Freedom can mean so many things. To many people it means throwing off political tyranny. To some it means tossing aside all moral restraints. To others it means a total absence of responsibilities.

Most people probably agree that *freedom* essentially means "being the kind of people we are meant to be." That is exactly the kind of freedom the Bible promises. But according to the Bible, the thing that keeps us from being the kind of people we are meant to be is ourselves. Or, to use a word that has gone out of style, *sin.* The Bible locates our lack of freedom in our own heart. Bound by our own selfishness, our pride, our sense of lacking purpose, we are not free—not until something, or someone, shows us the way out.

According to the Bible, that someone is Christ. The kind of freedom promised is not political, but it is possible to have Christ's freedom under any form of government. Christ's freedom is not freedom from morality but freedom to live for something higher than rules. It is freedom to be good, great, joyous, beautiful in spirit, kind, even able to forget ourselves.

You will know the truth, and the truth will set you free.
So if the Son sets you free, you will indeed be free. JOHN 8:32, 36

You are not slaves; you are free. But your freedom is not an excuse to do evil. You are free to live as God's slaves. Show respect for everyone. Love your Christian brothers and sisters. 1 PETER 2:16-17

God in his gracious kindness declares us not guilty. He has done this through Christ Jesus, who has freed us by taking away our sins. ROMANS 3:24

We died and were buried with Christ by baptism. And just as Christ was raised from the dead by the glorious power of the Father, now we also may live new lives.
Since we have been united with him in his death, we will also be raised as he was. Our old sinful selves were crucified with Christ so that sin might lose its power in our lives. We are no longer slaves to sin. For when we died with Christ we were set free from the power of sin. And since we died with Christ, we know we will also share his new life.
Sin is no longer your master, for you are no longer subject to the law, which enslaves you to sin. Instead, you are free by God's grace.
Don't you realize that whatever you choose to obey becomes your master? You can choose sin, which leads to death, or you can choose to obey God and receive his approval. Thank God! Once you were slaves of sin, but now you have obeyed with all your heart the new teaching God has given you. Now you are free from sin, your old master, and you have become slaves to your new master, righteousness. ROMANS 6:4-8, 14, 16-18

If you will help me, I will run to follow your commands. PSALM 119:32

I love God's law with all my heart. But there is another law at
work within me that is at war with my mind. This law wins the
fight and makes me a slave to the sin that is still within me. Oh,
what a miserable person I am! Who will free me from this life that
is dominated by sin? Thank God! The answer is in Jesus Christ
our Lord. So you see how it is: In my mind I really want to obey
God's law, but because of my sinful nature I am a slave to sin.
ROMANS 7:22-25

In my distress I prayed to the LORD, and the LORD answered me
and rescued me. PSALM 118:5

Oh, what joy for those whose rebellion is forgiven, whose sin is
put out of sight! Yes, what joy for those whose record the LORD
has cleared of sin, whose lives are lived in complete honesty!
PSALM 32:1-2

All creation is waiting eagerly for that future day when God will
reveal who his children really are. Against its will, everything on
earth was subjected to God's curse. All creation anticipates the
day when it will join God's children in glorious freedom from
death and decay. ROMANS 8:19-21

Now, the Lord is the Spirit, and wherever the Spirit of the Lord is,
he gives freedom. 2 CORINTHIANS 3:17

So Christ has really set us free. Now make sure that you stay free,
and don't get tied up again in slavery to the law. GALATIANS 5:1

You, dear friends, have been called to live in freedom—not
freedom to satisfy your sinful nature, but freedom to serve one
another in love. For the whole law can be summed up in this one
command: "Love your neighbor as yourself." GALATIANS 5:13-14

Just as you accepted Christ Jesus as your Lord, you must continue
to live in obedience to him.

Don't let anyone lead you astray with empty philosophy and
high-sounding nonsense that come from human thinking and
from the evil powers of this world, and not from Christ.
COLOSSIANS 2:6, 8

You have died with Christ, and he has set you free from the evil
powers of this world. So why do you keep on following rules of
the world, such as, "Don't handle, don't eat, don't touch." Such
rules are mere human teaching about things that are gone as soon
as we use them. These rules may seem wise because they require
strong devotion, humility, and severe bodily discipline. But they
have no effect when it comes to conquering a person's evil
thoughts and desires. COLOSSIANS 2:20-23

If you keep looking steadily into God's perfect law—the law that
sets you free—and if you do what it says and don't forget what
you heard, then God will bless you for doing it. JAMES 1:25

Whenever you speak, or whatever you do, remember that you
will be judged by the law of love, the law that set you free.
JAMES 2:12

*See also Contentment, Sin and Redemption, Temptation, Worldly Cares, Worry
and Anxiety.*

Friends

If loneliness is a problem in the modern world (and it is, definitely), friendship ought to be highly valued. It is, but many struggle with a "loyalty gap"—the feeling that relationships (marriage, friendship, employer-employee, etc.) are temporary at best, to be dissolved whenever one feels like it. This situation isn't new, as this verse makes clear:

Many will say they are loyal friends, but who can find one who is really faithful? PROVERBS 20:6

Of course, the Bible gives some examples of "really faithful" friends. The classic example is that Old Testament pair, David and Jonathan.

After David had finished talking with Saul, he met Jonathan, the king's son. There was an immediate bond of love between them, and they became the best of friends. . . . And Jonathan made a special vow to be David's friend, and he sealed the pact by giving him his robe, tunic, sword, bow, and belt. 1 SAMUEL 18:1-4

Touching and beautiful—but all too rare. We value our friends, yet all too often find ourselves puzzling over why friendships end instead of endure. The great English author Samuel Johnson, who loved company and valued his friends, stated that "a man, sir, should keep his friendships in constant repair."

The Bible is primarily concerned with our relationship to God—our greatest and most faithful friend—yet it has much to say about friends and keeping friendships in "constant repair." The book of Proverbs in particular is an excellent "Friendship Repair Manual."

A friend is always loyal, and a brother is born to help in time of need. PROVERBS 17:17

There are "friends" who destroy each other, but a real friend sticks closer than a brother. PROVERBS 18:24

Wounds from a friend are better than many kisses from an enemy.
The heartfelt counsel of a friend is as sweet as perfume and incense.
Never abandon a friend—either yours or your father's. Then in your time of need, you won't have to ask your relatives for assistance.
As iron sharpens iron, a friend sharpens a friend.
PROVERBS 27:6, 9-10, 17

It's harder to make amends with an offended friend than to capture a fortified city. Arguments separate friends like a gate locked with iron bars. PROVERBS 18:19

Don't visit your neighbors too often, or you will wear out your welcome. PROVERBS 25:17

Proverbs is "pro-friendship" but makes it clear that bad companions are worse than no friends at all.

The godly give good advice to their friends; the wicked lead them astray. PROVERBS 12:26

Keep away from angry, short-tempered people, or you will learn to be like them and endanger your soul. PROVERBS 22:24-25

Wicked people are an abomination to the LORD, but he offers his friendship to the godly. PROVERBS 3:32

> The New Testament introduces something new in the concept of friendship: Jesus' followers are not just pupils or servants but *friends.* As such, they are (or should be) friends of all other believers. *Love,* something almost always associated with man-woman or parent-child relationships, becomes key in the whole notion of friendship.

I command you to love each other in the same way that I love you. And here is how to measure it—the greatest love is shown when people lay down their lives for their friends. You are my friends if you obey me. I no longer call you servants, because a master doesn't confide in his servants. Now you are my friends, since I have told you everything the Father told me. JOHN 15:12-15

We know what real love is because Christ gave up his life for us. And so we also ought to give up our lives for our Christian friends. 1 JOHN 3:16

> In the Bible, *church* refers to a *community* of brothers and sisters in the faith—in other words, friends—not to a building. This doesn't mean every Christian is going to be the best friend and companion of every other Christian. It does mean we have a stake in each other's welfare. We are both friends and family.

Think of ways to encourage one another to outbursts of love and good deeds. And let us not neglect our meeting together, as

some people do, but encourage and warn each other, especially now that the day of his coming back again is drawing near.
HEBREWS 10:24-25

I don't need to write to you about the Christian love that should be shown among God's people. For God himself has taught you to love one another. Indeed, your love is already strong toward all the Christians. . . . Even so, dear friends, we beg you to love them more and more. 1 THESSALONIANS 4:9-10

Finally, all of you should be of one mind, full of sympathy toward each other, loving one another with tender hearts and humble minds. Don't repay evil for evil. Don't retaliate when people say unkind things about you. Instead, pay them back with a blessing. That is what God wants you to do, and he will bless you for it.
1 PETER 3:8-9

Continue to love each other with true Christian love. Don't forget to show hospitality to strangers, for some who have done this have entertained angels without realizing it! Don't forget about those in prison. Suffer with them as though you were there yourself. Share the sorrow of those being mistreated, as though you feel their pain in your own bodies. HEBREWS 13:1-3

> The Letter of James is the Bible's "practice what you preach" book. James pulled no punches in reminding Christians that all talk about love, faithfulness, and Christian community is wasted unless we actually *show* love to Christian brothers and sisters.

Dear brothers and sisters, what's the use of saying you have faith if you don't prove it by your actions? That kind of faith can't save anyone. Suppose you see a brother or sister who needs food or clothing, and you say, "Well, good-bye and God bless you; stay warm and eat well"—but then you don't give that person any food or clothing. What good does that do?

So you see, it isn't enough just to have faith. Faith that doesn't show itself by good deeds is no faith at all—it is dead and useless. JAMES 2:14-17

James made it clear (as does the book of Proverbs) that nothing harms friendship and community more than that small, deadly part of the body, the tongue.

Don't grumble about each other, my brothers and sisters, or God will judge you. For look! The great Judge is coming. He is standing at the door! JAMES 5:9

Evil words destroy one's friends; wise discernment rescues the godly. PROVERBS 11:9

A troublemaker plants seeds of strife; gossip separates the best of friends. PROVERBS 16:28

Disregarding another person's faults preserves love; telling about them separates close friends. PROVERBS 17:9

Just as damaging as a mad man shooting a lethal weapon is someone who lies to a friend and then says, "I was only joking." PROVERBS 26:18-19

James also emphasized the greatest quality in friendship or any human relationship: forgiveness and mercy.

My dear brothers and sisters, if anyone among you wanders away from the truth and is brought back again, you can be sure that the one who brings that person back will save that sinner from death and bring about the forgiveness of many sins. JAMES 5:19-20

See also Bad Company, Fellowship with God, Fellowship with Other Believers, Loneliness.

Generosity

The biblical view of generosity was neatly summarized by Winston Churchill: "We make a living by what we get, but we make a life by what we give." The Bible makes no bones about this: Good people are generous. A person of faith is a giver—not only of money, but of time, of energy, of himself. There are no promises of present or future peace to people who are stingy with their possessions or with themselves.

Good people will be generous to others and will be blessed for all they do. ISAIAH 32:8

It is sin to despise one's neighbors; blessed are those who help the poor. PROVERBS 14:21

A curse will come upon those who close their eyes to poverty. PROVERBS 28:27

Give generously, for your gifts will return to you later. Divide your gifts among many, for you do not know what risks might lie ahead. ECCLESIASTES 11:1-2

If there are any poor people in your towns when you arrive in the land the LORD your God is giving you, do not be hard-hearted or tightfisted toward them. Instead, be generous and lend them whatever they need. Do not be mean-spirited and refuse someone a loan because the year of release is close at hand. If you refuse to make the loan and the needy person cries out to the LORD, you will be considered guilty of sin. Give freely without begrudging it, and the LORD your God will bless you in everything you do.

DEUTERONOMY 15:7-10

If you give, you will receive. Your gift will return to you in full measure, pressed down, shaken together to make room for more, and running over. Whatever measure you use in giving—large or small—it will be used to measure what is given back to you.

LUKE 6:38

I tell you, use your worldly resources to benefit others and make friends. In this way, your generosity stores up a reward for you in heaven. LUKE 16:9

> A key point in the Bible is that everything in our life comes from God. It is only appropriate that he tells us bluntly what to do with what we have.

Honor the LORD with your wealth and with the best part of everything your land produces. PROVERBS 3:9

> The expression "cheerful giver" comes from the Bible. In the following passage, Paul emphasizes that the act of giving, which is a good deed, needs to flow from a generous heart also. It is good to do the deed, but it is even better when it is done willingly, not just from a sense of duty.

Remember this—a farmer who plants only a few seeds will get a small crop. But the one who plants generously will get a generous crop. You must each make up your own mind as to how much you should give. Don't give reluctantly or in response to pressure. For God loves the person who gives cheerfully. And God will generously provide all you need. Then you will always have everything you need and plenty left over to share with others. . . . God is the one who gives seed to the farmer and then bread to eat. In the same way, he will give you many opportunities to do good, and he will produce a great harvest of generosity in you.

Yes, you will be enriched so that you can give even more generously. And when we take your gifts to those who need them, they will break out in thanksgiving to God.
2 CORINTHIANS 9:6-11

God is not unfair. He will not forget how hard you have worked for him and how you have shown your love to him by caring for other Christians, as you still do.   HEBREWS 6:10

It is possible to give freely and become more wealthy, but those who are stingy will lose everything.

The generous prosper and are satisfied; those who refresh others will themselves be refreshed.   PROVERBS 11:24-25

If you help the poor, you are lending to the LORD—and he will repay you!   PROVERBS 19:17

Blessed are those who are generous, because they feed the poor.
PROVERBS 22:9

> Jesus knew that some people are seemingly generous because they want to be admired, not because they really care for others. He warned against this, assuring his followers that the best acts of generosity were done for their own sake, not to win applause.

Take care! Don't do your good deeds publicly, to be admired, because then you will lose the reward from your Father in heaven.

When you give a gift to someone in need, don't shout about it as the hypocrites do—blowing trumpets in the synagogues and streets to call attention to their acts of charity! I assure you, they have received all the reward they will ever get. But when you give to someone, don't tell your left hand what your right hand is doing. Give your gifts in secret, and your Father, who knows all secrets, will reward you. MATTHEW 6:1-4

> Jesus followed this same thought in his parable of the Last Judgment. He promises that the judgment will bring surprise for many people. Those who are truly generous will be surprised—because they acted from a generous heart, not to win a reward or score points with God.

When the Son of Man comes in his glory, and all the angels with him, then he will sit upon his glorious throne. All the nations will be gathered in his presence, and he will separate them as a shepherd separates the sheep from the goats. He will place the sheep at his right hand and the goats at his left. Then the King will say to those on the right, "Come, you who are blessed by my Father, inherit the Kingdom prepared for you from the foundation of the world. For I was hungry, and you fed me. I was thirsty, and you gave me a drink. I was a stranger, and you invited me into your home. I was naked, and you gave me clothing. I was sick, and you cared for me. I was in prison, and you visited me."

Then these righteous ones will reply, "Lord, when did we ever see you hungry and feed you? Or thirsty and give you something to drink? Or a stranger and show you hospitality? Or naked and give you clothing? When did we ever see you sick or in prison, and visit you?" And the King will tell them, "I assure you, when you did it to one of the least of these my brothers and sisters, you were doing it to me!"

Then the King will turn to those on the left and say, "Away with you, you cursed ones, into the eternal fire prepared for the Devil and his demons! For I was hungry, and you didn't feed me. I was thirsty, and you didn't give me anything to drink. I was a stranger, and you didn't invite me into your home. I was naked, and you gave me no clothing. I was sick and in prison, and you didn't visit me."

Then they will reply, "Lord, when did we ever see you hungry or thirsty or a stranger or naked or sick or in prison, and not help you?"

And he will answer, "I assure you, when you refused to help the least of these my brothers and sisters, you were refusing to help me." And they will go away into eternal punishment, but the righteous will go into eternal life. MATTHEW 25:31-46

Love your enemies! Do good to them! Lend to them! And don't be concerned that they might not repay. Then your reward from heaven will be very great, and you will truly be acting as children of the Most High, for he is kind to the unthankful and to those who are wicked. You must be compassionate, just as your Father is compassionate. LUKE 6:35-36

> Do we have to be rich to be generous? Hardly. Jesus commended those who had little to give but who gave generously anyway.

While Jesus was in the Temple, he watched the rich people putting their gifts into the collection box. Then a poor widow came by and dropped in two pennies. "I assure you," he said, "this poor widow has given more than all the rest of them. For they have given a tiny part of their surplus, but she, poor as she is, has given everything she has." LUKE 21:1-4

Then [Jesus] turned to his host. "When you put on a luncheon or a dinner," he said, "don't invite your friends, brothers, relatives, and rich neighbors. For they will repay you by inviting you back. Instead, invite the poor, the crippled, the lame, and the blind. Then at the resurrection of the godly, God will reward you for inviting those who could not repay you." LUKE 14:12-14

Tell those who are rich in this world not to be proud and not to trust in their money, which will soon be gone. But their trust should be in the living God, who richly gives us all we need for our enjoyment. Tell them to use their money to do good. They should be rich in good works and should give generously to those in need, always being ready to share with others whatever God has given them. By doing this they will be storing up their treasure as a good foundation for the future so that they may take hold of real life. 1 TIMOTHY 6:17-19

> "Charity begins at home" is an old cliché but a true one. The Bible agrees that we should take care of our own families. And, the Bible extends that to include our "faith family" of fellow Christians.

If one of you has enough money to live well, and sees a brother or sister in need and refuses to help—how can God's love be in that person? 1 JOHN 3:17

Whenever we have the opportunity, we should do good to everyone, especially to our Christian brothers and sisters. GALATIANS 6:10

Those who won't care for their own relatives, especially those living in the same household, have denied what we believe. Such people are worse than unbelievers. 1 TIMOTHY 5:8

See also Duty to the Poor, Kindness, Money.

God as Judge

*J*udgmental has become a dirty word in our day as we are pressed to be "open-minded" and "accepting." Small wonder people don't like the idea of God as the cosmic Judge who keeps account of our deeds. But the idea ought to give us comfort. It reminds us that our actions and our words matter. Would we really be faithful people if we thought of God as a big softy who pays no mind to our behavior?

We cannot imagine the power of the Almighty, yet he is so just and merciful that he does not oppress us. No wonder people everywhere fear him. People who are truly wise show him reverence. JOB 37:23-24

Unfailing love, O Lord, is yours. Surely you judge all people according to what they have done. PSALM 62:12

People may be pure in their own eyes, but the LORD examines their motives. PROVERBS 16:2

People may think they are doing what is right, but the LORD examines the heart.

The LORD is more pleased when we do what is just and right than when we give him sacrifices. PROVERBS 21:2-3

God will judge us for everything we do, including every secret thing, whether good or bad. ECCLESIASTES 12:14

The human heart is most deceitful and desperately wicked. Who really knows how bad it is? But I know! I, the LORD, search all hearts and examine secret motives. I give all people their due rewards, according to what their actions deserve.
JEREMIAH 17:9-10

How do you benefit if you gain the whole world but lose your own soul in the process? Is anything worth more than your soul? For I, the Son of Man, will come in the glory of my Father with his angels and will judge all people according to their deeds.
MATTHEW 16:26-27

God is not unfair. He will not forget how hard you have worked for him and how you have shown your love to him by caring for other Christians, as you still do. HEBREWS 6:10

You may be saying, "What terrible people you have been talking about!" But you are just as bad, and you have no excuse! When you say they are wicked and should be punished, you are condemning yourself, for you do these very same things. And we know that God, in his justice, will punish anyone who does such things. Do you think that God will judge and condemn others for doing them and not judge you when you do them, too? Don't you realize how kind, tolerant, and patient God is with you? Or don't you care? Can't you see how kind he has been in giving you time to turn from your sin? ROMANS 2:1-4

Have I been faithful? Well, it matters very little what you or
anyone else thinks. I don't even trust my own judgment on this
point. My conscience is clear, but that isn't what matters. It is the
Lord himself who will examine me and decide.

So be careful not to jump to conclusions before the Lord returns
as to whether or not someone is faithful. When the Lord comes, he
will bring our deepest secrets to light and will reveal our private
motives. And then God will give to everyone whatever praise is
due. 1 CORINTHIANS 4:3-5

If we examine ourselves, we will not be examined by God and
judged in this way. But when we are judged and disciplined by
the Lord, we will not be condemned with the world.
1 CORINTHIANS 11:31-32

Remember that the heavenly Father to whom you pray has no
favorites when he judges. He will judge or reward you according
to what you do. So you must live in reverent fear of him during
your time as foreigners here on earth. 1 PETER 1:17

As we live in God, our love grows more perfect. So we will not be
afraid on the day of judgment, but we can face him with
confidence because we are like Christ here in this world.

Such love has no fear because perfect love expels all fear. If we
are afraid, it is for fear of judgment, and this shows that his love
has not been perfected in us. 1 JOHN 4:17-18

A good person produces good words from a good heart, and an
evil person produces evil words from an evil heart. And I tell you
this, that you must give an account on judgment day of every idle
word you speak. The words you say now reflect your fate then;
either you will be justified by them or you will be condemned.
MATTHEW 12:35-37

Knowing that God is the great Judge gives another kind of comfort: the security of knowing that the injustice in this world will not go unpunished forever. If God is not a judge—the only completely fair judge in the universe—then who will bring justice to innocent people?

End the wickedness of the ungodly, but help all those who obey you. For you look deep within the mind and heart, O righteous God. PSALM 7:9

At last everyone will say, "There truly is a reward for those who live for God; surely there is a God who judges justly here on earth." PSALM 58:11

The Lord knows how to rescue godly people from their trials, even while punishing the wicked right up until the day of judgment. 2 PETER 2:9

We must all stand before Christ to be judged. We will each receive whatever we deserve for the good or evil we have done in our bodies. 2 CORINTHIANS 5:10

It is destined that each person dies only once and after that comes judgment. HEBREWS 9:27

God has also commanded that the heavens and the earth will be consumed by fire on the day of judgment, when ungodly people will perish.

But you must not forget, dear friends, that a day is like a thousand years to the Lord, and a thousand years is like a day. The Lord isn't really being slow about his promise to return, as some people think. No, he is being patient for your sake. He does not want anyone to perish, so he is giving more time for everyone to repent. 2 PETER 3:7-9

The Bible reminds us again and again that God is in charge of the universe, and he alone is fit to be Judge. This ought to make us aware that we should leave the judging to God.

It isn't my responsibility to judge outsiders, but it certainly is your job to judge those inside the church who are sinning in these ways. God will judge those on the outside; but as the Scriptures say, "You must remove the evil person from among you." 1 CORINTHIANS 5:12-13

Don't grumble about each other, my brothers and sisters, or God will judge you. For look! The great Judge is coming. He is standing at the door! JAMES 5:9

Your former friends are very surprised when you no longer join them in the wicked things they do, and they say evil things about you. But just remember that they will have to face God, who will judge everyone, both the living and the dead. 1 PETER 4:4-5

The Bible ends with John's vision of the Last Judgment in the book of Revelation. Some have called this a gruesome vision, but it is only gruesome if we have some reason to fear God's judgment.

I saw a great white throne, and I saw the one who was sitting on it. The earth and sky fled from his presence, but they found no place to hide. I saw the dead, both great and small, standing before God's throne. And the books were opened, including the Book of Life. And the dead were judged according to the things written in the books, according to what they had done. . . . And death and the grave were thrown into the lake of fire. This is the second death—the lake of fire. And anyone whose name was not found recorded in the Book of Life was thrown into the lake of fire. REVELATION 20:11-15

See also God's Fairness, God's Mercy.

God's Concern for the Poor

Throughout history, the poor of this world have been ignored at best and victimized at worst. In our day, they continue to feel like a political football as politicians and taxpayers fight over government aid and social programs. Above the fray, the Bible reminds us that these people are not political pawns, nor are they nobodies. They are special objects of God's attention, and even if they are forgotten by their fellow human beings, they are not forgotten by the Father.

The LORD hears the cries of his needy ones; he does not despise his people who are oppressed.   PSALM 69:33

He will rescue the poor when they cry to him; he will help the oppressed, who have no one to defend them. He feels pity for the weak and the needy, and he will rescue them. He will save them from oppression and from violence, for their lives are precious to him.   PSALM 72:12-14

He will listen to the prayers of the destitute. He will not reject their pleas.   PSALM 102:17

He satisfies the thirsty and fills the hungry with good things. But he rescues the poor from their distress and increases their families like vast flocks of sheep. PSALM 107:9, 41

He stands beside the needy, ready to save them from those who condemn them. PSALM 109:31

He lifts the poor from the dirt and the needy from the garbage dump. PSALM 113:7

I know the LORD will surely help those they persecute; he will maintain the rights of the poor. PSALM 140:12

Do not rob the poor because they are poor or exploit the needy in court. For the LORD is their defender. He will injure anyone who injures them. PROVERBS 22:22-23

When the poor and needy search for water and there is none, and their tongues are parched from thirst, then I, the LORD, will answer them. I, the God of Israel, will never forsake them. ISAIAH 41:17

Listen to me, dear brothers and sisters. Hasn't God chosen the poor in this world to be rich in faith? Aren't they the ones who will inherit the kingdom God promised to those who love him? JAMES 2:5

See also Duty to the Poor.

God's Fairness

Have you ever been unfairly passed over for a promotion, for a job, for anything? Most people have. Sometimes it seems unfair to the person passed over, while the person making the judgment may have felt it was a fair decision. But the sad truth is, there is injustice in the world. Some people play favorites, and others can be bribed and blackmailed. And, it's not unheard of for Christians to be unjustly treated for their beliefs.

While there is not much justice in this world, there is complete justice with our heavenly Father. He is totally impartial.

The LORD your God is the God of gods and Lord of lords. He is the great God, mighty and awesome, who shows no partiality and takes no bribes. He gives justice to orphans and widows. He shows love to the foreigners living among you and gives them food and clothing. DEUTERONOMY 10:17-18

God is mighty, yet he does not despise anyone! He is mighty in both power and understanding. JOB 36:5

Peter replied, "I see very clearly that God doesn't show partiality. In every nation he accepts those who fear him and do what is right." ACTS 10:34-35

> We should be thankful that God is impartial. We should also be terrified if our life isn't as it should be. Several New Testament passages promise that our wrongs will be judged, with no favoritism shown. God does not play favorites with the wealthy, the educated, the attractive, or even regular churchgoers. He is merciful to all, but he is also the fair judge of all.

There is going to come a day of judgment when God, the just judge of all the world, will judge all people according to what they have done. He will give eternal life to those who persist in doing what is good, seeking after the glory and honor and immortality that God offers. But he will pour out his anger and wrath on those who live for themselves, who refuse to obey the truth and practice evil deeds. There will be trouble and calamity for everyone who keeps on sinning—for the Jew first and also for the Gentile. But there will be glory and honor and peace from God for all who do good—for the Jew first and also for the Gentile. For God does not show favoritism.
ROMANS 2:5-11

Remember that the Lord will reward each one of us for the good we do, whether we are slaves or free.
And in the same way, you masters must treat your slaves right. Don't threaten them; remember, you both have the same Master in heaven, and he has no favorites. EPHESIANS 6:8-9

If you do what is wrong, you will be paid back for the wrong you have done. For God has no favorites who can get away with evil.
COLOSSIANS 3:25

Remember that the heavenly Father to whom you pray has no favorites when he judges. He will judge or reward you according to what you do. So you must live in reverent fear of him during your time as foreigners here on earth. 1 PETER 1:17

See also Forgiving Others, God as Judge, Revenge.

God's Guidance

There is no lack of experts in the world. Many TV and radio broadcasts as well as every bookstore are well supplied with people who present themselves as experts in just about everything—career, dieting, exercise, politics, and even spiritual matters.

But what about *reliability?* Isn't the important thing that we are guided by someone who truly wants what is best for us and who understands our deepest needs? The sad thing about all the self-appointed experts out there is that they are capable of failing us. And life is too short and too precious to be put in the hands of hucksters and fools.

But the Bible promises us an Expert whose guidance is never in doubt.

He is our God forever and ever, and he will be our guide until we die. PSALM 48:14

O LORD, you are my light; yes, LORD, you light up my darkness. In your strength I can crush an army; with my God I can scale any wall. 2 SAMUEL 22:29-30

I will lead blind Israel down a new path, guiding them along an unfamiliar way. I will make the darkness bright before them and smooth out the road ahead of them. Yes, I will indeed do these things; I will not forsake them. ISAIAH 42:16

"I know the plans I have for you," says the LORD. "They are plans for good and not for disaster, to give you a future and a hope. In those days when you pray, I will listen. If you look for me in earnest, you will find me when you seek me." JEREMIAH 29:11-13

Jesus gave the world a new promise: the Holy Spirit as guide. The beautiful thing about this is that the Holy Spirit has a role that touches every area of our life every day. Since Jesus cannot physically be with us, as believers we have the presence of God through the Holy Spirit always.

I will ask the Father, and he will give you another Counselor, who will never leave you. He is the Holy Spirit, who leads into all truth. The world at large cannot receive him, because it isn't looking for him and doesn't recognize him. But you do, because he lives with you now and later will be in you.

When the Father sends the Counselor as my representative—and by the Counselor I mean the Holy Spirit—he will teach you everything and will remind you of everything I myself have told you. JOHN 14:16-17, 26

The Psalms paint vivid pictures of God walking with us. In particular, Psalm 23 is famous as the "shepherd psalm." It is an assurance of God's leading even in the worst of times.

The LORD is my shepherd; I have everything I need.
He lets me rest in green meadows; he leads me beside peaceful streams. He renews my strength. He guides me along right paths, bringing honor to his name.
Even when I walk through the dark valley of death, I will not be

afraid, for you are close beside me. Your rod and your staff protect and comfort me.

You prepare a feast for me in the presence of my enemies. You welcome me as a guest, anointing my head with oil. My cup overflows with blessings. Surely your goodness and unfailing love will pursue me all the days of my life, and I will live in the house of the LORD forever. PSALM 23

The LORD says, "I will guide you along the best pathway for your life. I will advise you and watch over you." PSALM 32:8

The steps of the godly are directed by the LORD. He delights in every detail of their lives. Though they stumble, they will not fall, for the LORD holds them by the hand. PSALM 37:23-24

We can make our plans, but the LORD determines our steps. PROVERBS 16:9

I was so foolish and ignorant—I must have seemed like a senseless animal to you. Yet I still belong to you; you are holding my right hand. You will keep on guiding me with your counsel, leading me to a glorious destiny. Whom have I in heaven but you? I desire you more than anything on earth. My health may fail, and my spirit may grow weak, but God remains the strength of my heart; he is mine forever. PSALM 73:22-26

Fearing people is a dangerous trap, but to trust the LORD means safety. PROVERBS 29:25

Though the Lord gave you adversity for food and affliction for drink, he will still be with you to teach you. You will see your teacher with your own eyes, and you will hear a voice say, "This is the way; turn around and walk here." ISAIAH 30:20-21

I can never escape from your spirit! I can never get away from your presence! If I go up to heaven, you are there; if I go down to the place of the dead, you are there. If I ride the wings of the morning, if I dwell by the farthest oceans, even there your hand will guide me, and your strength will support me.   PSALM 139:7-10

> Jesus understood that the world is full of self-appointed guides, whose advice is worse than having no guide at all. He warned his followers what happens to these false leaders and those who follow them.

They are blind guides leading the blind, and if one blind person guides another, they will both fall into a ditch.   MATTHEW 15:14

> Thankfully, our greatest Guide is not blind, and we are not dependent solely on human leaders. People who seek direction from the Lord can take comfort in knowing he is happy to give it.

The godly are directed by their honesty; the wicked fall beneath their load of sin.   PROVERBS 11:5

Seek his will in all you do, and he will direct your paths.
PROVERBS 3:6

See also Faith, Hope, Obeying God, Trusting God.

God's Love for Us

Love is such an overused word—don't we "love" hot dogs and apple pie, and "love" going to the beach? But *love* in the Bible has a much richer meaning, particularly when applied to God's feeling toward his people. The Bible describes a kind of love that goes far beyond the greatest human capacity.

The LORD watches over those who fear him, those who rely on his unfailing love.

We depend on the LORD alone to save us. Only he can help us, protecting us like a shield.   PSALM 33:18, 20

The LORD says, "Then I will heal you of your idolatry and faithlessness, and my love will know no bounds, for my anger will be gone forever! I will be to Israel like a refreshing dew from heaven."   HOSEA 14:4-5

I have loved you, my people, with an everlasting love. With unfailing love I have drawn you to myself.   JEREMIAH 31:3

Can anything ever separate us from Christ's love? Does it mean he no longer loves if we have trouble or calamity, or are persecuted, or are hungry or cold or in danger or threatened with death? (Even the Scriptures say, "For your sake we are killed every day; we are being slaughtered like sheep.") No, despite all these things, overwhelming victory is ours through Christ, who loved us.

And I am convinced that nothing can ever separate us from his love. Death can't, and life can't. The angels can't, and the demons can't. Our fears for today, our worries about tomorrow, and even the powers of hell can't keep God's love away. Whether we are high above the sky or in the deepest ocean, nothing in all creation will ever be able to separate us from the love of God that is revealed in Christ Jesus our Lord. ROMANS 8:35-39

May you experience the love of Christ, though it is so great you will never fully understand it. Then you will be filled with the fullness of life and power that comes from God. EPHESIANS 3:19

See how very much our heavenly Father loves us, for he allows us to be called his children, and we really are! But the people who belong to this world don't know God, so they don't understand that we are his children. 1 JOHN 3:1

> In the New Testament this overwhelming love God has for us takes human form itself in the self-sacrificing love of Jesus.

The Word became human and lived here on earth among us. He was full of unfailing love and faithfulness. And we have seen his glory, the glory of the only Son of the Father. JOHN 1:14

God so loved the world that he gave his only Son, so that everyone who believes in him will not perish but have eternal life. God did not send his Son into the world to condemn it, but to save it. JOHN 3:16-17

We know how dearly God loves us, because he has given us the Holy Spirit to fill our hearts with his love.

But God showed his great love for us by sending Christ to die for us while we were still sinners. And since we have been made right in God's sight by the blood of Christ, he will certainly save us from God's judgment. For since we were restored to friendship with God by the death of his Son while we were still his enemies, we will certainly be delivered from eternal punishment by his life. So now we can rejoice in our wonderful new relationship with God—all because of what our Lord Jesus Christ has done for us in making us friends of God. ROMANS 5:5, 8-11

Whatever we do, it is because Christ's love controls us. Since we believe that Christ died for everyone, we also believe that we have all died to the old life we used to live. 2 CORINTHIANS 5:14

God is so rich in mercy, and he loved us so very much, that even while we were dead because of our sins, he gave us life when he raised Christ from the dead. (It is only by God's special favor that you have been saved!) For he raised us from the dead along with Christ, and we are seated with him in the heavenly realms—all because we are one with Christ Jesus. And so God can always point to us as examples of the incredible wealth of his favor and kindness toward us, as shown in all he has done for us through Christ Jesus. EPHESIANS 2:4-7

Anyone who does not love does not know God—for God is love.

God showed how much he loved us by sending his only Son into the world so that we might have eternal life through him. This is real love. It is not that we loved God, but that he loved us and sent his Son as a sacrifice to take away our sins.

Dear friends, since God loved us that much, we surely ought to love each other. No one has ever seen God. But if we love each other, God lives in us, and his love has been brought to full expression through us.

And God has given us his Spirit as proof that we live in him and he in us. 1 JOHN 4:8-13

> Does God love all people? Of course. But remember the old cliché, "Don't hate people, hate their ways"? This is the Bible's view of God: He hates evil and sees it for what it is. And while he doesn't hate wicked people (after all, he wants everyone to repent and lead a good life), he does show a special concern for people who love and obey him.

The LORD opens the eyes of the blind. The LORD lifts the burdens of those bent beneath their loads. The LORD loves the righteous. PSALM 146:8

The LORD despises the way of the wicked, but he loves those who pursue godliness. PROVERBS 15:9

"I know the plans I have for you," says the LORD. "They are plans for good and not for disaster, to give you a future and a hope. In those days when you pray, I will listen. If you look for me in earnest, you will find me when you seek me. I will be found by you," says the LORD. JEREMIAH 29:11-14

Many sorrows come to the wicked, but unfailing love surrounds those who trust the LORD.
So rejoice in the LORD and be glad, all you who obey him! Shout for joy, all you whose hearts are pure! PSALM 32:10-11

Those who obey my commandments are the ones who love me. And because they love me, my Father will love them, and I will love them. And I will reveal myself to each one of them.
All those who love me will do what I say. My Father will love them, and we will come to them and live with them.
JOHN 14:21, 23

We know that God causes everything to work together for the good of those who love God and are called according to his purpose for them. ROMANS 8:28

> The last book of the Bible, Revelation, reminds us that love and discipline are not separate. Knowing that this present world must end someday, the author of Revelation exhorts readers to be watchful, for the God of love is also the one who presides at the world's last judgment.

I am the one who corrects and disciplines everyone I love. Be diligent and turn from your indifference. REVELATION 3:19

See also Comfort in Times of Trouble, Discipline and Correction, God's Guidance.

God's Mercy

Don't get mad—get even." This seems to be the usual way people view conflict. We should be thankful that God takes a different view of things. Although the Bible makes it clear that God is the great Judge who hates all evildoing, he is also the Merciful One who forgives and accepts people who turn to him.

Give thanks to the LORD, for he is good! His faithful love endures forever. 1 CHRONICLES 16:34

Let the people turn from their wicked deeds. Let them banish from their minds the very thought of doing wrong! Let them turn to the LORD that he may have mercy on them. Yes, turn to our God, for he will abundantly pardon. ISAIAH 55:7

As surely as I live, says the Sovereign LORD, I take no pleasure in the death of wicked people. I only want them to turn from their wicked ways so they can live. Turn! Turn from your wickedness, O people of Israel! Why should you die? EZEKIEL 33:11

To the faithful you show yourself faithful; to those with integrity you show integrity. 2 SAMUEL 22:26

The Lord does not abandon anyone forever. Though he brings grief, he also shows compassion according to the greatness of his unfailing love. For he does not enjoy hurting people or causing them sorrow. LAMENTATIONS 3:31-33

God is so rich in mercy, and he loved us so very much, that even while we were dead because of our sins, he gave us life when he raised Christ from the dead. (It is only by God's special favor that you have been saved!) For he raised us from the dead along with Christ, and we are seated with him in the heavenly realms—all because we are one with Christ Jesus. EPHESIANS 2:4-6

You are a God of forgiveness, gracious and merciful, slow to become angry, and full of unfailing love and mercy.
NEHEMIAH 9:17

Where is another God like you, who pardons the sins of the survivors among his people? You cannot stay angry with your people forever, because you delight in showing mercy. Once again you will have compassion on us. You will trample our sins under your feet and throw them into the depths of the ocean! You will show us your faithfulness and unfailing love as you promised with an oath to our ancestors Abraham and Jacob long ago.
MICAH 7:18-20

I, the Son of Man, have come to save the lost. If a shepherd has one hundred sheep, and one wanders away and is lost, what will he do? Won't he leave the ninety-nine others and go out into the hills to search for the lost one? And if he finds it, he will surely rejoice over it more than over the ninety-nine that didn't wander away! In the same way, it is not my heavenly Father's will that even one of these little ones should perish. MATTHEW 18:11-14

He saved us, not because of the good things we did, but because
of his mercy. He washed away our sins and gave us a new life
through the Holy Spirit. TITUS 3:5

Let us come boldly to the throne of our gracious God. There we
will receive his mercy, and we will find grace to help us when we
need it. HEBREWS 4:16

> Is God's promise of mercy completely unconditional? Not exactly.
> Jesus let his followers know that receiving God's mercy requires that
> they be merciful themselves. According to the Bible, all of us are in
> the same boat: We are sinners, needing to be forgiven by God and
> to come into a right relationship with him. So none of us is in a
> position to be haughty and unforgiving toward others.

If you forgive those who sin against you, your heavenly Father
will forgive you. But if you refuse to forgive others, your Father
will not forgive your sins. MATTHEW 6:14-15

His mercy goes on from generation to generation, to all who fear
him. LUKE 1:50

Now turn from your sins and turn to God, so you can be cleansed
of your sins. Then wonderful times of refreshment will come from
the presence of the Lord, and he will send Jesus your Messiah to
you again. ACTS 3:19-20

God overlooked people's former ignorance about these things, but
now he commands everyone everywhere to turn away from idols
and turn to him. ACTS 17:30

The Lord isn't really being slow about his promise to return, as
some people think. No, he is being patient for your sake. He does
not want anyone to perish, so he is giving more time for everyone
to repent. 2 PETER 3:9

Nothing demonstrates forgiveness better than Jesus' wonderful parable about a forgiven person who was stingy with his own forgiveness.

The Kingdom of Heaven can be compared to a king who decided to bring his accounts up to date with servants who had borrowed money from him. In the process, one of his debtors was brought in who owed him millions of dollars. He couldn't pay, so the king ordered that he, his wife, his children, and everything he had be sold to pay the debt. But the man fell down before the king and begged him, "Oh, sir, be patient with me, and I will pay it all." Then the king was filled with pity for him, and he released him and forgave his debt.

But when the man left the king, he went to a fellow servant who owed him a few thousand dollars. He grabbed him by the throat and demanded instant payment. His fellow servant fell down before him and begged for a little more time. "Be patient and I will pay it," he pleaded. But his creditor wouldn't wait. He had the man arrested and jailed until the debt could be paid in full.

When some of the other servants saw this, they were very upset. They went to the king and told him what had happened. Then the king called in the man he had forgiven and said, "You evil servant! I forgave you that tremendous debt because you pleaded with me. Shouldn't you have mercy on your fellow servant, just as I had mercy on you?" Then the angry king sent the man to prison until he had paid every penny.

That's what my heavenly Father will do to you if you refuse to forgive your brothers and sisters in your heart.

MATTHEW 18:23-35

Psalm 103 is a song of praise for God's mercy. Nothing else in the Bible quite equals it. No wonder it has been set to music many times.

He forgives all my sins and heals all my diseases. He ransoms me from death and surrounds me with love and tender mercies. He fills my life with good things. My youth is renewed like the eagle's! The LORD gives righteousness and justice to all who are treated unfairly. He revealed his character to Moses and his deeds to the people of Israel. The LORD is merciful and gracious; he is slow to get angry and full of unfailing love. He will not constantly accuse us, nor remain angry forever. He has not punished us for all our sins, nor does he deal with us as we deserve. For his unfailing love toward those who fear him is as great as the height of the heavens above the earth. He has removed our rebellious acts as far away from us as the east is from the west. The LORD is like a father to his children, tender and compassionate to those who fear him. For he understands how weak we are; he knows we are only dust. Our days on earth are like grass; like wildflowers, we bloom and die. The wind blows, and we are gone—as though we had never been here. But the love of the LORD remains forever with those who fear him.   PSALM 103:3-17

See also Confessing Sin, Guilt, Repentance.

Guilt

Secular psychologists like to talk about—and try to get rid of—patients' guilt feelings. Often the assumption is that the *feeling* is the problem. If this can be gotten rid of, the problem is solved—or so they say. They overlook the fact that people often experience genuine guilt over having wronged someone—another person, or God himself. Getting rid of the *feeling* isn't the problem, then, is it? The problem is that a precious relationship has been broken. It needs mending.

Happily, the Bible holds out more promise than mental-health professionals do. It asserts that much of our guilt isn't just a feeling—it is a real awareness of harm done to someone. It also assures us that, if we approach him humbly, God willingly and eagerly forgives us, cleanses us of our guilt, and restores joy to our life.

O God, you know how foolish I am; my sins cannot be hidden from you. PSALM 69:5

He has not punished us for all our sins, nor does he deal with us as we deserve. For his unfailing love toward those who fear him is as great as the height of the heavens above the earth. He has removed our rebellious acts as far away from us as the east is from the west. The LORD is like a father to his children, tender and compassionate to those who fear him. For he understands how weak we are; he knows we are only dust.   PSALM 103:10-14

Oh, what joy for those whose rebellion is forgiven, whose sin is put out of sight! Yes, what joy for those whose record the LORD has cleared of sin, whose lives are lived in complete honesty!

When I refused to confess my sin, I was weak and miserable, and I groaned all day long. Day and night your hand of discipline was heavy on me. My strength evaporated like water in the summer heat.

Finally, I confessed all my sins to you and stopped trying to hide them. I said to myself, "I will confess my rebellion to the LORD." And you forgave me! All my guilt is gone.

Therefore, let all the godly confess their rebellion to you while there is time, that they may not drown in the floodwaters of judgment. For you are my hiding place; you protect me from trouble. You surround me with songs of victory.   PSALM 32:1-7

Let the people turn from their wicked deeds. Let them banish from their minds the very thought of doing wrong! Let them turn to the LORD that he may have mercy on them. Yes, turn to our God, for he will abundantly pardon.   ISAIAH 55:7

If wicked people turn away from all their sins and begin to obey my laws and do what is just and right, they will surely live and not die. All their past sins will be forgotten, and they will live because of the righteous things they have done.   EZEKIEL 18:21-22

All have sinned; all fall short of God's glorious standard. Yet now God in his gracious kindness declares us not guilty. He has done this through Christ Jesus, who has freed us by taking away our sins.   ROMANS 3:23-24

Those who become Christians become new persons. They are not the same anymore, for the old life is gone. A new life has begun! All this newness of life is from God, who brought us back to himself through what Christ did. And God has given us the task of reconciling people to him. For God was in Christ, reconciling the world to himself, no longer counting people's sins against them. 2 CORINTHIANS 5:17-19

Since we have a great High Priest who rules over God's people, let us go right into the presence of God, with true hearts fully trusting him. For our evil consciences have been sprinkled with Christ's blood to make us clean, and our bodies have been washed with pure water. HEBREWS 10:21-22

It is by our actions that we know we are living in the truth, so we will be confident when we stand before the Lord, even if our hearts condemn us. For God is greater than our hearts, and he knows everything.

Dear friends, if our conscience is clear, we can come to God with bold confidence. 1 JOHN 3:19-21

If we are living in the light of God's presence, just as Christ is, then we have fellowship with each other, and the blood of Jesus, his Son, cleanses us from every sin. 1 JOHN 1:7

See also Confessing Sin, God's Mercy, Repentance, Sin and Redemption.

Hate

Turn on the daily news and you can't help but notice how hate-filled the world is. One nation against another, one ethnic group hating another, one political group spouting hateful half-truths about another. It is easy to get the impression that some people actually *enjoy* hating others. The more aware we are of this, the more normal it seems. Whatever happened to our grandparents' advice: "Don't hate people—hate their *ways*"?

The Bible has one basic word regarding hatred of people: *don't*. It's normal and right for a person of faith to hate evil. But we are not to hate people, not even bad people, and we especially are not to hate fellow Christians. In the Kingdom of God, the impulse to hate has no place.

Hatred stirs up quarrels, but love covers all offenses.
PROVERBS 10:12

You have heard that the law of Moses says, "Love your neighbor" and hate your enemy. But I say, love your enemies! Pray for those who persecute you! In that way, you will be acting as true children of your Father in heaven. For he gives his sunlight to both the evil and the good, and he sends rain on the just and on the unjust, too. MATTHEW 5:43-45

Anyone who says, "I am in the light" but rejects another Christian is still in darkness. But anyone who loves other Christians is walking in the light and does not cause anyone to stumble. Those who reject other Christians are wandering in spiritual darkness and don't know where they are going, for the darkness has made them blind. 1 JOHN 2:9-11

If someone says, "I love God," but hates another Christian, that person is a liar; for if we don't love people we can see, how can we love God, whom we have not seen? And God himself has commanded that we must love not only him but our Christian brothers and sisters, too. 1 JOHN 4:20-21

> These words from 1 John remind us of a painful reality: Christians do fight each other. It happens within denominations, individual churches, and even friendships of Christians. Believers fight each other, snub each other, act as if they had no spiritual kinship whatever. Is it any wonder the world sometimes laughs at us?

So now we can tell who are children of God and who are children of the Devil. Anyone who does not obey God's commands and does not love other Christians does not belong to God.

This is the message we have heard from the beginning: We should love one another. We must not be like Cain, who belonged to the evil one and killed his brother. And why did he kill him? Because Cain had been doing what was evil, and his brother had been doing what was right. So don't be surprised, dear brothers and sisters, if the world hates you.

If we love other Christians, it proves that we have passed from death to eternal life. But a person who doesn't love them is still dead. Anyone who hates another Christian is really a murderer at heart. And you know that murderers don't have eternal life within them.   1 JOHN 3:10-15

See also Anger, Enemies, Envy, Forgiving Others, Mercy.

Heaven

Times change, and so do people's attitudes toward the afterlife. Reincarnation, astral projection, near-death encounters . . . unbelievers are fascinated by what happens after the body dies. Yet Christians, even preachers, seem to talk very little about heaven.

Christians of the past felt differently. In spite of the stereotype of Christians constantly preaching about the fires of hell, many preachers focused on heaven—God's rest and joy and complete satisfaction for us after enduring the troubles of this earthly life. It is mentioned again and again in the New Testament, not as an afterthought but as a key element in Christian belief. C. S. Lewis observed that belief in heaven is "not a form of escapism or wishful thinking, but one of the things a Christian is meant to do."

Does being otherworldly mean we are of no use in this life? Hardly. Lewis also noted that Christians who have a genuine belief in the joys of heaven seem to be the happiest people here on earth—and also the most likely to make the earth a more livable place.

I know that my Redeemer lives, and that he will stand upon the earth at last. And after my body has decayed, yet in my body I will see God! I will see him for myself. Yes, I will see him with my own eyes. I am overwhelmed at the thought! JOB 19:25-27

You will show me the way of life, granting me the joy of your presence and the pleasures of living with you forever. PSALM 16:11

Surely your goodness and unfailing love will pursue me all the days of my life, and I will live in the house of the LORD forever. PSALM 23:6

> Writing to the Corinthians, Paul assured them that heaven isn't just an "additive" to the gospel message; it is part and parcel of the whole message. A gospel without the promise of heaven is no gospel at all.

If we have hope in Christ only for this life, we are the most miserable people in the world.

But the fact is that Christ has been raised from the dead. He has become the first of a great harvest of those who will be raised to life again. 1 CORINTHIANS 15:19-20

I give them eternal life, and they will never perish. No one will snatch them away from me, for my Father has given them to me, and he is more powerful than anyone else. So no one can take them from me. JOHN 10:28-29

There are many rooms in my Father's home, and I am going to prepare a place for you. If this were not so, I would tell you plainly. When everything is ready, I will come and get you, so that you will always be with me where I am. JOHN 14:2-3

> Are you dissatisfied with the way you look? So many people are, even people who are extremely attractive. Interestingly, the Bible gives us a pleasant bit of news: In heaven we will have a new body.

Whatever gripe we had about life in our earthly body, our new body
will be wonderful.

We know that when this earthly tent we live in is taken
down—when we die and leave these bodies—we will have a
home in heaven, an eternal body made for us by God himself and
not by human hands. We grow weary in our present bodies, and
we long for the day when we will put on our heavenly bodies like
new clothing. For we will not be spirits without bodies, but we
will put on new heavenly bodies. 2 CORINTHIANS 5:1-3

We are citizens of heaven, where the Lord Jesus Christ lives. And
we are eagerly waiting for him to return as our Savior. He will take
these weak mortal bodies of ours and change them into glorious
bodies like his own, using the same mighty power that he will use
to conquer everything, everywhere. PHILIPPIANS 3:20-21

The Lord will deliver me from every evil attack and will bring me
safely to his heavenly Kingdom. To God be the glory forever and
ever. Amen. 2 TIMOTHY 4:18

All these faithful ones died without receiving what God had
promised them, but they saw it all from a distance and welcomed
the promises of God. They agreed that they were no more than
foreigners and nomads here on earth. And obviously people who
talk like that are looking forward to a country they can call their
own. If they had meant the country they came from, they would
have found a way to go back. But they were looking for a better
place, a heavenly homeland. That is why God is not ashamed to
be called their God, for he has prepared a heavenly city for them.
HEBREWS 11:13-16

You have come to Mount Zion, to the city of the living God, the
heavenly Jerusalem, and to thousands of angels in joyful
assembly. You have come to the assembly of God's firstborn

children, whose names are written in heaven. You have come to
God himself, who is the judge of all people. And you have come
to the spirits of the redeemed in heaven who have now been made
perfect. HEBREWS 12:22-23

This world is not our home; we are looking forward to our city in
heaven, which is yet to come. HEBREWS 13:14

Whatever is good and perfect comes to us from God above, who
created all heaven's lights. Unlike them, he never changes or casts
shifting shadows. JAMES 1:17

We live with a wonderful expectation because Jesus Christ rose
again from the dead. For God has reserved a priceless inheritance
for his children. It is kept in heaven for you, pure and undefiled.
1 PETER 1:3-4

Anyone who is willing to hear should listen to the Spirit and
understand what the Spirit is saying to the churches. Everyone
who is victorious will eat from the tree of life in the paradise of
God. REVELATION 2:7

All who are victorious will become pillars in the Temple of
my God, and they will never have to leave it. And I will write
my God's name on them, and they will be citizens in the city
of my God—the new Jerusalem that comes down from heaven
from my God. And they will have my new name inscribed upon
them. REVELATION 3:12

Since we believe in this wonderful home, our ultimate destiny, how
does this affect our present-day priorities? In a big way, naturally.
Nothing puts our everyday affairs into their true perspective like
thoughts about the long haul.

Don't store up treasures here on earth, where they can be eaten by moths and get rusty, and where thieves break in and steal. Store your treasures in heaven, where they will never become moth-eaten or rusty and where they will be safe from thieves. Wherever your treasure is, there your heart and thoughts will also be. MATTHEW 6:19-21

Since you have been raised to new life with Christ, set your sights on the realities of heaven, where Christ sits at God's right hand in the place of honor and power. Let heaven fill your thoughts. Do not think only about things down here on earth. For you died when Christ died, and your real life is hidden with Christ in God. And when Christ, who is your real life, is revealed to the whole world, you will share in all his glory. COLOSSIANS 3:1-4

The day of the Lord will come as unexpectedly as a thief. Then the heavens will pass away with a terrible noise, and everything in them will disappear in fire, and the earth and everything on it will be exposed to judgment.

Since everything around us is going to melt away, what holy, godly lives you should be living! You should look forward to that day and hurry it along—the day when God will set the heavens on fire and the elements will melt away in the flames. But we are looking forward to the new heavens and new earth he has promised, a world where everyone is right with God. 2 PETER 3:10-13

Revelation could be called the Book of Heaven. The book ends appropriately: with a vision of heaven, the new Jerusalem. People often avoid reading Revelation because some of its visions and symbols are difficult to grasp. But the last two chapters are clear. They are a vivid promise of bliss for the people of God.

I saw a new heaven and a new earth, for the old heaven and the old earth had disappeared. And the sea was also gone. And I saw the holy city, the new Jerusalem, coming down from God out of heaven like a beautiful bride prepared for her husband.

I heard a loud shout from the throne saying, "Look, the home of God is now among his people! He will live with them, and they will be his people. God himself will be with them. He will remove all of their sorrows, and there will be no more death or sorrow or crying or pain. For the old world and its evils are gone forever."

And the one sitting on the throne said, "Look, I am making all things new!" And then he said to me, "Write this down, for what I tell you is trustworthy and true." And he also said, "It is finished! I am the Alpha and the Omega—the Beginning and the End. To all who are thirsty I will give the springs of the water of life without charge! All who are victorious will inherit all these blessings, and I will be their God, and they will be my children. But cowards who turn away from me, and unbelievers, and the corrupt, and murderers, and the immoral, and those who practice witchcraft, and idol worshipers, and all liars—their doom is in the lake that burns with fire and sulfur. This is the second death."

Then one of the seven angels . . . took me in spirit to a great, high mountain, and he showed me the holy city, Jerusalem, descending out of heaven from God.

No temple could be seen in the city, for the Lord God Almighty and the Lamb are its temple. And the city has no need of sun or moon, for the glory of God illuminates the city, and the Lamb is its light. The nations of the earth will walk in its light, and the rulers of the world will come and bring their glory to it. Its gates never close at the end of day because there is no night. And all the nations will bring their glory and honor into the city. Nothing evil will be allowed to enter—no one who practices shameful idolatry and dishonesty—but only those whose names are written in the Lamb's Book of Life. REVELATION 21:1-10, 22-27

No longer will anything be cursed. For the throne of God and of the Lamb will be there, and his servants will worship him. And they will see his face, and his name will be written on their foreheads. And there will be no night there—no need for lamps or sun—for the Lord God will shine on them. And they will reign forever and ever. REVELATION 22:3-5

See also Eternal Life, Hell, Jesus' Second Coming.

Hell

Now here is an unpopular topic, one that even very faithful people tend to avoid. In our age when nothing seems permanent, the idea of being permanently separated from God strikes people as too—well, *final.* We wonder, *Shouldn't there be, perhaps, a second chance?* No wonder belief in reincarnation is so popular. It gives people the comfort of believing that if they ruin this life, they will get another chance, and another, and . . .

This isn't the picture the Bible shows. It presents us with one life per person, a life that can be used in the service and worship of God—or a life lived without God. God made us free, able to make moral and spiritual choices. So he can't really be accused of "sending people to hell," as if he took some delight in punishing us. Far from it! But since we are free, we can, finally and forever, say no to God.

Billy Graham summed it up very well: "Hell is essentially and basically banishment from the presence of God for deliberately rejecting Jesus Christ as Lord and Savior."

The doctrine of hell isn't supposed to make people *happy,* by the way. Happiness comes from knowing that we not only avoided hell but that we live forever in the presence of a loving God.

As surely as I live, says the Sovereign LORD, I take no pleasure in the death of wicked people. I only want them to turn from their wicked ways so they can live. Turn! Turn from your wickedness, O people of Israel! Why should you die? EZEKIEL 33:11

God shows his anger from heaven against all sinful, wicked people who push the truth away from themselves. For the truth about God is known to them instinctively. God has put this knowledge in their hearts. From the time the world was created, people have seen the earth and sky and all that God made. They can clearly see his invisible qualities—his eternal power and divine nature. So they have no excuse whatsoever for not knowing God.

Yes, they knew God, but they wouldn't worship him as God or even give him thanks. And they began to think up foolish ideas of what God was like. The result was that their minds became dark and confused. Claiming to be wise, they became utter fools instead. ROMANS 1:18-22

You can enter God's Kingdom only through the narrow gate. The highway to hell is broad, and its gate is wide for the many who choose the easy way. But the gateway to life is small, and the road is narrow, and only a few ever find it. MATTHEW 7:13-14

I, the Son of Man, will send my angels, and they will remove from my Kingdom everything that causes sin and all who do evil, and they will throw them into the furnace and burn them. There will be weeping and gnashing of teeth. Then the godly will shine like the sun in their Father's Kingdom. Anyone who is willing to hear should listen and understand! MATTHEW 13:41-43

The Kingdom of Heaven is like a fishing net that is thrown into the water and gathers fish of every kind. When the net is full, they drag it up onto the shore, sit down, sort the good fish into crates, and throw the bad ones away. That is the way it will be at the end of the world. The angels will come and separate the wicked people from the godly, throwing the wicked into the fire. There will be weeping and gnashing of teeth. MATTHEW 13:47-50

He will come with his mighty angels, in flaming fire, bringing judgment on those who don't know God and on those who refuse to obey the Good News of our Lord Jesus. They will be punished with everlasting destruction, forever separated from the Lord and from his glorious power when he comes to receive glory and praise from his holy people. And you will be among those praising him on that day, for you believed what we testified about him. 2 THESSALONIANS 1:7-10

God did not spare even the angels when they sinned; he threw them into hell, in gloomy caves and darkness until the judgment day. 2 PETER 2:4

Then the Devil, who betrayed them, was thrown into the lake of fire that burns with sulfur, joining the beast and the false prophet. There they will be tormented day and night forever and ever.

And death and the grave were thrown into the lake of fire. This is the second death—the lake of fire. And anyone whose name was not found recorded in the Book of Life was thrown into the lake of fire. REVELATION 20:10, 14-15

Cowards who turn away from me, and unbelievers, and the corrupt, and murderers, and the immoral, and those who practice witchcraft, and idol worshipers, and all liars—their doom is in the lake that burns with fire and sulfur. This is the second death. REVELATION 21:8

See also Eternal Life, Heaven, Jesus' Second Coming.

The Holy Spirit

Recent years have seen a renewed interest in the Holy Spirit, and rightly so. For too long the Spirit was a neglected part of our belief, something people tacked on to their creed (". . . and I believe in the Holy Spirit"), but did not understand very well. People across the globe have gone back to the Bible and sparked a renewed interest in the Spirit and his role in their lives.

There is a separate chapter devoted to "Baptism of the Spirit and Gifts of the Spirit," but as you will see from the Bible promises in this chapter, the Spirit himself *is* God's great gift to all believers. The gift was prophesied in the Old Testament, fulfilled in the New, and—praise God!—the Spirit is still active today among God's children.

"This is my covenant with them," says the LORD. "My Spirit will not leave them, and neither will these words I have given you. They will be on your lips and on the lips of your children and your children's children forever. I, the LORD, have spoken!"
ISAIAH 59:21

I will give you a new heart with new and right desires, and I will
put a new spirit in you. I will take out your stony heart of sin and
give you a new, obedient heart. And I will put my Spirit in you so
you will obey my laws and do whatever I command.

And you will . . . be my people, and I will be your God.
EZEKIEL 36:26-28

I will pour out my Spirit upon all people. Your sons and
daughters will prophesy. Your old men will dream dreams. Your
young men will see visions. In those days, I will pour out my
Spirit even on servants, men and women alike. JOEL 2:28-29

[John the Baptist:] "I baptize with water those who turn from their
sins and turn to God. But someone is coming soon who is far
greater than I am—so much greater that I am not even worthy to
be his slave. He will baptize you with the Holy Spirit and with
fire." MATTHEW 3:11

Everyone who asks, receives. Everyone who seeks, finds. And the
door is opened to everyone who knocks.

You fathers—if your children ask for a fish, do you give them a
snake instead? Or if they ask for an egg, do you give them a
scorpion? Of course not! If you sinful people know how to give
good gifts to your children, how much more will your heavenly
Father give the Holy Spirit to those who ask him. LUKE 11:10-13

The truth is, no one can enter the Kingdom of God without being
born of water and the Spirit. Humans can reproduce only human
life, but the Holy Spirit gives new life from heaven. JOHN 3:5-6

I will ask the Father, and he will give you another Counselor, who
will never leave you. He is the Holy Spirit, who leads into all
truth. The world at large cannot receive him, because it isn't
looking for him and doesn't recognize him. But you do, because
he lives with you now and later will be in you.

But when the Father sends the Counselor as my representative—
and by the Counselor I mean the Holy Spirit—he will teach you
everything and will remind you of everything I myself have told
you. JOHN 14:16-17, 26

It is the Spirit who gives eternal life. Human effort accomplishes
nothing. And the very words I have spoken to you are spirit and
life. JOHN 6:63

When the Spirit of truth comes, he will guide you into all truth.
He will not be presenting his own ideas; he will be telling you
what he has heard. He will tell you about the future. He will
bring me glory by revealing to you whatever he receives from
me. All that the Father has is mine; this is what I mean when I
say that the Spirit will reveal to you whatever he receives from
me. JOHN 16:13-15

When you are arrested, don't worry about what to say in your
defense, because you will be given the right words at the right
time. For it won't be you doing the talking—it will be the Spirit of
your Father speaking through you. MATTHEW 10:19-20

Go and make disciples of all the nations, baptizing them in the
name of the Father and the Son and the Holy Spirit. Teach these
new disciples to obey all the commands I have given you. And be
sure of this: I am with you always, even to the end of the age.
MATTHEW 28:19-20

When the Holy Spirit has come upon you, you will receive
power and will tell people about me everywhere—in Jerusalem,
throughout Judea, in Samaria, and to the ends of the earth.
ACTS 1:8

Suddenly, there was a sound from heaven like the roaring of a
mighty windstorm in the skies above them, and it filled the house

where they were meeting. Then, what looked like flames or
tongues of fire appeared and settled on each of them. And
everyone present was filled with the Holy Spirit and began
speaking in other languages, as the Holy Spirit gave them this
ability. ACTS 2:2-4

> Paul and the other New Testament writers felt the Spirit working in
> their own lives and in the lives of other Christians. Constantly they
> speak of the Spirit as a *power,* as an *enabler,* leading believers to
> accomplish great things with their lives.

We know how dearly God loves us, because he has given us the
Holy Spirit to fill our hearts with his love. ROMANS 5:5

The power of the life-giving Spirit has freed you through Christ
Jesus from the power of sin that leads to death.

Those who are dominated by the sinful nature think about sinful
things, but those who are controlled by the Holy Spirit think
about things that please the Spirit. If your sinful nature controls
your mind, there is death. But if the Holy Spirit controls your
mind, there is life and peace.

The Spirit of God, who raised Jesus from the dead, lives in you.
And just as he raised Christ from the dead, he will give life to
your mortal body by this same Spirit living within you.

For all who are led by the Spirit of God are children of God.

So you should not be like cowering, fearful slaves. You should
behave instead like God's very own children, adopted into his
family—calling him "Father, dear Father." For his Holy Spirit
speaks to us deep in our hearts and tells us that we are God's
children. ROMANS 8:2, 5-6, 11, 14-16

God has actually given us his Spirit (not the world's spirit) so we
can know the wonderful things God has freely given us.

But people who aren't Christians can't understand these truths
from God's Spirit. It all sounds foolish to them because only those

who have the Spirit can understand what the Spirit means. We
who have the Spirit understand these things, but others can't
understand us at all. How could they? For, "Who can know what
the Lord is thinking? Who can give him counsel?" But we can
understand these things, for we have the mind of Christ.
1 CORINTHIANS 2:12, 14-16

> The old religion of the Jews centered around worshiping God in the
> Temple at Jerusalem. The apostle Paul saw something new at work:
> Instead of God being in the Temple, God the Spirit now dwells
> within and among his people.

Don't you realize that all of you together are the temple of God
and that the Spirit of God lives in you? God will bring ruin upon
anyone who ruins this temple. For God's temple is holy, and you
Christians are that temple. 1 CORINTHIANS 3:16-17

Don't you know that your body is the temple of the Holy Spirit,
who lives in you and was given to you by God? You do not belong
to yourself, for God bought you with a high price. So you must
honor God with your body. 1 CORINTHIANS 6:19-20

I want you to know how to discern what is truly from God: No
one speaking by the Spirit of God can curse Jesus, and no one is
able to say, "Jesus is Lord," except by the Holy Spirit.
1 CORINTHIANS 12:3

Clearly, you are a letter from Christ prepared by us. It is written
not with pen and ink, but with the Spirit of the living God. It is
carved not on stone, but on human hearts.

He is the one who has enabled us to represent his new covenant.
This is a covenant, not of written laws, but of the Spirit. The old
way ends in death; in the new way, the Holy Spirit gives life.

Now, the Lord is the Spirit, and wherever the Spirit of the Lord
is, he gives freedom. 2 CORINTHIANS 3:3, 6, 17

Our dying bodies make us groan and sigh, but it's not that we want to die and have no bodies at all. We want to slip into our new bodies so that these dying bodies will be swallowed up by everlasting life. God himself has prepared us for this, and as a guarantee he has given us his Holy Spirit. 2 CORINTHIANS 5:4-5

> Paul spoke of the Spirit as a *guarantee,* a sort of "down payment" on heaven. When believers see God the Spirit working in their lives and the lives of others, they are seeing the guarantee that their eternal life with God has already begun.

We who live by the Spirit eagerly wait to receive everything promised to us who are right with God through faith.

The old sinful nature loves to do evil, which is just opposite from what the Holy Spirit wants. And the Spirit gives us desires that are opposite from what the sinful nature desires. These two forces are constantly fighting each other, and your choices are never free from this conflict. But when you are directed by the Holy Spirit, you are no longer subject to the law.

But when the Holy Spirit controls our lives, he will produce this kind of fruit in us: love, joy, peace, patience, kindness, goodness, faithfulness, gentleness, and self-control. Here there is no conflict with the law.

If we are living now by the Holy Spirit, let us follow the Holy Spirit's leading in every part of our lives.
GALATIANS 5:5, 17-18, 22-23, 25

This light within you produces only what is good and right and true.

Don't be drunk with wine, because that will ruin your life. Instead, let the Holy Spirit fill and control you.
EPHESIANS 5:9, 18

With the help of the Holy Spirit who lives within us, carefully guard what has been entrusted to you. 2 TIMOTHY 1:14

He saved us, not because of the good things we did, but because of his mercy. He washed away our sins and gave us a new life through the Holy Spirit. He generously poured out the Spirit upon us because of what Jesus Christ our Savior did. TITUS 3:5-6

Those who obey God's commandments live in fellowship with him, and he with them. And we know he lives in us because the Holy Spirit lives in us. 1 JOHN 3:24

> One other forgotten aspect of the Spirit's work is the Bible itself. It is not the product of human authors alone but is also the result of the Spirit's power:

No prophecy in Scripture ever came from the prophets themselves or because they wanted to prophesy. It was the Holy Spirit who moved the prophets to speak from God. 2 PETER 1:20-21

See Baptism of the Spirit and Gifts of the Spirit, God's Guidance.

Hope

"High Hopes" could be a subtitle of the Bible, the New Testament in particular. The Bible authors understood that people aren't content to live but need to have something to live *for*. Salesmen and politicians understand this, too, so they make promises (most of which they cannot keep). Solomon understood this aspect of human nature when he wrote the following:

Hope deferred makes the heart sick, but when dreams come true, there is life and joy. PROVERBS 13:12

Hope is never an afterthought in the Bible. It is a key component of the good life. As far as the authors of the Bible were concerned, hope was as vital to life as oxygen.

O Lord, you alone are my hope. I've trusted you, O LORD, from childhood. Yes, you have been with me from birth; from my mother's womb you have cared for me. No wonder I am always praising you! PSALM 71:5-6

Blessed are those who trust in the LORD and have made the LORD their hope and confidence. JEREMIAH 17:7

There are three things that will endure—faith, hope, and love. 1 CORINTHIANS 13:13

We who live by the Spirit eagerly wait to receive everything promised to us who are right with God through faith. GALATIANS 5:5

What is faith? It is the confident assurance that what we hope for is going to happen. It is the evidence of things we cannot yet see. HEBREWS 11:1

> The world makes lots of promises and offers lots of hopes—physical beauty, wealth, fame, long life. There is nothing wrong with hoping for these things, but the Bible offers a much higher hope: endurance through life's bad days and life beyond this life. The Bible offers us a hope that persists when we are completely disillusioned with this world and its broken promises.

Why am I discouraged? Why so sad? I will put my hope in God! I will praise him again—my Savior and my God! PSALM 42:11

The hopes of the godly result in happiness, but the expectations of the wicked are all in vain. PROVERBS 10:28

The needy will not be forgotten forever; the hopes of the poor will not always be crushed. PSALM 9:18

Such things were written in the Scriptures long ago to teach us. They give us hope and encouragement as we wait patiently for God's promises. ROMANS 15:4

We are pressed on every side by troubles, but we are not crushed and broken. We are perplexed, but we don't give up and quit. We are hunted down, but God never abandons us. We get knocked down, but we get up again and keep going. Through suffering, these bodies of ours constantly share in the death of Jesus so that the life of Jesus may also be seen in our bodies. 2 CORINTHIANS 4:8-10

> Failure is a constant factor in human life. We fall short of our own expectations, and we fall short of God's. This could lead us to despair, but in the Bible's view, today's disillusionment is the raw material of the Christian's hope for the future.

O Israel, hope in the LORD; for with the LORD there is unfailing love and an overflowing supply of salvation. He himself will free Israel from every kind of sin. PSALM 130:7-8

In those days you were living apart from Christ. You were excluded from God's people, Israel, and you did not know the promises God had made to them. You lived in this world without God and without hope. But now you belong to Christ Jesus. Though you once were far away from God, now you have been brought near to him because of the blood of Christ. EPHESIANS 2:12-13

He declared us not guilty because of his great kindness. And now we know that we will inherit eternal life. TITUS 3:7

> Hope serves to sustain us today, but its focal point is the future. As wonderful as life on earth can be when we live the life of faith, the center of hope is something beyond this earthly life. People without faith may see only a hopeless end, but the believer rejoices in an endless hope.

If we have hope in Christ only for this life, we are the most miserable people in the world. 1 CORINTHIANS 15:19

We are all one body, we have the same Spirit, and we have all been called to the same glorious future. EPHESIANS 4:4

We have heard that you trust in Christ Jesus and that you love all of God's people. You do this because you are looking forward to the joys of heaven—as you have been ever since you first heard the truth of the Good News. This same Good News that came to you is going out all over the world. It is changing lives everywhere, just as it changed yours that very first day you heard and understood the truth about God's great kindness to sinners. COLOSSIANS 1:4-6

This is the secret: Christ lives in you, and this is your assurance that you will share in his glory. COLOSSIANS 1:27

Brothers and sisters, I want you to know what will happen to the Christians who have died so you will not be full of sorrow like people who have no hope. For since we believe that Jesus died and was raised to life again, we also believe that when Jesus comes, God will bring back with Jesus all the Christians who have died. 1 THESSALONIANS 4:13-14

I have been sent to bring faith to those God has chosen and to teach them to know the truth that shows them how to live godly lives. This truth gives them the confidence of eternal life, which God promised them before the world began—and he cannot lie. TITUS 1:1-2

All honor to the God and Father of our Lord Jesus Christ, for it is by his boundless mercy that God has given us the privilege of being born again. Now we live with a wonderful expectation because Jesus Christ rose again from the dead. For God has reserved a priceless inheritance for his children. It is kept in heaven for you, pure and undefiled, beyond the reach of change and decay. And God, in his mighty power, will protect you until you receive this salvation, because you are trusting him. It will be revealed on the last day for all to see. So be truly glad! There is wonderful joy ahead, even though it is necessary for you to endure many trials for a while. 1 PETER 1:3-6

> The great songwriter Oscar Hammerstein II claimed that he "just couldn't write anything without hope in it." No wonder his happy, sunny songs are still popular. The Bible presents something even more substantial than a cheerful, upbeat song, though. It gives a picture of an endless, joyous life with God, a conviction that happiness will one day triumph completely over sadness.

We should live in this evil world with self-control, right conduct, and devotion to God, while we look forward to that wonderful event when the glory of our great God and Savior, Jesus Christ, will be revealed. TITUS 2:12-13

Look forward to the special blessings that will come to you at the return of Jesus Christ.

Through Christ you have come to trust in God. And because God raised Christ from the dead and gave him great glory, your faith and hope can be placed confidently in God. 1 PETER 1:13, 21

The LORD watches over those who fear him, those who rely on his unfailing love. PSALM 33:18

"I know the plans I have for you," says the LORD. "They are plans for good and not for disaster, to give you a future and a hope. In those days when you pray, I will listen. If you look for me in earnest, you will find me when you seek me." JEREMIAH 29:11-13

The unfailing love of the LORD never ends! By his mercies we have been kept from complete destruction. Great is his faithfulness; his mercies begin afresh each day. I say to myself, "The LORD is my inheritance; therefore, I will hope in him!"

The LORD is wonderfully good to those who wait for him and seek him. So it is good to wait quietly for salvation from the LORD. LAMENTATIONS 3:22-26

> We can't really hope unless we trust, can we? In a world of selfish people, we sometimes wonder: Is there anyone we can trust? How can we make plans when the people we rely on are so fickle and unreliable? For that matter, can we even trust ourselves? But the Bible presents us with one who can be relied on totally—God. The basis for our hope is complete trust in the one who is reliable.

Love the LORD, all you faithful ones! For the LORD protects those who are loyal to him, but he harshly punishes all who are arrogant. So be strong and take courage, all you who put your hope in the LORD! PSALM 31:23-24

God has given us both his promise and his oath. These two things are unchangeable because it is impossible for God to lie. Therefore, we who have fled to him for refuge can take new courage, for we can hold on to his promise with confidence.

This confidence is like a strong and trustworthy anchor for our souls. It leads us through the curtain of heaven into God's inner sanctuary. HEBREWS 6:18-19

Without wavering, let us hold tightly to the hope we say we have, for God can be trusted to keep his promise. HEBREWS 10:23

See also Ambition, Eternal Life, Faith, Heaven, Trusting God.

Hypocrisy

The old joke about hypocrites involves someone who said, "I don't go to church. Churches are full of hypocrites." The punch line is, "Come on in, there's always room for one more!"

Truth is, there is no room in the church for hypocrites. God's promises are for believers, not for those who only pretend to believe. Some of the harshest warnings in the Bible are reserved for the great pretenders in religion, the ones who act out a life of faith but inwardly deny it.

Smooth words may hide a wicked heart, just as a pretty glaze covers a common clay pot.

People with hate in their hearts may sound pleasant enough, but don't believe them. Though they pretend to be kind, their hearts are full of all kinds of evil. While their hatred may be concealed by trickery, it will finally come to light for all to see. PROVERBS 26:23-26

I will not allow deceivers to serve me, and liars will not be allowed to enter my presence. My daily task will be to ferret out criminals and free the city of the LORD from their grip. PSALM 101:7-8

I, the LORD, will punish all those, both Israelites and foreigners, who reject me and set up idols in their hearts so they fall into sin, and who then come to a prophet asking for my advice.
EZEKIEL 14:7

> No biblical author was more severe in his words to hypocrites than the prophet Amos. He looked around and saw a religion filled with outward show, but inside was hypocrisy, a sham. His promises apply to religious hypocrites of every age.

I [God] hate all your show and pretense—the hypocrisy of your religious festivals and solemn assemblies. I will not accept your burnt offerings and grain offerings. I won't even notice all your choice peace offerings. Away with your hymns of praise! They are only noise to my ears. I will not listen to your music, no matter how lovely it is. Instead, I want to see a mighty flood of justice, a river of righteous living that will never run dry. AMOS 5:21-24

Listen to this, you who rob the poor and trample the needy! You can't wait for the Sabbath day to be over and the religious festivals to end so you can get back to cheating the helpless. You measure out your grain in false measures and weigh it out on dishonest scales. And you mix the wheat you sell with chaff swept from the floor! Then you enslave poor people for a debt of one piece of silver or a pair of sandals.

Now the LORD has sworn this oath by his own name, the Pride of Israel: "I will never forget the wicked things you have done! The earth will tremble for your deeds, and everyone will mourn." AMOS 8:4-8

> Jesus' words to hypocrites are as stern as Amos's. For Jesus, the important thing is to please God, not the desire to be admired as a "religious person."

Take care! Don't do your good deeds publicly, to be admired, because then you will lose the reward from your Father in heaven. When you give a gift to someone in need, don't shout about it as the hypocrites do—blowing trumpets in the synagogues and streets to call attention to their acts of charity! I assure you, they have received all the reward they will ever get. But when you give to someone, don't tell your left hand what your right hand is doing.

And now about prayer. When you pray, don't be like the hypocrites who love to pray publicly on street corners and in the synagogues where everyone can see them. I assure you, that is all the reward they will ever get.

And when you fast, don't make it obvious, as the hypocrites do, who try to look pale and disheveled so people will admire them for their fasting. I assure you, that is the only reward they will ever get. MATTHEW 6:1-3, 5, 16

Why worry about a speck in your friend's eye when you have a log in your own? How can you think of saying, "Friend, let me help you get rid of that speck in your eye," when you can't see past the log in your own eye? Hypocrite! First get rid of the log from your own eye; then perhaps you will see well enough to deal with the speck in your friend's eye. MATTHEW 7:3-5

> Some of Jesus' words were directed against Pharisees, people who were admired for their strict observance of Jewish laws. Jesus criticized them, not for observing the law, but for losing sight of the really important things of the Spirit.

How terrible it will be for you teachers of religious law and you Pharisees. Hypocrites! For you are careful to tithe even the tiniest part of your income, but you ignore the important things of the law—justice, mercy, and faith. You should tithe, yes, but you should not leave undone the more important things.

How terrible it will be for you teachers of religious law and you

Pharisees. Hypocrites! You are like whitewashed tombs—
beautiful on the outside but filled on the inside with dead
people's bones and all sorts of impurity. You try to look like
upright people outwardly, but inside your hearts are filled with
hypocrisy and lawlessness.

How terrible it will be for you teachers of religious law and you
Pharisees. Hypocrites! For you build tombs for the prophets your
ancestors killed and decorate the graves of the godly people your
ancestors destroyed. Then you say, "We never would have joined
them in killing the prophets." MATTHEW 23:23, 27-30

> In a nutshell, the promise to hypocrites is this: Although you fool
> many and are considered very religious, God is aware of the real
> state of your hearts.

The time is coming when everything will be revealed; all that is
secret will be made public. Whatever you have said in the dark
will be heard in the light, and what you have whispered behind
closed doors will be shouted from the housetops for all to hear!
LUKE 12:2-3

Why do you call me "Lord," when you won't obey me?
LUKE 6:46

Those who keep on sinning have never known [Christ] or
understood who he is.

So now we can tell who are children of God and who are
children of the Devil. Anyone who does not obey God's
commands and does not love other Christians does not belong to
God. 1 JOHN 3:6, 10

If someone says, "I belong to God," but doesn't obey God's
commandments, that person is a liar and does not live in the
truth. 1 JOHN 2:4

They will act as if they are religious, but they will reject the power
that could make them godly. You must stay away from people like
that. 2 TIMOTHY 3:5

> The Bible contains no promises of reward for active church
> members. We're all aware that churches are full of pastors, teachers,
> and other leaders who "talk the talk but don't walk the walk." It is
> not our place to judge these people, but the New Testament makes
> it plain that God will judge them:

If you teach others, why don't you teach yourself? You tell others
not to steal, but do you steal? You say it is wrong to commit
adultery, but do you do it? You condemn idolatry, but do you steal
from pagan temples? You are so proud of knowing the law, but
you dishonor God by breaking it. No wonder the Scriptures say,
"The world blasphemes the name of God because of you."
ROMANS 2:21-24

> Faithful church attendance does not guarantee a reward, either.
> How many powerful sermons have rolled past the ears—and
> hearts—of the person who fills a space in a pew every Sunday. The
> apostle James had some words of warning to those who hear
> without paying heed:

Remember, it is a message to obey, not just to listen to. If you don't
obey, you are only fooling yourself. For if you just listen and don't
obey, it is like looking at your face in a mirror but doing nothing
to improve your appearance. You see yourself, walk away, and
forget what you look like. But if you keep looking steadily into
God's perfect law—the law that sets you free—and if you do what
it says and don't forget what you heard, then God will bless you for
doing it.

If you claim to be religious but don't control your tongue, you
are just fooling yourself, and your religion is worthless. Pure
and lasting religion in the sight of God our Father means that

we must care for orphans and widows in their troubles, and refuse to let the world corrupt us.   JAMES 1:22-27

See also Fellowship with Other Believers, Judging Others, Self-Righteousness.

Jesus' Second Coming

People sometimes accuse Christians of being "otherworldly."
They have a point. Christianity *does* focus on eternal life with God.
But, that belief affects our life in *this* world. Some of the noblest and
kindest deeds have been done by people who believed that their
final destination was heaven, not earth.

Unfortunately, all too often it appears Christians are "this worldly,"
forgetting how much the Bible has to say about the end of this
present life. In the past, Christians took great comfort from the Lord's
promise that he would return in glory. We still can.

Billy Graham summarized the belief quite well: "Our world is filled
with fear, hate, lust, greed, war, and utter despair. Surely the second
coming of Jesus Christ is the only hope of replacing these depressing
features with trust, love, universal peace, and prosperity."

We are citizens of heaven, where the Lord Jesus Christ lives. And
we are eagerly waiting for him to return as our Savior. He will take
these weak mortal bodies of ours and change them into glorious
bodies like his own, using the same mighty power that he will use
to conquer everything, everywhere. PHILIPPIANS 3:20-21

When Christ, who is your real life, is revealed to the whole world, you will share in all his glory. COLOSSIANS 3:4

I can tell you this directly from the Lord: We who are still living when the Lord returns will not rise to meet him ahead of those who are in their graves. For the Lord himself will come down from heaven with a commanding shout, with the call of the archangel, and with the trumpet call of God. First, all the Christians who have died will rise from their graves. Then, together with them, we who are still alive and remain on the earth will be caught up in the clouds to meet the Lord in the air and remain with him forever. So comfort and encourage each other with these words. 1 THESSALONIANS 4:15-18

You know quite well that the day of the Lord will come unexpectedly, like a thief in the night. When people are saying, "All is well; everything is peaceful and secure," then disaster will fall upon them as suddenly as a woman's birth pains begin when her child is about to be born. And there will be no escape.
1 THESSALONIANS 5:2-3

These trials will make you partners with Christ in his suffering, and afterward you will have the wonderful joy of sharing his glory when it is displayed to all the world. 1 PETER 4:13

When the head Shepherd comes, your reward will be a never-ending share in his glory and honor. 1 PETER 5:4

Dear friends, we are already God's children, and we can't even imagine what we will be like when Christ returns. But we do know that when he comes we will be like him, for we will see him as he really is. 1 JOHN 3:2

Look! He comes with the clouds of heaven. And everyone will see him—even those who pierced him. And all the nations of the earth will weep because of him. Yes! Amen! REVELATION 1:7

> In the Gospels, Jesus promises his return but names no specific time. This is intended to give people hope, but Jesus makes it clear that it should do more than that: The possibility of his returning at any time means that we should be living a godly life so that we will always be ready. We ought to behave as if the "inspector" might arrive at any moment.

When the Son of Man comes in his glory, and all the angels with him, then he will sit upon his glorious throne. All the nations will be gathered in his presence, and he will separate them as a shepherd separates the sheep from the goats. He will place the sheep at his right hand and the goats at his left. Then the King will say to those on the right, "Come, you who are blessed by my Father, inherit the Kingdom prepared for you from the foundation of the world. For I was hungry, and you fed me. I was thirsty, and you gave me a drink. I was a stranger, and you invited me into your home. I was naked, and you gave me clothing. I was sick, and you cared for me. I was in prison, and you visited me."

Then these righteous ones will reply, "Lord, when did we ever see you hungry and feed you? Or thirsty and give you something to drink? Or a stranger and show you hospitality? Or naked and give you clothing? When did we ever see you sick or in prison, and visit you?" And the King will tell them, "I assure you, when you did it to one of the least of these my brothers and sisters, you were doing it to me!"

Then the King will turn to those on the left and say, "Away with you, you cursed ones, into the eternal fire prepared for the Devil and his demons! For I was hungry, and you didn't feed me. I was thirsty, and you didn't give me anything to drink. I was a stranger, and you didn't invite me into your home. I was naked, and you gave me no clothing. I was sick and in prison, and you didn't visit me."

Then they will reply, "Lord, when did we ever see you hungry or thirsty or a stranger or naked or sick or in prison, and not help you?" And he will answer, "I assure you, when you refused to help the least of these my brothers and sisters, you were refusing to help me."

And they will go away into eternal punishment, but the righteous will go into eternal life. MATTHEW 25:31-46

I, the Son of Man, will come in the glory of my Father with his angels and will judge all people according to their deeds. MATTHEW 16:27-28

If a person is ashamed of me and my message, I, the Son of Man, will be ashamed of that person when I return in my glory and in the glory of the Father and the holy angels. LUKE 9:26

No one knows the day or the hour when these things will happen, not even the angels in heaven or the Son himself. Only the Father knows.

When the Son of Man returns, it will be like it was in Noah's day. In those days before the Flood, the people were enjoying banquets and parties and weddings right up to the time Noah entered his boat. People didn't realize what was going to happen until the Flood came and swept them all away. That is the way it will be when the Son of Man comes.

Two men will be working together in the field; one will be taken, the other left. Two women will be grinding flour at the mill; one will be taken, the other left. So be prepared, because you don't know what day your Lord is coming. MATTHEW 24:36-42

The coming of the Son of Man can be compared with that of a man who left home to go on a trip. He gave each of his employees instructions about the work they were to do, and he told the gatekeeper to watch for his return. So keep a sharp lookout! For you do not know when the homeowner will return—at evening,

midnight, early dawn, or late daybreak. Don't let him find you
sleeping when he arrives without warning. MARK 13:34-36

"Everyone will see the Son of Man arrive on the clouds with
power and great glory. So when all these things begin to happen,
stand straight and look up, for your salvation is near!"
    Then he gave them this illustration: "Notice the fig tree, or any
other tree. When the leaves come out, you know without being
told that summer is near. Just so, when you see the events I've
described taking place, you can be sure that the Kingdom of God
is near.
    "Watch out! Don't let me find you living in careless ease and
drunkenness, and filled with the worries of this life. Don't let that
day catch you unaware, as in a trap. For that day will come upon
everyone living on the earth. Keep a constant watch. And pray
that, if possible, you may escape these horrors and stand before
the Son of Man." LUKE 21:27-31, 34-36

> The Bible ends, appropriately, with both a prayer and a promise:
> Jesus is coming.

"See, I am coming soon, and my reward is with me, to repay all
according to their deeds."
    He who is the faithful witness to all these things says, "Yes, I am
coming soon!"
    Amen! Come, Lord Jesus! REVELATION 22:12, 20

See also Eternal Life, Heaven, Hell.

Joy

Christian author C. S. Lewis titled his autobiography
Surprised by Joy. He believed that joy was a key part of the Christian
life, one too often neglected.

Christianity has a reputation for being the "don't" religion—a
killjoy faith designed to keep people from enjoying their lives.
Nothing could be more untrue. The Old and New Testaments
promise us joy—not a temporary, fleeting "high," but something that
endures through both good and bad days.

This is the day the LORD has made. We will rejoice and be glad in
it. PSALM 118:24

I am overwhelmed with joy in the LORD my God! For he has
dressed me with the clothing of salvation and draped me in a robe
of righteousness. I am like a bridegroom in his wedding suit or a
bride with her jewels. The Sovereign LORD will show his justice to
the nations of the world. Everyone will praise him! His
righteousness will be like a garden in early spring, filled with
young plants springing up everywhere. ISAIAH 61:10-11

His anger lasts for a moment, but his favor lasts a lifetime!
Weeping may go on all night, but joy comes with the morning.
You have turned my mourning into joyful dancing. You have
taken away my clothes of mourning and clothed me with joy.
PSALM 30:5, 11

In him our hearts rejoice, for we are trusting in his holy name.
PSALM 33:21

A river brings joy to the city of our God, the sacred home of the
Most High. PSALM 46:4

The godly will rejoice in the LORD and find shelter in him. And
those who do what is right will praise him. PSALM 64:10

You satisfy me more than the richest of foods. I will praise you
with songs of joy. PSALM 63:5

Let the godly rejoice. Let them be glad in God's presence. Let
them be filled with joy. PSALM 68:3

Happy are those who hear the joyful call to worship, for they will
walk in the light of your presence, LORD. They rejoice all day long
in your wonderful reputation. They exult in your righteousness.
PSALM 89:15-16

Light shines on the godly, and joy on those who do right. May all
who are godly be happy in the LORD and praise his holy name!
PSALM 97:11-12

You will live in joy and peace. The mountains and hills will
burst into song, and the trees of the field will clap their hands!
ISAIAH 55.12

I have loved you even as the Father has loved me. Remain in my love. When you obey me, you remain in my love, just as I obey my Father and remain in his love. I have told you this so that you will be filled with my joy. Yes, your joy will overflow!
JOHN 15:9-11

The Kingdom of God is not a matter of what we eat or drink, but of living a life of goodness and peace and joy in the Holy Spirit. If you serve Christ with this attitude, you will please God. And other people will approve of you, too.   ROMANS 14:17-18

When the Holy Spirit controls our lives, he will produce this kind of fruit in us: love, joy, peace, patience, kindness, goodness, faithfulness, gentleness, and self-control. Here there is no conflict with the law.   GALATIANS 5:22-23

Don't be drunk with wine, because that will ruin your life. Instead, let the Holy Spirit fill and control you. Then you will sing psalms and hymns and spiritual songs among yourselves, making music to the Lord in your hearts.   EPHESIANS 5:18-19

Always be full of joy in the Lord. I say it again—rejoice! Let everyone see that you are considerate in all you do. Remember, the Lord is coming soon.
   Don't worry about anything; instead, pray about everything. Tell God what you need and thank him for all he has done. If you do this, you will experience God's peace, which is far more wonderful than the human mind can understand. His peace will guard your hearts and minds as you live in Christ Jesus.
PHILIPPIANS 4:4-7

You have come to Mount Zion, to the city of the living God, the heavenly Jerusalem, and to thousands of angels in joyful assembly.   HEBREWS 12:22

The words of Jesus and the apostle Paul assure believers that we can
experience joy in the midst of trouble. Their promises have helped
Christians through many centuries of persecution and abuse.

God blesses you who are hated and excluded and mocked and
cursed because you are identified with me, the Son of Man.
When that happens, rejoice! Yes, leap for joy! For a great reward
awaits you in heaven. And remember, the ancient prophets were
also treated that way by your ancestors.   LUKE 6:22-23

Because of our faith, Christ has brought us into this place of
highest privilege where we now stand, and we confidently and
joyfully look forward to sharing God's glory.
We can rejoice, too, when we run into problems and trials, for
we know that they are good for us—they help us learn to endure.
And endurance develops strength of character in us, and
character strengthens our confident expectation of salvation.
ROMANS 5:2-4

We serve God whether people honor us or despise us, whether
they slander us or praise us. We are honest, but they call us
impostors. We are well known, but we are treated as unknown.
We live close to death, but here we are, still alive. We have been
beaten within an inch of our lives. Our hearts ache, but we always
have joy. 2 CORINTHIANS 6:8-10

See also Eternal Life, Faith, Hope, Worldly Cares, Worry and Anxiety.

Judging Others

Is there anything more amusing than discussing someone else's faults? This shouldn't be so, especially for Christians. Yet most people, including Christians, act as though it is an acceptable form of entertainment. Is it any surprise that most TV sitcoms are built around people tearing each other down, either behind their back or right to their face? It's terribly funny on TV—but not at all funny in real life, especially if you are the person being degraded.

The Bible has a lot to say about being judgmental. Jesus and the apostles understood clearly the human tendency to put down others. Among Christians, this sometimes even takes the form of questioning another's spiritual condition. The Bible promises a rude awakening for people who make a hobby out of judging others. Such promises come from the only impartial Judge of human behavior, God himself.

The LORD doesn't make decisions the way you do! People judge by outward appearance, but the LORD looks at a person's thoughts and intentions. 1 SAMUEL 16:7

Stop judging others, and you will not be judged. For others will treat you as you treat them. Whatever measure you use in judging others, it will be used to measure how you are judged. And why worry about a speck in your friend's eye when you have a log in your own? How can you think of saying, "Friend, let me help you get rid of that speck in your eye," when you can't see past the log in your own eye? Hypocrite! First get rid of the log from your own eye; then perhaps you will see well enough to deal with the speck in your friend's eye. MATTHEW 7:1-5

We have stopped evaluating others by what the world thinks about them. Once I mistakenly thought of Christ that way, as though he were merely a human being. How differently I think about him now! What this means is that those who become Christians become new persons. They are not the same anymore, for the old life is gone. A new life has begun! 2 CORINTHIANS 5:16-17

Don't grumble about each other, my brothers and sisters, or God will judge you. For look! The great Judge is coming. He is standing at the door! JAMES 5:9

Don't speak evil against each other, my dear brothers and sisters. If you criticize each other and condemn each other, then you are criticizing and condemning God's law. But you are not a judge who can decide whether the law is right or wrong. Your job is to obey it. God alone, who made the law, can rightly judge among us. He alone has the power to save or to destroy. So what right do you have to condemn your neighbor? JAMES 4:11-12

Whenever you speak, or whatever you do, remember that you will be judged by the law of love, the law that set you free. For there will be no mercy for you if you have not been merciful to others. But if you have been merciful, then God's mercy toward you will win out over his judgment against you. JAMES 2:12-13

In his letter to the Romans, Paul begins by describing the immorality of people who do not know God. But as he continues his argument, he warns Christians about any feelings of superiority.

You may be saying, "What terrible people you have been talking about!" But you are just as bad, and you have no excuse! When you say they are wicked and should be punished, you are condemning yourself, for you do these very same things. And we know that God, in his justice, will punish anyone who does such things. Do you think that God will judge and condemn others for doing them and not judge you when you do them, too? Don't you realize how kind, tolerant, and patient God is with you? Or don't you care? Can't you see how kind he has been in giving you time to turn from your sin?

But no, you won't listen. So you are storing up terrible punishment for yourself because of your stubbornness in refusing to turn from your sin. For there is going to come a day of judgment when God, the just judge of all the world, will judge all people according to what they have done.
ROMANS 2:1-6

It's true that the Bible has harsh words against people who judge others. At the same time, though, believers are expected to maintain godly moral standards. In the fellowship of the faithful there is no place for self-righteousness, but there is a place for pointing out flagrant sin for what it is. As Paul observed, Christians without moral standards are not Christians at all.

It isn't my responsibility to judge outsiders, but it certainly is your job to judge those inside the church who are sinning in these ways. God will judge those on the outside; but as the Scriptures say, "You must remove the evil person from among you."
1 CORINTHIANS 5:12-13

The apostle Paul raised an interesting question: Can we even judge ourselves fairly? His conclusion was that God alone can judge a person fairly.

What about me? Have I been faithful? Well, it matters very little what you or anyone else thinks. I don't even trust my own judgment on this point. My conscience is clear, but that isn't what matters. It is the Lord himself who will examine me and decide.

So be careful not to jump to conclusions before the Lord returns as to whether or not someone is faithful. When the Lord comes, he will bring our deepest secrets to light and will reveal our private motives. And then God will give to everyone whatever praise is due. 1 CORINTHIANS 4:3-5

One of the greatest temptations a Christian faces is comparing his own spiritual life to another Christian's. It is so easy, and so tempting, to look down on another person who seems to have less faith. But the Bible has something to say about this habit.

Accept Christians who are weak in faith, and don't argue with them about what they think is right or wrong. For instance, one person believes it is all right to eat anything. But another believer who has a sensitive conscience will eat only vegetables. Those who think it is all right to eat anything must not look down on those who won't. And those who won't eat certain foods must not condemn those who do, for God has accepted them. Who are you to condemn God's servants? They are responsible to the Lord, so let him tell them whether they are right or wrong. The Lord's power will help them do as they should.

In the same way, some think one day is more holy than another day, while others think every day is alike. Each person should have a personal conviction about this matter. Those who have a special day for worshiping the Lord are trying to honor him. Those who eat all kinds of food do so to honor the Lord, since they give thanks to God before eating. And those who won't eat

everything also want to please the Lord and give thanks to God. For we are not our own masters when we live or when we die.
ROMANS 14:1-7

See also Anger, Envy, God's Fairness, Hate, Hypocrisy, Self-Righteousness, The Tongue.

Justification

Signs reading Get Right with God once appeared on roadsides throughout America. Over time the signs have almost disappeared and so has the feeling that we ought to get right with God.

Being "right with God" is what *justification* means. God hasn't changed, and neither has human nature. We still need to be justified, and all our moral efforts and self-esteem boosters won't do it. But the New Testament promises that we don't have to rely on our own efforts. Someone else has enabled us to "get right with God," to be accepted by him.

We are made right in God's sight when we trust in Jesus Christ to take away our sins. And we all can be saved in this same way, no matter who we are or what we have done.

For all have sinned; all fall short of God's glorious standard. Yet now God in his gracious kindness declares us not guilty. He has done this through Christ Jesus, who has freed us by taking away our sins.   ROMANS 3:22-24

Brothers, listen! In this man Jesus there is forgiveness for your sins. Everyone who believes in him is freed from all guilt and declared right with God.   ACTS 13:38-39

I assure you, those who listen to my message and believe in God who sent me have eternal life. They will never be condemned for their sins, but they have already passed from death into life.
JOHN 5:24

Since we have been made right in God's sight by faith, we have peace with God because of what Jesus Christ our Lord has done for us.

And since we have been made right in God's sight by the blood of Christ, he will certainly save us from God's judgment.

So now we can rejoice in our wonderful new relationship with God—all because of what our Lord Jesus Christ has done for us in making us friends of God.

And the result of God's gracious gift is very different from the result of that one man's sin. For Adam's sin led to condemnation, but we have the free gift of being accepted by God, even though we are guilty of many sins. ROMANS 5:1, 9, 11, 16

Now there is no condemnation for those who belong to Christ Jesus.

And having chosen them, he called them to come to him. And he gave them right standing with himself, and he promised them his glory.

What can we say about such wonderful things as these? If God is for us, who can ever be against us? Since God did not spare even his own Son but gave him up for us all, won't God, who gave us Christ, also give us everything else?

Who dares accuse us whom God has chosen for his own? Will God? No! He is the one who has given us right standing with himself. Who then will condemn us? Will Christ Jesus? No, for he is the one who died for us and was raised to life for us and is sitting at the place of highest honor next to God, pleading for us.

Can anything ever separate us from Christ's love? Does it mean he no longer loves us if we have trouble or calamity, or are persecuted, or are hungry or cold or in danger or threatened with death? ROMANS 8:1, 30-35

God was in Christ, reconciling the world to himself, no longer counting people's sins against them. This is the wonderful message he has given us to tell others. We are Christ's ambassadors, and God is using us to speak to you. We urge you, as though Christ himself were here pleading with you, "Be reconciled to God!" For God made Christ, who never sinned, to be the offering for our sin, so that we could be made right with God through Christ. 2 CORINTHIANS 5:19-21

He declared us not guilty because of his great kindness. And now we know that we will inherit eternal life. TITUS 3:7

It is by believing in your heart that you are made right with God, and it is by confessing with your mouth that you are saved. ROMANS 10:10

> Paul, who preached the message of justification, holds out a wonderful promise: No matter how a person has wasted life, it is possible to change, to be made right with God and to start a new life.

Don't you know that those who do wrong will have no share in the Kingdom of God? Don't fool yourselves. Those who indulge in sexual sin, who are idol worshipers, adulterers, male prostitutes, homosexuals, thieves, greedy people, drunkards, abusers, and swindlers—none of these will have a share in the Kingdom of God. There was a time when some of you were just like that, but now your sins have been washed away, and you have been set apart for God. You have been made right with God because of what the Lord Jesus Christ and the Spirit of our God have done for you. 1 CORINTHIANS 6:9-11

See also Guilt; New Birth, New Life; Repentance; Salvation; Sin and Redemption.

Kindness

A great Christian hymn writer wrote that "kindness has converted more sinners than zeal, eloquence, or learning." Remarkable, isn't it, that when we think of "good people," "saints," or "model Christians," we think first of kindness, not intelligence or cleverness. Jesus, who is not only the Savior but also the one we are called to imitate, was wise and eloquent, too. Yet, what we remember about Jesus is mercy, kindness, compassion.

God blesses those who are merciful, for they will be shown mercy. MATTHEW 5:7

Since the Bible is an extremely practical book, the idea of mercy is not just an abstract concept. In the same chapter in which Jesus tells people to be merciful, he puts the idea of kindness in very concrete terms:

Give to those who ask, and don't turn away from those who want to borrow. MATTHEW 5:42

The King will say to those on the right, "Come, you who are blessed by my Father, inherit the Kingdom prepared for you from the foundation of the world. For I was hungry, and you fed me. I was thirsty, and you gave me a drink. I was a stranger, and you invited me into your home. I was naked, and you gave me clothing. I was sick, and you cared for me. I was in prison, and you visited me." MATTHEW 25:34-36

If you lend money only to those who can repay you, what good is that? Even sinners will lend to their own kind for a full return.
Love your enemies! Do good to them! Lend to them! And don't be concerned that they might not repay. Then your reward from heaven will be very great, and you will truly be acting as children of the Most High, for he is kind to the unthankful and to those who are wicked. You must be compassionate, just as your Father is compassionate. LUKE 6:34-36

If your gift is to encourage others, do it! If you have money, share it generously. If God has given you leadership ability, take the responsibility seriously. And if you have a gift for showing kindness to others, do it gladly.
Don't just pretend that you love others. Really love them. Hate what is wrong. Stand on the side of the good. Love each other with genuine affection, and take delight in honoring each other.
ROMANS 12:8-10

Love is patient and kind. Love is not jealous or boastful or proud or rude. Love does not demand its own way. Love is not irritable, and it keeps no record of when it has been wronged. It is never glad about injustice but rejoices whenever the truth wins out. Love never gives up, never loses faith, is always hopeful, and endures through every circumstance. 1 CORINTHIANS 13:4-7

Kindness is hard to separate from the issue of forgiveness. In fact, the Bible constantly places the two together. Life in this world brings us in continuous contact with people who irritate us, frustrate us, even drive us to the brink of frenzy. Despite this, the Bible repeats this theme: Be forgiving, for God is a forgiving God, and we are to be like him.

Since God chose you to be the holy people whom he loves, you must clothe yourselves with tenderhearted mercy, kindness, humility, gentleness, and patience. You must make allowance for each other's faults and forgive the person who offends you. Remember, the Lord forgave you, so you must forgive others. And the most important piece of clothing you must wear is love. Love is what binds us all together in perfect harmony. And let the peace that comes from Christ rule in your hearts. For as members of one body you are all called to live in peace. And always be thankful. COLOSSIANS 3:12-15

All of you should be of one mind, full of sympathy toward each other, loving one another with tender hearts and humble minds. 1 PETER 3:8

It is sin to despise one's neighbors; blessed are those who help the poor. PROVERBS 14:21

If one of you has enough money to live well, and sees a brother or sister in need and refuses to help—how can God's love be in that person? 1 JOHN 3:17

See also Forgiving Others, Generosity.

Laziness

The Bible doesn't say much about workaholics. Worshiping one's work has a way of keeping people away from God, which is wrong. But the Bible does have a lot to say about idleness. In those days, before the welfare state, the lazy person could only look forward to poverty. The Bible's promises about laziness still apply today, for the Bible authors understood that the lazy person's life harms not only himself but others—even society—as well.

A lazy person is as bad as someone who destroys things.
PROVERBS 18:9

Lazy people are a pain to their employer. They are like smoke in the eyes or vinegar that sets the teeth on edge.   PROVERBS 10:26

The desires of lazy people will be their ruin, for their hands refuse to work.   PROVERBS 21:25

Take a lesson from the ants, you lazybones. Learn from their ways and be wise!
But you, lazybones, how long will you sleep? When will you

wake up? I want you to learn this lesson: A little extra sleep, a little more slumber, a little folding of the hands to rest—and poverty will pounce on you like a bandit; scarcity will attack you like an armed robber. PROVERBS 6:6, 9-11

Lazy people don't even cook the game they catch, but the diligent make use of everything they find. PROVERBS 12:27

Hard work means prosperity; only fools idle away their time. PROVERBS 12:11

Lazy people want much but get little, but those who work hard will prosper and be satisfied. PROVERBS 13:4

Work brings profit, but mere talk leads to poverty! PROVERBS 14:23

A lazy person has trouble all through life; the path of the upright is easy! PROVERBS 15:19

A lazy person sleeps soundly—and goes hungry. PROVERBS 19:15

If you are too lazy to plow in the right season, you will have no food at the harvest.
    If you love sleep, you will end in poverty. Keep your eyes open, and there will be plenty to eat! PROVERBS 20:4, 13

Good planning and hard work lead to prosperity, but hasty shortcuts lead to poverty. PROVERBS 21:5

Too much sleep clothes a person with rags. PROVERBS 23:21

I walked by the field of a lazy person, the vineyard of one lacking sense. I saw that it was overgrown with thorns. It was covered with weeds, and its walls were broken down. PROVERBS 24:30-31

Hard workers have plenty of food; playing around brings poverty. PROVERBS 28:19

It is good for people to eat well, drink a good glass of wine, and enjoy their work—whatever they do under the sun—for however long God lets them live. And it is a good thing to receive wealth from God and the good health to enjoy it. To enjoy your work and accept your lot in life—that is indeed a gift from God. ECCLESIASTES 5:18-19

Laziness lets the roof leak, and soon the rafters begin to rot. ECCLESIASTES 10:18

> The apostle Paul, an industrious, energetic man, had no kind words for lazy people. He thought it especially improper that people calling themselves Christians should be lazy, relying on the charity of others and putting their idle hours to bad use rather than good.

Dear brothers and sisters, we give you this command with the authority of our Lord Jesus Christ: Stay away from any Christian who lives in idleness and doesn't follow the tradition of hard work we gave you. For you know that you ought to follow our example. We were never lazy when we were with you.

Even while we were there with you, we gave you this rule: "Whoever does not work should not eat."

Yet we hear that some of you are living idle lives, refusing to work and wasting time meddling in other people's business. In the name of the Lord Jesus Christ we appeal to such people—no, we command them: Settle down and get to work. Earn your own living. And I say to the rest of you, dear brothers and sisters, never get tired of doing good. 2 THESSALONIANS 3:6-7, 10-13

> Paul reminded people of a basic fact of the Christian life: Everything we do, including our work, whatever it is, should be done for the glory of God.

Never be lazy in your work, but serve the Lord enthusiastically.
ROMANS 12:11

My dear brothers and sisters, be strong and steady, always
enthusiastic about the Lord's work, for you know that nothing
you do for the Lord is ever useless. 1 CORINTHIANS 15:58

See also Ambition, The Sabbath, Work.

Loneliness

One TV talk show host claims that loneliness is *the* great problem in our society—not poverty or homelessness, not drugs or crime, but just plain *loneliness,* that achy feeling of not being connected closely to someone.

One of the Bible's first observations on human nature is that loneliness is a bad thing.

> The LORD God said, "It is not good for the man to be alone. I will make a companion who will help him." So the LORD God formed from the soil every kind of animal and bird. He brought them to Adam to see what he would call them, and Adam chose a name for each one. He gave names to all the livestock, birds, and wild animals. But still there was no companion suitable for him.
>
> GENESIS 2:18-20

The right solution to Adam's loneliness was another human being. But, sadly, loneliness occurs not only to single people but also to married people, to parents, to people who work all day with others. Unfortunately, it is possible to be lonely even when surrounded by others. Perhaps the worst part is, it's a burden few people are willing to admit to carrying.

How many suicides occur because of loneliness? A neighbor, a coworker, someone in our own family—even we ourselves—can ache on the inside, sometimes hiding it under outward pleasantness. Burying the ache only adds another burden.

Interestingly, the Bible—the book of Psalms in particular—includes many instances of lonely people who poured out their sorrow to God.

Turn to me and have mercy on me, for I am alone and in deep distress.

May integrity and honesty protect me, for I put my hope in you. PSALM 25:16, 21

As for me, I am poor and needy, but the Lord is thinking about me right now. You are my helper and my savior. Do not delay, O my God. PSALM 40:17

Painful words to read, but comforting also, knowing that God is thinking about us. It is also a comfort knowing that God's Son experienced all the pains of human life, even loneliness, especially at the time of his arrest and crucifixion.

All the disciples deserted him and fled. MATTHEW 26:56

Surely a Savior who experienced this part of human life has sympathy for those of us who feel the same pain. We can be thankful because not only does he sympathize, he is the *answer* to our pain.

Sing praises to God and to his name! Sing loud praises to him who rides the clouds. His name is the LORD—rejoice in his presence! Father to the fatherless, defender of widows—this is God, whose

dwelling is holy. God places the lonely in families; he sets the
prisoners free and gives them joy.   PSALM 68:4-6

> Does God really "place the lonely in families"? Not in the sense that
> every person will have a spouse and children to provide
> companionship. But there is that greatest of all families, the
> community of God's people. A person with no family at all can find
> a place in the family of God. Every fellow believer is a brother and
> sister, all with one and the same Father. The Bible's greatest promise
> for the lonely person is this promise written by the apostle Paul:

I will be your Father, and you will be my sons and daughters, says
the Lord Almighty.   2 CORINTHIANS 6:18

See also Fellowship with God, Fellowship with Other Believers, Friends.

Loving God

C. S. Lewis said that "a man's spiritual health is exactly proportional to his love for God." It's true that God is concerned about our morals and our conduct, but he is mostly concerned with our heart. Are we devoted to him? Although we love other things—our family, our spouse, our friends—do we still love God *more?* If not, then, as Lewis noted, we may not be spiritually healthy.

Perhaps the key to it all is *need.* We know we need God more than anything else. When we forget this, our love wanes. Then, when we feel it, as in times of sorrow, we run back to God, aware of our need. It is a great comfort to know that God understands this.

Take delight in the LORD, and he will give you your heart's desires. PSALM 37:4

I love all who love me. Those who search for me will surely find me. PROVERBS 8:17

The LORD says, "I will rescue those who love me. I will protect those who trust in my name. When they call on me, I will answer;

I will be with them in trouble. I will rescue them and honor them.
I will satisfy them with a long life and give them my salvation."
PSALM 91:14-16

The LORD is close to all who call on him, yes, to all who call on
him sincerely. He fulfills the desires of those who fear him; he
hears their cries for help and rescues them. The LORD protects
all those who love him, but he destroys the wicked.
PSALM 145:18-20

> Jesus himself had a lot to say about loving God. What he said about
> our love for the Father outdoes anything ever said about love in pop
> songs and poetry.

The most important commandment is this:" Hear, O Israel! The
Lord our God is the one and only Lord. And you must love the
Lord your God with all your heart, all your soul, all your mind,
and all your strength." The second is equally important: "Love
your neighbor as yourself." No other commandment is greater
than these. MARK 12:29-31

> It is much easier to talk about love than actually do it. How often do
> we gleefully tell other people we love them, but then prove by our
> actions that we don't? We do the same to God. Jesus understood
> this, and he warned his followers about "talking the talk" and not
> "walking the walk."

If you love me, obey my commandments. And I will ask the
Father, and he will give you another Counselor, who will never
leave you.
  Those who obey my commandments are the ones who love me.
And because they love me, my Father will love them, and I will
love them. And I will reveal myself to each one of them.
  All those who love me will do what I say. My Father will love
them, and we will come to them and live with them. Anyone who

doesn't love me will not do what I say. And remember, my words are not my own. This message is from the Father who sent me. JOHN 14:15-16, 21, 23-24

Great crowds were following Jesus. He turned around and said to them, "If you want to be my follower you must love me more than your own father and mother, wife and children, brothers and sisters—yes, more than your own life. Otherwise, you cannot be my disciple." LUKE 14:25-26

No eye has seen, no ear has heard, and no mind has imagined what God has prepared for those who love him. 1 CORINTHIANS 2:9

> In the Bible, two kinds of love are never separated: love for God and love for other people. One without the other is—well, incomplete.

One day an expert in religious law stood up to test Jesus by asking him this question: "Teacher, what must I do to receive eternal life?"

Jesus replied, "What does the law of Moses say? How do you read it?"

The man answered, "'You must love the Lord your God with all your heart, all your soul, all your strength, and all your mind.' And, 'Love your neighbor as yourself.'"

"Right!" Jesus told him. "Do this and you will live!" LUKE 10:25-28

If someone says, "I love God," but hates another Christian, that person is a liar; for if we don't love people we can see, how can we love God, whom we have not seen? And God himself has commanded that we must love not only him but our Christian brothers and sisters, too. 1 JOHN 4:20-21

God is not unfair. He will not forget how hard you have worked for him and how you have shown your love to him by caring for other Christians, as you still do. HEBREWS 6:10

While knowledge may make us feel important, it is love that really builds up the church. Anyone who claims to know all the answers doesn't really know very much. But the person who loves God is the one God knows and cares for. 1 CORINTHIANS 8:1-3

See also Fellowship with God, Obeying God.

Loving Others

Loving other human beings doesn't mean being "in love" with everyone. That kind of warm-fuzzy love is easy—that is, until the emotion starts to fade. But the human love the Bible talks about isn't just a passing emotional state. It's something based on *choice.* We *choose* to care about another person's welfare, even if that person has hurt us, called us names, ignored us. Parents understand this kind of love, for they keep loving their children even when the children don't act as though they love them back. It is similar but not as steadfast, as God's love for us. He loves us when we aren't at all lovable and gives this command: "Love other people the way I love you. Make *giving,* not *getting,* the goal of your love." Is this hard? Only because we haven't made it a habit.

Hatred stirs up quarrels, but love covers all offenses.
PROVERBS 10:12

Disregarding another person's faults preserves love; telling about them separates close friends. PROVERBS 17:9

A friend is always loyal, and a brother is born to help in time of
need. PROVERBS 17:17

Do for others as you would like them to do for you.
   Do you think you deserve credit merely for loving those who
love you? Even the sinners do that! And if you do good only to
those who do good to you, is that so wonderful? Even sinners
do that much! And if you lend money only to those who can
repay you, what good is that? Even sinners will lend to their
own kind for a full return. Love your enemies! Do good to them!
Lend to them! And don't be concerned that they might not
repay. Then your reward from heaven will be very great, and
you will truly be acting as children of the Most High, for he is
kind to the unthankful and to those who are wicked. You must
be compassionate, just as your Father is compassionate.
LUKE 6:31-36

If you welcome a prophet as one who speaks for God, you will
receive the same reward a prophet gets. And if you welcome good
and godly people because of their godliness, you will be given a
reward like theirs. And if you give even a cup of cold water to one
of the least of my followers, you will surely be rewarded.
MATTHEW 10:41-42

One day an expert in religious law stood up to test Jesus by
asking him this question: "Teacher, what must I do to receive
eternal life?"
   Jesus replied, "What does the law of Moses say? How do you
read it?"
   The man answered; "'You must love the Lord your God with
all your heart, all your soul, all your strength, and all your
mind.' And, 'Love your neighbor as yourself.'"
   "Right!" Jesus told him. "Do this and you will live!" LUKE
10:25-28

I am giving you a new commandment: Love each other. Just as I have loved you, you should love each other. Your love for one another will prove to the world that you are my disciples.
JOHN 13:34-35

God has given each of us the ability to do certain things well. So if God has given you the ability to prophesy, speak out when you have faith that God is speaking through you. If your gift is that of serving others, serve them well. If you are a teacher, do a good job of teaching. If your gift is to encourage others, do it! If you have money, share it generously. If God has given you leadership ability, take the responsibility seriously. And if you have a gift for showing kindness to others, do it gladly.

Don't just pretend that you love others. Really love them. Hate what is wrong. Stand on the side of the good. Love each other with genuine affection, and take delight in honoring each other.
ROMANS 12:6-10

Pay all your debts, except the debt of love for others. You can never finish paying that! If you love your neighbor, you will fulfill all the requirements of God's law. For the commandments against adultery and murder and stealing and coveting—and any other commandment—are all summed up in this one commandment: "Love your neighbor as yourself." Love does no wrong to anyone, so love satisfies all of God's requirements. ROMANS 13:8-10

> Chapter 13 of Paul's first letter to the Corinthians is considered the Bible's great "love chapter." Paul had been writing to a quarrelsome group of Christians about their spiritual gifts and how to use them to everyone's benefit. Paul was wise enough to know that in any group of people, the greatest gift they can share with each other is love—not just warm feelings, but the kind of amazing love described here:

If I could speak in any language in heaven or on earth but didn't love others, I would only be making meaningless noise like a loud gong or a clanging cymbal. If I had the gift of prophecy, and if I knew all the mysteries of the future and knew everything about everything, but didn't love others, what good would I be? And if I had the gift of faith so that I could speak to a mountain and make it move, without love I would be no good to anybody. If I gave everything I have to the poor and even sacrificed my body, I could boast about it; but if I didn't love others, I would be of no value whatsoever.

Love is patient and kind. Love is not jealous or boastful or proud or rude. Love does not demand its own way. Love is not irritable, and it keeps no record of when it has been wronged. It is never glad about injustice but rejoices whenever the truth wins out. Love never gives up, never loses faith, is always hopeful, and endures through every circumstance.

Love will last forever, but prophecy and speaking in unknown languages and special knowledge will all disappear. Now we know only a little, and even the gift of prophecy reveals little! But when the end comes, these special gifts will all disappear.

It's like this: When I was a child, I spoke and thought and reasoned as a child does. But when I grew up, I put away childish things. Now we see things imperfectly as in a poor mirror, but then we will see everything with perfect clarity. All that I know now is partial and incomplete, but then I will know everything completely, just as God knows me now.

There are three things that will endure—faith, hope, and love—and the greatest of these is love. 1 CORINTHIANS 13

> Paul and the other New Testament authors had much more to say on this subject. They portray love as the greatest of duties, but not a burdensome, unpleasant duty. It is a duty we can actually enjoy, knowing that we are passing on God's love for us to other people.

When we place our faith in Christ Jesus, it makes no difference to God whether we are circumcised or not circumcised. What is important is faith expressing itself in love.

For you, dear friends, have been called to live in freedom—not
freedom to satisfy your sinful nature, but freedom to serve one
another in love. For the whole law can be summed up in this
one command: "Love your neighbor as yourself."

When the Holy Spirit controls our lives, he will produce this
kind of fruit in us: love, joy, peace, patience, kindness, goodness,
faithfulness, gentleness, and self-control.
GALATIANS 5:6, 13-14, 22-23

Be humble and gentle. Be patient with each other, making
allowance for each other's faults because of your love. Always
keep yourselves united in the Holy Spirit, and bind yourselves
together with peace.

We are all one body, we have the same Spirit, and we have all
been called to the same glorious future.   EPHESIANS 4:2-4

Don't be selfish; don't live to make a good impression on others.
Be humble, thinking of others as better than yourself. Don't think
only about your own affairs, but be interested in others, too, and
what they are doing.

Your attitude should be the same that Christ Jesus had.
PHILIPPIANS 2:3-5

I don't need to write to you about the Christian love that should
be shown among God's people. For God himself has taught you to
love one another.   1 THESSALONIANS 4:9

Continue to love each other with true Christian love. Don't forget
to show hospitality to strangers, for some who have done this
have entertained angels without realizing it! Don't forget about
those in prison. Suffer with them as though you were there
yourself. Share the sorrow of those being mistreated, as though
you feel their pain in your own bodies.   HEBREWS 13:1-3

Yes indeed, it is good when you truly obey our Lord's royal
command found in the Scriptures: "Love your neighbor as
yourself." JAMES 2:8

> Jesus told his followers they must love their enemies. This is often
> difficult. Curiously, it is also difficult at times to love other
> Christians. Every group of Christians that has ever lived has seen its
> share of bickering and hostility. Why so, when we are supposed to
> be brothers and sisters in God's family? Perhaps, like any human
> family, we just quarrel now and then. But the New Testament holds
> up an ideal for us: If we truly love God, we will love each other.

God is not unfair. He will not forget how hard you have worked
for him and how you have shown your love to him by caring for
other Christians, as you still do. Our great desire is that you will
keep right on loving others as long as life lasts, in order to make
certain that what you hope for will come true. HEBREWS 6:10-11

Anyone who loves other Christians is walking in the light and
does not cause anyone to stumble. 1 JOHN 2:10

Anyone who does not obey God's commands and does not love
other Christians does not belong to God.

This is the message we have heard from the beginning: We
should love one another. . . .

If we love other Christians, it proves that we have passed from
death to eternal life. But a person who doesn't love them is still
dead. Anyone who hates another Christian is really a murderer at
heart. And you know that murderers don't have eternal life within
them. We know what real love is because Christ gave up his life
for us. And so we also ought to give up our lives for our Christian
friends. But if one of you has enough money to live well, and sees
a brother or sister in need and refuses to help—how can God's
love be in that person?

Dear children, let us stop just saying we love each other; let us really show it by our actions. It is by our actions that we know we are living in the truth, so we will be confident when we stand before the Lord. 1 JOHN 3:10-19

Everyone who believes that Jesus is the Christ is a child of God. And everyone who loves the Father loves his children, too. We know we love God's children if we love God and obey his commandments. 1 JOHN 5:1-2

Now you can have sincere love for each other as brothers and sisters because you were cleansed from your sins when you accepted the truth of the Good News. So see to it that you really do love each other intensely with all your hearts. 1 PETER 1:22

See also Forgiving Others, Mercy.

Lying

Astand-up comic told his audience, "I wanted to go into politics, but I have this bad habit of telling the truth." Dishonesty has become so commonplace in politics, in business, and in the world in general that it seems downright normal. But people *know* instinctively that they should tell the truth. We certainly expect it from others, knowing that the world can't function if no one is trustworthy.

The Bible takes lying so seriously that one of the Ten Commandments forbids it:

Do not testify falsely against your neighbor. EXODUS 20:16

Specifically, this forbids giving a false testimony in court. But in a nutshell it sums up the whole biblical teaching on honesty. Lying has no part in the life of faith. In fact, the Bible has some dire warnings against deceivers.

The LORD hates cheating, but he delights in honesty. PROVERBS 11:1

Truth stands the test of time; lies are soon exposed. PROVERBS 12:19

The buyer haggles over the price, saying, "It's worthless," then brags about getting a bargain!

The LORD despises double standards; he is not pleased by dishonest scales. PROVERBS 20:14, 23

Telling lies about others is as harmful as hitting them with an ax, wounding them with a sword, or shooting them with a sharp arrow. PROVERBS 25:18

A false witness will not go unpunished, nor will a liar escape. PROVERBS 19:5

A truthful witness does not lie; a false witness breathes lies. PROVERBS 14:5

Though everyone else in the world is a liar, God is true. ROMANS 3:4

Do not testify spitefully against innocent neighbors; don't lie about them. And don't say, "Now I can pay them back for all their meanness to me! I'll get even!" PROVERBS 24:28-29

You will destroy those who tell lies. The LORD detests murderers and deceivers. PSALM 5:6

Neighbors lie to each other, speaking with flattering lips and insincere hearts. May the LORD bring their flattery to an end and silence their proud tongues. They say, "We will lie to our hearts' content. Our lips are our own—who can stop us?"

The LORD replies, "I have seen violence done to the helpless, and I have heard the groans of the poor. Now I will rise up to rescue them, as they have longed for me to do." PSALM 12:2-5

People with integrity have firm footing, but those who follow crooked paths will slip and fall.

The godly person gives wise advice, but the tongue that deceives will be cut off. PROVERBS 10:9, 31

> The New Testament introduces a different aspect: an emphasis on telling the truth to fellow Christians. Not that we are to be truthful *only* to Christians, but that we especially owe Christians the truth since we are part of one body, the church.

Put away all falsehood and "tell your neighbor the truth" because we belong to each other. EPHESIANS 4:25

Don't lie to each other, for you have stripped off your old evil nature and all its wicked deeds. COLOSSIANS 3:9

> Lying is such a serious offense in God's eyes that the Bible's final book, Revelation, contains a shocking conclusion: Liars are excluded from heaven along with murderers and idol worshipers. In the New Jerusalem, the heavenly city, they have no place. This doesn't mean that anyone who ever told a lie will be kept out of heaven. God is willing and eager to receive people who repent of their sins, including dishonesty. But the Revelation passage does communicate that dishonesty—which most people think of as a relatively *minor* sin—is not minor at all.

"All who are victorious will inherit all these blessings, and I will be their God, and they will be my children. But cowards who turn away from me, and unbelievers, and the corrupt, and murderers, and the immoral, and those who practice witchcraft, and idol worshipers, and all liars—their doom is in the lake that burns with fire and sulfur. This is the second death."
Outside the city are the dogs—the sorcerers, the sexually immoral, the murderers, the idol worshipers, and all who love to live a lie. REVELATION 21:7-8; 22:15

See also The Tongue.

Marriage

The wisecracking Mae West was quoted as saying, "Marriage is a great institution, but I'm not ready for an institution." Sometimes it appears that most people share Mae's cynical view of marriage. Divorce is so common that many people have ceased to think of it as a tragedy—except, perhaps, the ones experiencing it. It has, alas, become run-of-the mill—"normal." It wasn't so long ago that it was rare and definitely *not* the norm. Somewhere along the line the idea of *permanence* was thrown aside. "Till death do us part" is still part of most wedding ceremonies, but we wonder if anyone takes the words seriously.

The Bible promises heaven to those who love and honor God. It does *not* promise that marriage is heaven, which is perhaps why marriage disappoints so many people. "I loved Tom, but it just hasn't worked out." Do people expect too much? Can two human beings expect perfection from each other?

The Bible does have a high view of marriage, particularly marriage between two Christians. It is to be a lifetime plan, not something that can conveniently be disposed of in a lawyer's office and a courtroom. The love of husband and wife is, at its best, a hint of the deeper love between a human being and God.

Give honor to marriage, and remain faithful to one another in marriage. God will surely judge people who are immoral and those who commit adultery. HEBREWS 13:4

Drink water from your own well—share your love only with your wife. Why spill the water of your springs in public, having sex with just anyone? You should reserve it for yourselves. Don't share it with strangers.

Let your wife be a fountain of blessing for you. Rejoice in the wife of your youth. . . . May you always be captivated by her love. PROVERBS 5:15-19

Live happily with the woman you love through all the meaningless days of life that God has given you in this world. The wife God gives you is your reward for all your earthly toil. ECCLESIASTES 9:9

The man who finds a wife finds a treasure and receives favor from the LORD. PROVERBS 18:22

The apostle Paul, who was single, recommended the single life for people like himself, dedicated to God's service. But Paul was realistic enough to know that many people, no matter how deep their faith, are better off married than facing the temptations of the single life:

Because there is so much sexual immorality, each man should have his own wife, and each woman should have her own husband.

The husband should not deprive his wife of sexual intimacy, which is her right as a married woman, nor should the wife deprive her husband.

I wish everyone could get along without marrying, just as I do. But we are not all the same. God gives some the gift of marriage, and to others he gives the gift of singleness.

Now I say to those who aren't married and to widows—it's better to stay unmarried, just as I am. But if they can't control themselves, they should go ahead and marry. It's better to marry than to burn with lust. 1 CORINTHIANS 7:2-3, 7-9

> The apostles Peter and Paul also addressed a ticklish situation that existed both in their day and in ours: What if a Christian's spouse is not a Christian?

Now, I will speak to the rest of you, though I do not have a direct command from the Lord. If a Christian man has a wife who is an unbeliever and she is willing to continue living with him, he must not leave her. And if a Christian woman has a husband who is an unbeliever, and he is willing to continue living with her, she must not leave him. For the Christian wife brings holiness to her marriage, and the Christian husband brings holiness to his marriage. Otherwise, your children would not have a godly influence, but now they are set apart for him. (But if the husband or wife who isn't a Christian insists on leaving, let them go. In such cases the Christian husband or wife is not required to stay with them, for God wants his children to live in peace.) You wives must remember that your husbands might be converted because of you. And you husbands must remember that your wives might be converted because of you. 1 CORINTHIANS 7:12-16

> As you can see, Paul had much to say on the subject of marriage. He has been accused of being against women because of his discussion of a wife's submission. The passage here will show that he did *not* have in mind an abusive or dominating relationship, but one based on mutual love.

You will submit to one another out of reverence for Christ. You wives will submit to your husbands as you do to the Lord. For a husband is the head of his wife as Christ is the head of his body, the church; he gave his life to be her Savior. As the church submits to Christ, so you wives must submit to your husbands in everything.

And you husbands must love your wives with the same love Christ showed the church. He gave up his life for her to make her holy and clean, washed by baptism and God's word. He did this to present her to himself as a glorious church without a spot or wrinkle or any other blemish. Instead, she will be holy and without fault. In the same way, husbands ought to love their wives as they love their own bodies. For a man is actually loving himself when he loves his wife. No one hates his own body but lovingly cares for it, just as Christ cares for his body, which is the church. And we are his body.

As the Scriptures say, "A man leaves his father and mother and is joined to his wife, and the two are united into one." This is a great mystery, but it is an illustration of the way Christ and the church are one. So again I say, each man must love his wife as he loves himself, and the wife must respect her husband.
EPHESIANS 5:21-33

You wives must accept the authority of your husbands, even those who refuse to accept the Good News. Your godly lives will speak to them better than any words. They will be won over by watching your pure, godly behavior. . . .

You should be known for the beauty that comes from within, the unfading beauty of a gentle and quiet spirit, which is so precious to God. That is the way the holy women of old made themselves beautiful. They trusted God and accepted the authority of their husbands. 1 PETER 3:1-5

You wives must submit to your husbands, as is fitting for those who belong to the Lord. And you husbands must love your wives and never treat them harshly. COLOSSIANS 3:18-19

God wants you to be holy, so you should keep clear of all sexual sin. Then each of you will control your body and live in holiness and honor—not in lustful passion as the pagans do, in their ignorance of God and his ways.

Never cheat another Christian in this matter by taking his wife, for the Lord avenges all such sins, as we have solemnly warned you before. God has called us to be holy, not to live impure lives.
1 THESSALONIANS 4:3-7

In the same way, you husbands must give honor to your wives. Treat her with understanding as you live together. She may be weaker than you are, but she is your equal partner in God's gift of new life. If you don't treat her as you should, your prayers will not be heard. 1 PETER 3:7

> The Bible reminds us in several places that marriage is God's idea—not just a human convenience but something ordered by God to bring us pleasure and companionship in this world. Anyone undergoing marital problems may have doubts about this, and it is easy to get cynical about marriage when all around us marriages are falling apart. But the Bible is clear: Human beings, with all their faults and failings, can thank God for the institution of marriage.

The Holy Spirit tells us clearly that in the last times some will turn away from what we believe; they will follow lying spirits and teachings that come from demons. These teachers are hypocrites and liars. They pretend to be religious, but their consciences are dead.

They will say it is wrong to be married and wrong to eat certain foods. But God created those foods to be eaten with thanksgiving by people who know and believe the truth. Since everything God created is good, we should not reject any of it. We may receive it gladly, with thankful hearts. For we know it is made holy by the word of God and prayer. 1 TIMOTHY 4:1-5

See also Adultery, Children, Parents.

Meekness, Humility, Gentleness

Meekness is not weakness, nor does it mean letting oneself be a doormat or a milksop. It refers to our attitude toward insults and injuries. Instead of getting mad and getting even, the meek person says, "This shall pass." A meek person can have healthy self-esteem (to use our modern terms) yet not be a vain, arrogant, chip-on-the-shoulder type of person, always concerned about being slighted.

Do we have any meekness role models? The media give us entertainers, sports stars, and politicians strutting their egos in front of the cameras and microphones. Meek people don't normally seek the limelight, but they exist in the world, doing more good than all the egomaniacs combined.

If we seek role models, the Bible has many of them. It is also full of promises for those who follow those role models.

God blesses those who are gentle and lowly, for the whole earth will belong to them. MATTHEW 5:5

He leads the humble in what is right, teaching them his way. PSALM 25:9

Those who are gentle and lowly will possess the land; they will live in prosperous security.   PSALM 37:11

The LORD delights in his people; he crowns the humble with salvation.   PSALM 149:4

A gentle answer turns away wrath, but harsh words stir up anger.   PROVERBS 15:1

Mockers can get a whole town agitated, but those who are wise will calm anger.   PROVERBS 29:8

Patience is better than pride.   ECCLESIASTES 7:8

The humble will be filled with fresh joy from the LORD. Those who are poor will rejoice in the Holy One of Israel.   ISAIAH 29:19

Beg the LORD to save you—all you who are humble, all you who uphold justice. Walk humbly and do what is right. Perhaps even yet the LORD will protect you from his anger on that day of destruction.   ZEPHANIAH 2:3

Rejoice. Change your ways. Encourage each other. Live in harmony and peace. Then the God of love and peace will be with you.   2 CORINTHIANS 13:11

> Religious people have gotten a bad reputation for being self-righteous. Some are. But, according to the Bible, the right attitude toward other people's sins should be one of gentle correction. Instead of shouting from our moral pedestals, we are told to get down in the trenches with our brothers and sisters, using kindness and humility to steer them back toward the right path.

Dear friends, if a Christian is overcome by some sin, you who are godly should gently and humbly help that person back onto the right path. And be careful not to fall into the same temptation yourself. Share each other's troubles and problems, and in this way obey the law of Christ. If you think you are too important to help someone in need, you are only fooling yourself. You are really a nobody. GALATIANS 6:1-3

Be humble and gentle. Be patient with each other, making allowance for each other's faults because of your love.
EPHESIANS 4:2

Since God chose you to be the holy people whom he loves, you must clothe yourselves with tenderhearted mercy, kindness, humility, gentleness, and patience. You must make allowance for each other's faults and forgive the person who offends you. Remember, the Lord forgave you, so you must forgive others. And the most important piece of clothing you must wear is love. Love is what binds us all together in perfect harmony.
COLOSSIANS 3:12-14

We are often so appearance conscious that we forget God has little concern for our outward self. The Bible authors urged Christians to put aside their pride and vanity over physical beauty and cultivate the less visible quality of gentleness.

Don't be concerned about the outward beauty that depends on fancy hairstyles, expensive jewelry, or beautiful clothes. You should be known for the beauty that comes from within, the unfading beauty of a gentle and quiet spirit, which is so precious to God. 1 PETER 3:3-4

Our great role model, Jesus himself, the Son of God, was not an arrogant egomaniac but quite the opposite. He described himself as *gentle* and *humble* and promised rest for people in this world of warring egos. And he demonstrated his gentleness and humility in a remarkable way.

Jesus said, "Come to me, all of you who are weary and carry heavy burdens, and I will give you rest. Take my yoke upon you. Let me teach you, because I am humble and gentle, and you will find rest for your souls. For my yoke fits perfectly, and the burden I give you is light." MATTHEW 11:28

Jesus knew that the Father had given him authority over everything and that he had come from God and would return to God. So he got up from the table, took off his robe, wrapped a towel around his waist, and poured water into a basin. Then he began to wash the disciples' feet and to wipe them with the towel he had around him.

When he came to Simon Peter, Peter said to him, "Lord, why are you going to wash my feet?"

Jesus replied, "You don't understand now why I am doing it; someday you will."

"No," Peter protested, "you will never wash my feet!"

Jesus replied, "But if I don't wash you, you won't belong to me."

After washing their feet, he put on his robe again and sat down and asked, "Do you understand what I was doing? You call me 'Teacher' and 'Lord,' and you are right, because it is true. And since I, the Lord and Teacher, have washed your feet, you ought to wash each other's feet. I have given you an example to follow. Do as I have done to you. How true it is that a servant is not greater than the master. Nor are messengers more important than the one who sends them. You know these things—now do them! That is the path of blessing." JOHN 13:3-8, 12-17

See also Pride and Conceit, Self-Esteem, Selfishness.

Mercy

Mercy's indeed the attribute of heaven," wrote an
English poet. The Bible promises not only that God shows mercy to
people, but that people can—*must*—show mercy to each other.
Grudges and getting even are a normal part of the worldly scene, but
they have no place in the life of someone who has enjoyed the
mercy of God.

The Bible promises blessing for people who can mirror God's
mercy. It promises something else for those who refuse.

God blesses those who are merciful, for they will be shown
mercy. MATTHEW 5:7

There will be no mercy for you if you have not been merciful to
others. But if you have been merciful, then God's mercy toward
you will win out over his judgment against you. JAMES 2:13

Your own soul is nourished when you are kind, but you destroy
yourself when you are cruel. PROVERBS 11:17

The godly are concerned for the welfare of their animals, but even the kindness of the wicked is cruel. PROVERBS 12:10

Since God chose you to be the holy people whom he loves, you must clothe yourselves with tenderhearted mercy, kindness, humility, gentleness, and patience. You must make allowance for each other's faults and forgive the person who offends you. Remember, the Lord forgave you, so you must forgive others. And the most important piece of clothing you must wear is love. Love is what binds us all together in perfect harmony. And let the peace that comes from Christ rule in your hearts. For as members of one body you are all called to live in peace. And always be thankful. COLOSSIANS 3:12-15

Don't repay evil for evil. Don't retaliate when people say unkind things about you. Instead, pay them back with a blessing. That is what God wants you to do, and he will bless you for it. 1 PETER 3:9

Show mercy to those whose faith is wavering. Rescue others by snatching them from the flames of judgment. There are still others to whom you need to show mercy, but be careful that you aren't contaminated by their sins. JUDE 22-23

Wherever there is jealousy and selfish ambition, there you will find disorder and every kind of evil.
   But the wisdom that comes from heaven is first of all pure. It is also peace loving, gentle at all times, and willing to yield to others. It is full of mercy and good deeds. It shows no partiality and is always sincere. And those who are peacemakers will plant seeds of peace and reap a harvest of goodness. JAMES 3:16-18

Love your enemies! Do good to them! Lend to them! And don't be concerned that they might not repay. Then your reward from heaven will be very great, and you will truly be acting as children

of the Most High, for he is kind to the unthankful and to those
who are wicked. You must be compassionate, just as your Father
is compassionate.

Stop judging others, and you will not be judged. Stop criticizing
others, or it will all come back on you. If you forgive others, you
will be forgiven. If you give, you will receive.   LUKE 6:35-38

> A great illustration of mercy is Jesus' parable of the Good Samaritan.
> Knowing how Jews and Samaritans despised each other, Jesus
> showed that the greatest human mercy is mercy shown to someone
> we are expected to detest.

He asked Jesus, "And who is my neighbor?"

Jesus replied with an illustration: "A Jewish man was traveling
on a trip from Jerusalem to Jericho, and he was attacked by
bandits. They stripped him of his clothes and money, beat him up,
and left him half dead beside the road.

"By chance a Jewish priest came along; but when he saw the
man lying there, he crossed to the other side of the road and
passed him by. A Temple assistant walked over and looked at him
lying there, but he also passed by on the other side.

"Then a despised Samaritan came along, and when he saw the
man, he felt deep pity. Kneeling beside him, the Samaritan
soothed his wounds with medicine and bandaged them. Then he
put the man on his own donkey and took him to an inn, where he
took care of him. The next day he handed the innkeeper two
pieces of silver and told him to take care of the man. 'If his bill
runs higher than that,' he said, 'I'll pay the difference the next
time I am here.'

"Now which of these three would you say was a neighbor to the
man who was attacked by bandits?" Jesus asked.

The man replied, "The one who showed him mercy."

Then Jesus said, "Yes, now go and do the same."   LUKE 10:29-37

See also Enemies, Forgiving Others, God's Mercy.

Money

The Bible is a spiritual book, but not so spiritual that money doesn't matter. It *does* matter, mostly because of the human inclination to worship money instead of God. It matters because from the beginning of time human relations have been soured by greed. The movie character who gave the notorious "Greed is good" speech in the movie *Wall Street* was echoing the world's wisdom, not the Word of God. In fact, the Bible takes a position that will shock no one: Money doesn't satisfy. And whether or not we have money ultimately doesn't matter to God—it's how we choose to live.

The rich and the poor have this in common: The LORD made them both. PROVERBS 22:2

It is better to be godly and have little than to be evil and possess much. PSALM 37:16

We are merely moving shadows, and all our busy rushing ends in nothing. We heap up wealth for someone else to spend. PSALM 39:6

Riches won't help on the day of judgment, but right living is a safeguard against death.

Trust in your money and down you go! But the godly flourish like leaves in spring. PROVERBS 11:4, 28

Those who are wise must finally die, just like the foolish and senseless, leaving all their wealth behind. The grave is their eternal home, where they will stay forever. They may name their estates after themselves, but they leave their wealth to others. They will not last long despite their riches—they will die like the animals. This is the fate of fools, though they will be remembered as being so wise.

People who boast of their wealth don't understand that they will die like the animals. PSALM 49:10-13, 20

It is better to have little with fear for the LORD than to have great treasure with turmoil.

A bowl of soup with someone you love is better than steak with someone you hate. PROVERBS 15:16-17

The hot sun rises and dries up the grass; the flower withers, and its beauty fades away. So also, wealthy people will fade away with all of their achievements. JAMES 1:11

Don't weary yourself trying to get rich. Why waste your time? For riches can disappear as though they had the wings of a bird!
PROVERBS 23:4-5

Riches don't last forever, and the crown might not be secure for the next generation. PROVERBS 27:24

Those who love money will never have enough. How absurd to think that wealth brings true happiness! The more you have, the more people come to help you spend it. So what is the advantage of wealth—except perhaps to watch it run through your fingers!

People who work hard sleep well, whether they eat little or
much. But the rich are always worrying and seldom get a good
night's sleep.

There is another serious problem I have seen in the world.
Riches are sometimes hoarded to the harm of the saver, or they are
put into risky investments that turn sour, and everything is lost. In
the end, there is nothing left to pass on to one's children. People
who live only for wealth come to the end of their lives as naked
and empty-handed as on the day they were born.

And this, too, is a very serious problem. As people come into
this world, so they depart. All their hard work is for nothing. They
have been working for the wind, and everything will be swept
away. ECCLESIASTES 5:10-16

The person who wants to get rich quick will only get into trouble.
A greedy person tries to get rich quick, but it only leads to
poverty. PROVERBS 28:20, 22

Wealth from get-rich-quick schemes quickly disappears; wealth
from hard work grows. PROVERBS 13:11

They will throw away their money, tossing it out like worthless
trash. It won't buy their deliverance in that day of the LORD's
anger. It will neither satisfy nor feed them, for their love of money
made them stumble into sin. EZEKIEL 7:19

> The Word of God confirms something we all know deep down:
> Money is something we desire, but it does not satisfy us deeply. This
> is true even of money we come by honestly. And the Word has
> some very harsh words about money that was gotten dishonestly or
> at the expense of the poor.

How terrible it will be for you who get rich by unjust means! You
believe your wealth will buy security, putting your families
beyond the reach of danger. But by the murders you committed,

you have shamed your name and forfeited your lives. The very stones in the walls of your houses cry out against you, and the beams in the ceilings echo the complaint.

How terrible it will be for you who build cities with money gained by murder and corruption! Has not the LORD Almighty promised that the wealth of nations will turn to ashes? They work so hard, but all in vain! For the time will come when all the earth will be filled, as the waters fill the sea, with an awareness of the glory of the LORD. HABAKKUK 2:9-14

A person who gets ahead by oppressing the poor or by showering gifts on the rich will end in poverty. PROVERBS 22:16

Do not rob the poor because they are poor or exploit the needy in court. For the LORD is their defender. He will injure anyone who injures them. PROVERBS 22:22-23

Those who mock the poor insult their Maker; those who rejoice at the misfortune of others will be punished. PROVERBS 17:5

Look here, you rich people, weep and groan with anguish because of all the terrible troubles ahead of you. Your wealth is rotting away, and your fine clothes are moth-eaten rags. Your gold and silver have become worthless. The very wealth you were counting on will eat away your flesh in hell. This treasure you have accumulated will stand as evidence against you on the day of judgment. For listen! Hear the cries of the field workers whom you have cheated of their pay. The wages you held back cry out against you. The cries of the reapers have reached the ears of the Lord Almighty.

You have spent your years on earth in luxury, satisfying your every whim. Now your hearts are nice and fat, ready for the slaughter. You have condemned and killed good people who had no power to defend themselves against you. JAMES 5:1-6

I have seen violence done to the helpless, and I have heard the groans of the poor. Now I will rise up to rescue them, as they have longed for me to do. PSALM 12:5

> Just as those who pursue ill-gotten gain are promised judgment, those of a kinder disposition are promised kindness from the Lord:

Those who do not charge interest on the money they lend, and who refuse to accept bribes to testify against the innocent.
Such people will stand firm forever. PSALM 15:5

Oh, the joys of those who are kind to the poor. The LORD rescues them in times of trouble. PSALM 41:1

> Jesus, who apparently owned very little, understood that the key problem with money is that we let it separate us from God. It isn't bad in and of itself, but we let it become an idol.

No one can serve two masters. For you will hate one and love the other, or be devoted to one and despise the other. You cannot serve both God and money. MATTHEW 6:24

Jesus said again, "Dear children, it is very hard to get into the Kingdom of God. It is easier for a camel to go through the eye of a needle than for a rich person to enter the Kingdom of God!"
The disciples were astounded. "Then who in the world can be saved?" they asked.
Jesus looked at them intently and said, "Humanly speaking, it is impossible. But not with God. Everything is possible with God."
MARK 10:24-27

> Jesus understood something else: Money itself isn't evil. It is something we can use for our own selfishness—or to aid people who have little. The Bible gives us the concept of *stewardship,* the idea that what we do with our money indicates our priorities in life.

If you are untrustworthy about worldly wealth, who will trust you with the true riches of heaven? LUKE 16:11

We are poor, but we give spiritual riches to others. We own nothing, and yet we have everything. 2 CORINTHIANS 6:10

You will be enriched so that you can give even more generously. And when we take your gifts to those who need them, they will break out in thanksgiving to God. 2 CORINTHIANS 9:11

> Paul and the other apostles knew that Christians, like human beings in general, forget that their money should be used to benefit others. It seems that the more we have, the more likely we are to neglect our fellow man and to neglect God.

The love of money is at the root of all kinds of evil. And some people, craving money, have wandered from the faith and pierced themselves with many sorrows.

Tell those who are rich in this world not to be proud and not to trust in their money, which will soon be gone. But their trust should be in the living God, who richly gives us all we need for our enjoyment. Tell them to use their money to do good. They should be rich in good works and should give generously to those in need, always being ready to share with others whatever God has given them. By doing this they will be storing up their treasure as a good foundation for the future so that they may take hold of real life. 1 TIMOTHY 6:10, 17-19

Stay away from the love of money; be satisfied with what you have. For God has said, "I will never fail you. I will never forsake you." HEBREWS 13:5

You say, "I am rich. I have everything I want. I don't need a thing!" And you don't realize that you are wretched and miserable and poor and blind and naked. I advise you to buy gold from me—gold that has been purified by fire. Then you will be rich. And also buy white garments so you will not be shamed by your nakedness. And buy ointment for your eyes so you will be able to see. I am the one who corrects and disciplines everyone I love. Be diligent and turn from your indifference.   REVELATION 3:17-19

> One final note: God's Word forbids favoritism toward the rich. But how common that is! Even Christians may be inclined to favor the rich and well dressed and to ignore and neglect the poor person. But this is not the Christian way.

Listen to me, dear brothers and sisters. Hasn't God chosen the poor in this world to be rich in faith? Aren't they the ones who will inherit the kingdom God promised to those who love him? And yet, you insult the poor man! Isn't it the rich who oppress you and drag you into court? Aren't they the ones who slander Jesus Christ, whose noble name you bear?

Yes indeed, it is good when you truly obey our Lord's royal command found in the Scriptures: "Love your neighbor as yourself." But if you pay special attention to the rich, you are committing a sin, for you are guilty of breaking that law.
JAMES 2:5-9

See also Ambition, Duty to the Poor, Generosity, Self-Esteem, Success, Worry and Anxiety.

New Birth, New Life

Benjamin Franklin, having gained a reputation for his experiments with electricity, received a letter from evangelist George Whitefield. In the letter Franklin was told that since he had made progress in the knowledge of electricity, he should now "pursue the knowledge of the new birth." Whitefield thought that giving a person a new life was more important than increased learning about science and nature. Christians, including the ones who wrote the New Testament, have always agreed.

The words *born again* have been repeated so often that we forget their meaning. When Jesus first told Nicodemus (a very wise and religious man, by the way) that he had to be "born again," he was misunderstood. The words still are, but there's no reason why they should be. What it means is that the heart—the inward person, not the outward—is made new. For the person who experiences this, it is, to borrow the old cliché, the first day of the rest of his life. The body is not new, but the inner person is. The slate is wiped clean, and God views the person as brand new. This is only the first step, of course. The newborn must grow, and some grow faster and healthier than others. But before there is growth, there must be this new birth.

A Jewish religious leader named Nicodemus, a Pharisee, came to speak with Jesus. "Teacher," he said, "we all know that God has sent you to teach us. Your miraculous signs are proof enough that God is with you."

Jesus replied, "I assure you, unless you are born again, you can never see the Kingdom of God."

"What do you mean?" exclaimed Nicodemus. "How can an old man go back into his mother's womb and be born again?"

Jesus replied, "The truth is, no one can enter the Kingdom of God without being born of water and the Spirit. Humans can reproduce only human life, but the Holy Spirit gives new life from heaven. So don't be surprised at my statement that you must be born again. Just as you can hear the wind but can't tell where it comes from or where it is going, so you can't explain how people are born of the Spirit."   JOHN 3:1-8

> The Old Testament authors understood the new birth. What they foresaw was fulfilled in the life of Jesus.

Though our hearts are filled with sins, you forgive them all.
PSALM 65:3

"Wash yourselves and be clean! Let me no longer see your evil deeds. Give up your wicked ways. Learn to do good. Seek justice. Help the oppressed. Defend the orphan. Fight for the rights of widows.

"Come now, let us argue this out," says the LORD. "No matter how deep the stain of your sins, I can remove it. I can make you as clean as freshly fallen snow. Even if you are stained as red as crimson, I can make you as white as wool."   ISAIAH 1:16-18

Is anyone thirsty? Come and drink—even if you have no money! Come, take your choice of wine or milk—it's all free! Why spend your money on food that does not give you strength? Why pay for food that does you no good? Listen, and I will tell you where to get food that is good for the soul!

Come to me with your ears wide open. Listen, for the life of
your soul is at stake. I am ready to make an everlasting covenant
with you. I will give you all the mercies and unfailing love that I
promised to David. ISAIAH 55:1-3

O LORD, the hope of Israel, all who turn away from you will be
disgraced and shamed. They will be buried in a dry and dusty
grave, for they have forsaken the LORD, the fountain of living
water.

O LORD, you alone can heal me; you alone can save.
JEREMIAH 17:13-14

Long ago the LORD said to Israel: "I have loved you, my people,
with an everlasting love. With unfailing love I have drawn you to
myself.

"But this is the new covenant I will make with the people of
Israel on that day," says the LORD. "I will put my laws in their
minds, and I will write them on their hearts. I will be their God,
and they will be my people. And they will not need to teach their
neighbors, nor will they need to teach their family, saying, 'You
should know the LORD.' For everyone, from the least to the
greatest, will already know me," says the LORD. "And I will
forgive their wickedness and will never again remember their
sins." JEREMIAH 31:3, 33-34

I will give them singleness of heart and put a new spirit within
them. I will take away their hearts of stone and give them tender
hearts instead, so they will obey my laws and regulations. Then
they will truly be my people, and I will be their God.
EZEKIEL 11:19-20

I will sprinkle clean water on you, and you will be clean. Your filth
will be washed away, and you will no longer worship idols. And I
will give you a new heart with new and right desires, and I will put
a new spirit in you. I will take out your stony heart of sin and give

you a new, obedient heart. And I will put my Spirit in you so you
will obey my laws and do whatever I command. . . .

You will be my people, and I will be your God.   EZEKIEL 36:25-28

> What was promised and prophesied in the Old Testament came to
> life vividly in the life and work of Jesus. The New Testament
> constantly repeats this key message: The age of the new birth has
> dawned. For everyone who has ever sensed failure or despair (and
> who hasn't?), it is still a stirring, life-changing message.

Jesus called a small child over to him and put the child among
them. Then he said, "I assure you, unless you turn from your sins
and become as little children, you will never get into the Kingdom
of Heaven. Therefore, anyone who becomes as humble as this little
child is the greatest in the Kingdom of Heaven."   MATTHEW 18:2-4

I assure you, those who listen to my message and believe in God
who sent me have eternal life. They will never be condemned for
their sins, but they have already passed from death into life.
JOHN 5:24

I assure you, anyone who believes in me already has eternal life.
JOHN 6:47

If the Son sets you free, you will indeed be free.   JOHN 8:36

We died and were buried with Christ by baptism. And just as
Christ was raised from the dead by the glorious power of the
Father, now we also may live new lives.

Since we have been united with him in his death, we will also be
raised as he was. Our old sinful selves were crucified with Christ
so that sin might lose its power in our lives. We are no longer
slaves to sin. For when we died with Christ we were set free from
the power of sin. And since we died with Christ, we know we will
also share his new life.   ROMANS 6:4-8

Everyone dies because all of us are related to Adam, the first man. But all who are related to Christ, the other man, will be given new life. 1 CORINTHIANS 15:22

Those who become Christians become new persons. They are not the same anymore, for the old life is gone. A new life has begun! 2 CORINTHIANS 5:17

Christ lives in me. So I live my life in this earthly body by trusting in the Son of God, who loved me and gave himself for me. GALATIANS 2:20

You have stripped off your old evil nature and all its wicked deeds. In its place you have clothed yourselves with a brand-new nature that is continually being renewed as you learn more and more about Christ, who created this new nature within you. COLOSSIANS 3:9-10

It is by his boundless mercy that God has given us the privilege of being born again. Now we live with a wonderful expectation because Jesus Christ rose again from the dead.

For you have been born again. Your new life did not come from your earthly parents because the life they gave you will end in death. But this new life will last forever because it comes from the eternal, living word of God. 1 PETER 1:3, 23

You are a chosen people. You are a kingdom of priests, God's holy nation, his very own possession. This is so you can show others the goodness of God, for he called you out of the darkness into his wonderful light. 1 PETER 2:9

God saved you by his special favor when you believed. And you can't take credit for this; it is a gift from God. Salvation is not a reward for the good things we have done, so none of us can boast about it. For we are God's masterpiece. He has created us anew in

Christ Jesus, so that we can do the good things he planned for us long ago. EPHESIANS 2:8-10

He saved us, not because of the good things we did, but because of his mercy. He washed away our sins and gave us a new life through the Holy Spirit. He generously poured out the Spirit upon us because of what Jesus Christ our Savior did. TITUS 3:5-6

> Can a person lie or be deceived about being born again? Certainly. Jesus and the apostles understood this. While they warned against judging another person's spiritual condition, they did promise that we can know from a person's "fruit" whether there had really been a new birth. So, new birth is not just a prayer. It is a commitment to love God and to live as he wills.

If we love other Christians, it proves that we have passed from death to eternal life. But a person who doesn't love them is still dead. 1 JOHN 3:14

Every child of God defeats this evil world by trusting Christ to give the victory. And the ones who win this battle against the world are the ones who believe that Jesus is the Son of God.
So whoever has God's Son has life; whoever does not have his Son does not have life. 1 JOHN 5:4-5, 12

A healthy tree produces good fruit, and an unhealthy tree produces bad fruit. A good tree can't produce bad fruit, and a bad tree can't produce good fruit. So every tree that does not produce good fruit is chopped down and thrown into the fire. Yes, the way to identify a tree or a person is by the kind of fruit that is produced.
Not all people who sound religious are really godly. They may refer to me as "Lord," but they still won't enter the Kingdom of Heaven. The decisive issue is whether they obey my Father in heaven. MATTHEW 7:17-21

Prove by the way you live that you have really turned from your sins and turned to God. MATTHEW 3:8

See also Baptism of the Spirit and Gifts of the Spirit, Justification, Repentance, Salvation.

Obeying God

Anyone who has had any dealings with children knows that *obey* is not a dirty word. It may seem that way to children, but adults know that a home, a school, a camp cannot function if a child is constantly asking, "Who says I have to?" *Trust* is part of the picture. If the one giving the command is trusted, he is more likely to be obeyed. No wonder the old hymn had the chorus

> *Trust and obey*
> *For there's no other way*
> *To be happy in Jesus*
> *Than to trust and obey.*

This goes against our natural instincts, of course. The theme song today isn't "Trust and Obey" but "I Did It My Way." Still, people do look for guidance. Many, if not most, bookstores have a section on "Self-Help" and "Self-Improvement" that is well stocked, proving that people aren't totally satisfied with themselves.

The Bible promises something shocking: We are never more free or more content than when we put aside our selfishness and petty

desires and submit to God. In doing so, we are not obeying a
cosmic tyrant but a loving Father.

The LORD leads with unfailing love and faithfulness all those who
keep his covenant and obey his decrees. PSALM 25:10

Praise the LORD!
  Happy are those who fear the LORD. Yes, happy are those who
delight in doing what he commands. PSALM 112:1

Happy are those who obey his decrees and search for him with all
their hearts. PSALM 119:2

Keep the commandments and keep your life; despising them
leads to death. PROVERBS 19:16

Anyone who listens to my teaching and obeys me is wise, like a
person who builds a house on solid rock. Though the rain comes
in torrents and the floodwaters rise and the winds beat against
that house, it won't collapse, because it is built on rock. But
anyone who hears my teaching and ignores it is foolish, like a
person who builds a house on sand. When the rains and floods
come and the winds beat against that house, it will fall with a
mighty crash. MATTHEW 7:24-27

The sinful nature is always hostile to God. It never did obey God's
laws, and it never will. That's why those who are still under the
control of their sinful nature can never please God.
  But you are not controlled by your sinful nature. You are
controlled by the Spirit if you have the Spirit of God living in you.
(And remember that those who do not have the Spirit of Christ
living in them are not Christians at all.) ROMANS 8:7-9

If you will obey me and keep my covenant, you will be my own
special treasure from among all the nations of the earth; for all the

earth belongs to me. And you will be to me a kingdom of priests, my holy nation. EXODUS 19:5-6

Keep putting into practice all you learned from me and heard from me and saw me doing, and the God of peace will be with you. PHILIPPIANS 4:9

> We hear a lot of talk today about unconditional love. We are told that we ought to love and accept people as they are, demanding nothing from them. Many people even think of God that way—and it's true, in a way. God does love us and accept us as we are, no matter what our faults and failings may have been. But the Bible is clear about one thing: A true child of God will obey God. We can't just say, "God accepts me as I am" without adding the important words "and so I must submit myself to his authority."

Not all people who sound religious are really godly. They may refer to me as "Lord," but they still won't enter the Kingdom of Heaven. The decisive issue is whether they obey my Father in heaven. MATTHEW 7:21

Don't you realize that whatever you choose to obey becomes your master? You can choose sin, which leads to death, or you can choose to obey God and receive his approval. Thank God! Once you were slaves of sin, but now you have obeyed with all your heart the new teaching God has given you. Now you are free from sin, your old master, and you have become slaves to your new master, righteousness. ROMANS 6:16-18

The love of the LORD remains forever with those who fear him. His salvation extends to the children's children of those who are faithful to his covenant, of those who obey his commandments!
The LORD has made the heavens his throne; from there he rules over everything. Praise the LORD, you angels of his, you mighty creatures who carry out his plans, listening for each of his

commands. Yes, praise the LORD, you armies of angels who serve him and do his will!   PSALM 103:17-21

All who believe in God's Son have eternal life. Those who don't obey the Son will never experience eternal life, but the wrath of God remains upon them.   JOHN 3:36

> The words *I love you* are so easy to say but not always easy to put into action. We can talk the talk of love but have difficulty walking the walk. This is true of our love for other people and for God as well. Each of us knows, deep down, that the words are meaningless unless we back them up with loving actions. There is no place in the Bible for "talk love."

Jesus said to the people who believed in him, "You are truly my disciples if you keep obeying my teachings. And you will know the truth, and the truth will set you free.
   "I assure you, anyone who obeys my teaching will never die!"
JOHN 8:31-32, 51

If you love me, obey my commandments.
   Those who obey my commandments are the ones who love me. And because they love me, my Father will love them, and I will love them. And I will reveal myself to each one of them.
JOHN 14:15, 21

When you obey me, you remain in my love, just as I obey my Father and remain in his love. I have told you this so that you will be filled with my joy. Yes, your joy will overflow! I command you to love each other in the same way that I love you. And here is how to measure it—the greatest love is shown when people lay down their lives for their friends. You are my friends if you obey me. I no longer call you servants, because a master doesn't confide in his servants. Now you are my friends, since I have told you everything the Father told me. You didn't choose me. I chose you.

I appointed you to go and produce fruit that will last, so that the Father will give you whatever you ask for, using my name.
JOHN 15:10-16

Those who obey God's word really do love him. That is the way to know whether or not we live in him. Those who say they live in God should live their lives as Christ did.

And this world is fading away, along with everything it craves. But if you do the will of God, you will live forever.
1 JOHN 2:5-6, 17

We know we love God's children if we love God and obey his commandments. Loving God means keeping his commandments, and really, that isn't difficult.   1 JOHN 5:2-3

If you wander beyond the teaching of Christ, you will not have fellowship with God. But if you continue in the teaching of Christ, you will have fellowship with both the Father and the Son.
2 JOHN 9

See also Faith, Fellowship with God, Trusting God.

Opportunities

The opportunities we are talking about here are opportunities to advance God's Kingdom. An old proverb says that "hell is paved with good intentions and roofed with lost opportunities." The New Testament warns against losing opportunities. It maintains that our whole life is an opportunity to witness to the graciousness of God.

Don't get tired of doing what is good. Don't get discouraged and give up, for we will reap a harvest of blessing at the appropriate time. Whenever we have the opportunity, we should do good to everyone, especially to our Christian brothers and sisters.
GALATIANS 6:9-10

So be careful how you live, not as fools but as those who are wise. Make the most of every opportunity for doing good in these evil days. EPHESIANS 5:15-16

Live wisely among those who are not Christians, and make the most of every opportunity. Let your conversation be gracious and

effective so that you will have the right answer for everyone.
COLOSSIANS 4:5-6

> Jesus preached the message of God's Kingdom and the need for
> repentance and told his followers to do the same. He promised that
> some people would respond joyfully to the gospel and others would
> not, but he urged them to continue the work anyway.

Go and announce to them that the Kingdom of Heaven is near.
Whenever you enter a city or village, search for a worthy man
and stay in his home until you leave for the next town. When you
are invited into someone's home, give it your blessing. If it turns
out to be a worthy home, let your blessing stand; if it is not, take
back the blessing. If a village doesn't welcome you or listen to
you, shake off the dust of that place from your feet as you leave.
MATTHEW 10:7, 11-14

A man prepared a great feast and sent out many invitations. When
all was ready, he sent his servant around to notify the guests that
it was time for them to come. But they all began making excuses.
One said he had just bought a field and wanted to inspect it, so he
asked to be excused. Another said he had just bought five pair of
oxen and wanted to try them out. Another had just been married,
so he said he couldn't come.
The servant returned and told his master what they had said.
His master was angry and said, "Go quickly into the streets and
alleys of the city and invite the poor, the crippled, the lame, and
the blind." After the servant had done this, he reported, "There is
still room for more." So his master said, "Go out into the country
lanes and behind the hedges and urge anyone you find to come,
so that the house will be full. For none of those I invited first will
get even the smallest taste of what I had prepared for them."
LUKE 14:16-24

See also Witnessing.

Oppression

We hear so much today about exploitation, abuse, and oppression that the words have almost lost their meaning. Sadly, there is still real oppression in the world, with innocent people being exploited by cruel governments, employers, and institutions that forget they are dealing with flesh-and-blood human beings.

People have grown cynical about governments, including their own. They often view politicians and employers as enemies, not loyal friends or protectors. The feeling of being victimized by one's own elected officials can lead to despair. Likewise, we can feel oppressed by employers, by creditors, or even by people in our own family. The painful truth is that any person in authority can abuse that authority. The human condition is this: We *can't* live without putting certain people in authority, but some of those people *can* and will do us harm. This is as old as civilization.

But the Bible reminds us we are not helpless—not as long as God rules. We may never find complete justice in this life, but make no mistake, there is a loving God who keeps account of his exploited people.

The LORD is a shelter for the oppressed, a refuge in times of trouble. PSALM 9:9

LORD, you know the hopes of the helpless. Surely you will listen to their cries and comfort them. You will bring justice to the orphans and the oppressed, so people can no longer terrify them. PSALM 10:17-18

Do not oppress foreigners in any way. Remember, you yourselves were once foreigners in the land of Egypt.

Do not exploit widows or orphans. If you do and they cry out to me, then I will surely help them. My anger will blaze forth against you. EXODUS 22:21-24

Never take advantage of poor laborers, whether fellow Israelites or foreigners living in your towns. Pay them their wages each day before sunset because they are poor and are counting on it. Otherwise they might cry out to the LORD against you, and it would be counted against you as sin. DEUTERONOMY 24:14-15

The LORD replies, "I have seen violence done to the helpless, and I have heard the groans of the poor. Now I will rise up to rescue them, as they have longed for me to do." PSALM 12:5

The ones who can live here are those who are honest and fair, who reject making a profit by fraud, who stay far away from bribes, who refuse to listen to those who plot murder, who shut their eyes to all enticement to do wrong. These are the ones who will dwell on high. The rocks of the mountains will be their fortress of safety. Food will be supplied to them, and they will have water in abundance. ISAIAH 33:15-16

This is what the LORD says to the dynasty of David: Give justice to the people you judge! Help those who have been robbed; rescue

them from their oppressors. Do what is right, or my anger will
burn like an unquenchable fire because of all your sins.
JEREMIAH 21:12

How terrible it will be for you who lie awake at night, thinking up
evil plans. You rise at dawn and hurry to carry out any of the
wicked schemes you have power to accomplish. When you want a
certain piece of land, you find a way to seize it. When you want
someone's house, you take it by fraud and violence. No one's
family or inheritance is safe with you around!

But this is what the LORD says: "I will reward your evil with evil;
you won't be able to escape! After I am through with you, none of
you will ever again walk proudly in the streets." MICAH 2:1-3

> The Old Testament prophets, Amos in particular, had a great deal to
> say about oppression. They were especially horrified that people
> considered themselves religious yet still exploited others. The Lord
> promised serious consequences for such behavior.

This is what the LORD says: "The people of Israel have sinned
again and again, and I will not forget it. I will not let them go
unpunished any longer! They have perverted justice by selling
honest people for silver and poor people for a pair of sandals.
They trample helpless people in the dust and deny justice to those
who are oppressed. Both father and son sleep with the same
woman, corrupting my holy name.

"So I will make you groan as a wagon groans when it is loaded
down with grain." AMOS 2:6-7, 13

How you hate honest judges! How you despise people who tell the
truth! You trample the poor and steal what little they have through
taxes and unfair rent. Therefore, you will never live in the beautiful
stone houses you are building. You will never drink wine from the
lush vineyards you are planting. For I know the vast number of

your sins and rebellions. You oppress good people by taking bribes and deprive the poor of justice in the courts. So those who are wise will keep quiet, for it is an evil time.

Do what is good and run from evil—that you may live! Then the LORD God Almighty will truly be your helper, just as you have claimed he is. Hate evil and love what is good; remodel your courts into true halls of justice. Perhaps even yet the LORD God Almighty will have mercy on his people who remain.   AMOS 5:10-15

The LORD your God has arrived to live among you. He is a mighty savior. He will rejoice over you with great gladness. With his love, he will calm all your fears. He will exult over you by singing a happy song.

I will deal severely with all who have oppressed you. I will save the weak and helpless ones.   ZEPHANIAH 3:17, 19

This is what the LORD Almighty says: Judge fairly and honestly, and show mercy and kindness to one another. Do not oppress widows, orphans, foreigners, and poor people. And do not make evil plans to harm each other.

Your ancestors would not listen to this message. They turned stubbornly away and put their fingers in their ears to keep from hearing. They made their hearts as hard as stone, so they could not hear the law or the messages that the LORD Almighty had sent them by his Spirit through the earlier prophets. That is why the LORD Almighty was so angry with them.

Since they refused to listen when I called to them, I would not listen when they called to me, says the LORD Almighty.
ZECHARIAH 7:9-13

"I will put you on trial. I will be a ready witness against all sorcerers and adulterers and liars. I will speak against those who cheat employees of their wages, who oppress widows and orphans, or who deprive the foreigners living among you of justice, for these people do not fear me," says the LORD Almighty.

"I am the LORD, and I do not change. That is why you descendants of Jacob are not already completely destroyed. Ever since the days of your ancestors, you have scorned my laws and failed to obey them. Now return to me, and I will return to you," says the LORD Almighty.   MALACHI 3:5-7

> On one occasion while he was at his hometown synagogue, Jesus read a passage from the prophet Isaiah that deals with freedom from oppression. Jesus added a shocking revelation when he finished reading: Because he, the Son of God, had come into the world, the passage had been fulfilled. He did not mean that all oppression immediately ceased. His words are a promise that every oppressed person now has a Savior.

"The Spirit of the Lord is upon me, for he has appointed me to preach Good News to the poor. He has sent me to proclaim that captives will be released, that the blind will see, that the downtrodden will be freed from their oppressors, and that the time of the Lord's favor has come."

He rolled up the scroll, handed it back to the attendant, and sat down. Everyone in the synagogue stared at him intently. Then he said, "This Scripture has come true today before your very eyes!"
LUKE 4:18-21

See also Kindness, Money.

Parents

What purpose do parents serve in the modern world? Sometimes parents feel like unpaid chauffeurs, driving the children to and from ball games, band practice, whatever. With families on the move, each member pursuing his own individual plans, and precious little time for family togetherness, parents might wonder if they're really necessary for their children. Surrounded by educational and psychological "experts" on child rearing, too many parents feel inadequate for the task. Odd, since parents have been raising their children for centuries and, usually, have been pretty successful at it.

The Bible gives parents a much more important role than chauffeurs. In fact, they are so important that one of the Ten Commandments concerns them:

Honor your father and mother. Then you will live a long, full life in the land the LORD your God will give you.   EXODUS 20:12

Going against the grain of the world, the Bible imposes an important role on parents: discipline. It is an unpopular word these days. When have you seen a TV sitcom family that had a sane view of discipline? But in fact, parental discipline is an imitation of God himself, the Father who disciplines—not to abuse or to injure, but to set his children on the right path. It is discipline done out of love.

The LORD is like a father to his children, tender and compassionate to those who fear him. For he understands how weak we are; he knows we are only dust. PSALM 103:13-14

The LORD corrects those he loves, just as a father corrects a child in whom he delights. PROVERBS 3:12

Teach your children to choose the right path, and when they are older, they will remain upon it. PROVERBS 22:6

A youngster's heart is filled with foolishness, but discipline will drive it away. PROVERBS 22:15

Don't fail to correct your children. They won't die if you spank them. Physical discipline may well save them from death.
PROVERBS 23:13-14

To discipline and reprimand a child produces wisdom, but a mother is disgraced by an undisciplined child.
    Discipline your children, and they will give you happiness and peace of mind. PROVERBS 29:15, 17

Does this sound harsh? It shouldn't—nothing in the Bible condones abuse of children. In fact, Christian parents are often reminded to temper discipline with kindness.

Now a word to you fathers. Don't make your children angry by the way you treat them. Rather, bring them up with the discipline and instruction approved by the Lord. EPHESIANS 6:4

Fathers, don't aggravate your children. If you do, they will become discouraged and quit trying. COLOSSIANS 3:21

In both the Old and New Testaments, people of faith are given a critical role: passing on the heritage of faith to their children.

We will not hide these truths from our children but will tell the next generation about the glorious deeds of the LORD. We will tell of his power and the mighty miracles he did. For he issued his decree to Jacob; he gave his law to Israel. He commanded our ancestors to teach them to their children, so the next generation might know them—even the children not yet born—that they in turn might teach their children. So each generation can set its hope anew on God, remembering his glorious miracles and obeying his commands. Then they will not be like their ancestors—stubborn, rebellious, and unfaithful, refusing to give their hearts to God. PSALM 78:4-8

See also Children, Marriage.

Patience

You may have seen the popular wall poster a few years ago with the words "Give me patience, and I want it right NOW!" Patience seems to be in small supply in our instant gratification world. Yet with the amount of stress we have in this world, it might be the most useful quality we could hope for.

God is described as patient, overlooking people's wrongs and giving them time to change, to turn to him, to do right. The Bible spurs us on to imitate this, overlooking other people's offenses and enduring insults. What are we promised in return for this? Not a life without trouble, but a life with less fretting and fuming—a life that pleases God.

Be still in the presence of the LORD, and wait patiently for him to act. Don't worry about evil people who prosper or fret about their wicked schemes.

Stop your anger! Turn from your rage! Do not envy others—it only leads to harm. For the wicked will be destroyed, but those who trust in the LORD will possess the land. PSALM 37:7-9

A hothead starts fights; a cool-tempered person tries to stop them. PROVERBS 15:18

It is better to be patient than powerful; it is better to have self-control than to conquer a city. PROVERBS 16:32

Patience can persuade a prince, and soft speech can crush strong opposition. PROVERBS 25:15

Patience is better than pride.
  Don't be quick-tempered, for anger is the friend of fools.
ECCLESIASTES 7:8-9

By standing firm, you will win your souls. LUKE 21:19

Love is patient and kind. Love is not jealous or boastful or proud or rude. Love does not demand its own way. Love is not irritable, and it keeps no record of when it has been wronged.
1 CORINTHIANS 13:4-5

We can rejoice, too, when we run into problems and trials, for we know that they are good for us—they help us learn to endure. And endurance develops strength of character in us, and character strengthens our confident expectation of salvation. ROMANS 5:3-4

If we look forward to something we don't have yet, we must wait patiently and confidently. ROMANS 8:25

The Scriptures say, "Those who insult you are also insulting me." Such things were written in the Scriptures long ago to teach us. They give us hope and encouragement as we wait patiently for God's promises.
  May God, who gives this patience and encouragement, help you live in complete harmony with each other—each with the attitude of Christ Jesus toward the other. ROMANS 15:3-5

We try to live in such a way that no one will be hindered from finding the Lord by the way we act, and so no one can find fault with our ministry. In everything we do we try to show that we are true ministers of God. We patiently endure troubles and hardships and calamities of every kind. We have been beaten, been put in jail, faced angry mobs, worked to exhaustion, endured sleepless nights, and gone without food. We have proved ourselves by our purity, our understanding, our patience, our kindness, our sincere love, and the power of the Holy Spirit. We have faithfully preached the truth. God's power has been working in us. We have righteousness as our weapon, both to attack and to defend ourselves. 2 CORINTHIANS 6:3-7

We also pray that you will be strengthened with his glorious power so that you will have all the patience and endurance you need. May you be filled with joy, always thanking the Father, who has enabled you to share the inheritance that belongs to God's holy people, who live in the light. COLOSSIANS 1:11-12

Do not throw away this confident trust in the Lord, no matter what happens. Remember the great reward it brings you! Patient endurance is what you need now, so you will continue to do God's will. Then you will receive all that he has promised.
"For in just a little while, the Coming One will come and not delay. And a righteous person will live by faith. But I will have no pleasure in anyone who turns away." HEBREWS 10:35-38

Let us strip off every weight that slows us down, especially the sin that so easily hinders our progress. And let us run with endurance the race that God has set before us. We do this by keeping our eyes on Jesus, on whom our faith depends from start to finish. He was willing to die a shameful death on the cross because of the joy he knew would be his afterward. Now he is seated in the place of highest honor beside God's throne in heaven. Think about all he endured when sinful people did such terrible things to him, so that you don't become weary and give up. HEBREWS 12:1-3

Dear brothers and sisters, whenever trouble comes your way, let it be an opportunity for joy. For when your faith is tested, your endurance has a chance to grow. So let it grow, for when your endurance is fully developed, you will be strong in character and ready for anything. JAMES 1:2-4

If you suffer for doing right and are patient beneath the blows, God is pleased with you.
    This suffering is all part of what God has called you to. Christ, who suffered for you, is your example. Follow in his steps.
1 PETER 2:20-21

> One of the most touching promises in the Bible is Jesus' promise of rest for the weary. If you have ever heard these words set to music in Handel's *Messiah,* you know they are unforgettable.

Jesus said, "Come to me, all of you who are weary and carry heavy burdens, and I will give you rest. Take my yoke upon you. Let me teach you, because I am humble and gentle, and you will find rest for your souls. For my yoke fits perfectly, and the burden I give you is light." MATTHEW 11:28-30

> The first Christians eagerly awaited the return of Christ. It didn't happen in their lifetime (or in ours, yet), and some of them began to fret, particularly those who were being persecuted for their beliefs. *Has God forgotten us?* they wondered. *Has all our faithful living been in vain?* The apostles' response was a resounding no! Christ will return—according to his own plan, not ours. In the meantime, we continue living in this world, patiently enduring our hardships and looking forward to heaven.

Dear brothers and sisters, you must be patient as you wait for the Lord's return. Consider the farmers who eagerly look for the rains in the fall and in the spring. They patiently wait for the precious harvest to ripen. You, too, must be patient. And take courage, for the coming of the Lord is near.

Don't grumble about each other, my brothers and sisters, or God will judge you. For look! The great Judge is coming. He is standing at the door! JAMES 5:7-9

The Lord isn't really being slow about his promise to return, as some people think. No, he is being patient for your sake. He does not want anyone to perish, so he is giving more time for everyone to repent. 2 PETER 3:9

Don't get tired of doing what is good. Don't get discouraged and give up, for we will reap a harvest of blessing at the appropriate time. GALATIANS 6:9

See also Persecution, Perseverance, Worry and Anxiety.

Peace

It is curious that with all our timesaving and laborsaving devices (things our ancestors might have dreamed of), we still seem incredibly rushed, and often life seems to be a struggle with no end in sight. No wonder *peace* sounds so attractive to us.

Turn on the nightly news, and you'll notice that the politicians of the world haven't done well at bringing peace. Nor is this likely to happen. It is useless to wait for governments to bring peace. Anyway, peace doesn't mean just the absence of war. It means harmony, within individuals and between people. This kind of peace can be had even in the midst of war. It can be had—God has promised us this—in the midst of our own hectic, stress-filled life.

You will keep in perfect peace all who trust in you, whose thoughts are fixed on you! ISAIAH 26:3

"There is no peace for the wicked," says the LORD. ISAIAH 48:22

God blesses those who work for peace, for they will be called the children of God. MATTHEW 5:9

I will lie down in peace and sleep, for you alone, O LORD, will keep me safe. PSALM 4:8

Look at those who are honest and good, for a wonderful future lies before those who love peace. PSALM 37:37

Deceit fills hearts that are plotting evil; joy fills hearts that are planning peace! PROVERBS 12:20

I listen carefully to what God the LORD is saying, for he speaks peace to his people, his faithful ones. PSALM 85:8

When the ways of people please the LORD, he makes even their enemies live at peace with them. PROVERBS 16:7

A dry crust eaten in peace is better than a great feast with strife.
PROVERBS 17:1

Since we have been made right in God's sight by faith, we have peace with God because of what Jesus Christ our Lord has done for us. ROMANS 5:1

If your sinful nature controls your mind, there is death. But if the Holy Spirit controls your mind, there is life and peace. ROMANS 8:6

I pray that God, who gives you hope, will keep you happy and full of peace as you believe in him. May you overflow with hope through the power of the Holy Spirit. ROMANS 15:13

The God of peace will soon crush Satan under your feet.
ROMANS 16:20

God is not a God of disorder but of peace. 1 CORINTHIANS 14:33

When the Holy Spirit controls our lives, he will produce this kind of fruit in us: love, joy, peace, patience, kindness, goodness, faithfulness, gentleness, and self-control. Here there is no conflict with the law. GALATIANS 5:22-23

Always keep yourselves united in the Holy Spirit, and bind yourselves together with peace.

We are all one body, we have the same Spirit, and we have all been called to the same glorious future. EPHESIANS 4:3-4

The first Christians knew that one great enemy of peace is worry. We worry because we lack faith that God cares for us. So we often deprive ourselves of peace because of our lack of faith in God's continuous care. Paul assures Christians that God offers something greater than a life of worry.

Don't worry about anything; instead, pray about everything. Tell God what you need and thank him for all he has done. If you do this, you will experience God's peace, which is far more wonderful than the human mind can understand. His peace will guard your hearts and minds as you live in Christ Jesus.

Keep putting into practice all you learned from me and heard from me and saw me doing, and the God of peace will be with you. PHILIPPIANS 4:6-7, 9

Let the peace that comes from Christ rule in your hearts. For as members of one body you are all called to live in peace. And always be thankful. COLOSSIANS 3:15

So I tell you, don't worry about everyday life—whether you have enough food, drink, and clothes. Doesn't life consist of more than food and clothing? Look at the birds. They don't need to plant or harvest or put food in barns because your heavenly Father feeds them. And you are far more valuable to him than they are. Can all your worries add a single moment to your life? Of course not.

And why worry about your clothes? Look at the lilies and how they grow. They don't work or make their clothing, yet Solomon in all his glory was not dressed as beautifully as they are. And if God cares so wonderfully for flowers that are here today and gone tomorrow, won't he more surely care for you? You have so little faith!

So don't worry about having enough food or drink or clothing. Why be like the pagans who are so deeply concerned about these things? Your heavenly Father already knows all your needs, and he will give you all you need from day to day if you live for him and make the Kingdom of God your primary concern.

So don't worry about tomorrow, for tomorrow will bring its own worries. Today's trouble is enough for today. MATTHEW 6:25-34

A popular song gave the advice "Don't worry, be happy." Easier said than done, surely. The Bible gives the same advice but adds this: The God of peace is in charge of the world and is our only true source of lasting, worry-free peace. It also gives us some advice about how we can pursue a life of peace in this world.

If you want a happy life and good days, keep your tongue from speaking evil, and keep your lips from telling lies. 1 PETER 3:10

The LORD gives his people strength. The LORD blesses them with peace. PSALM 29:11

Those who trust in the LORD are as secure as Mount Zion; they will not be defeated but will endure forever.

Just as the mountains surround and protect Jerusalem, so the LORD surrounds and protects his people, both now and forever. PSALM 125:1-2

There will be glory and honor and peace from God for all who do good. ROMANS 2:10

Encourage each other. Live in harmony and peace. Then the God of love and peace will be with you.   2 CORINTHIANS 13:11

Try to live in peace with everyone, and seek to live a clean and holy life, for those who are not holy will not see the Lord. HEBREWS 12:14

> Jesus, who was persecuted to the point of death, knew that his followers would also face persecution. He gave them a promise: peace, even with persecution or the threat of persecution.

I am leaving you with a gift—peace of mind and heart. And the peace I give isn't like the peace the world gives. So don't be troubled or afraid.   JOHN 14:27

I have told you all this so that you may have peace in me. Here on earth you will have many trials and sorrows. But take heart, because I have overcome the world.   JOHN 16:33

> The prophet Isaiah had a vision of a world where peace reigned. He never saw this vision become a reality in his lifetime, and it has not happened in our own. Isaiah's vision was of something beyond this lifetime, the final and lasting peace that is heaven. Interestingly, he saw the peaceable Kingdom ushered in by a "Son." Isaiah didn't know it, but he was prophesying the Prince of Peace, Jesus himself.

A child is born to us, a son is given to us. And the government will rest on his shoulders. These will be his royal titles: Wonderful Counselor, Mighty God, Everlasting Father, Prince of Peace. His ever expanding, peaceful government will never end. He will rule forever with fairness and justice from the throne of his ancestor David. The passionate commitment of the LORD Almighty will guarantee this!   ISAIAH 9:6-7

Justice will rule in the wilderness and righteousness in the fertile field. And this righteousness will bring peace. Quietness and confidence will fill the land forever.

My people will live in safety, quietly at home. They will be at rest. ISAIAH 32:16-18

In that day the wolf and the lamb will live together; the leopard and the goat will be at peace. Calves and yearlings will be safe among lions, and a little child will lead them all. The cattle will graze among bears. Cubs and calves will lie down together. And lions will eat grass as the livestock do. Babies will crawl safely among poisonous snakes. Yes, a little child will put its hand in a nest of deadly snakes and pull it out unharmed. Nothing will hurt or destroy in all my holy mountain. And as the waters fill the sea, so the earth will be filled with people who know the LORD. ISAIAH 11:6-9

See also Contentment, Freedom, Trusting God, Worldly Cares, Worry and Anxiety.

Persecution

This chapter is about something the Bible is particularly concerned with—persecution of the righteous. One of humanity's sad ironies is that the wicked often do prosper and succeed while good people suffer. A great tragedy for any good person is not only suffering, but suffering *because of being a good person*. This happened in Bible days, and it still does. But a key theme in the Bible's promises is that God's eye is watching his people, and their persecution does not go unnoticed.

The bloodthirsty hate the honest, but the upright seek out the honest.

The godly despise the wicked; the wicked despise the godly.
PROVERBS 29:10, 27

God blesses those who are persecuted because they live for God, for the Kingdom of Heaven is theirs.

God blesses you when you are mocked and persecuted and lied about because you are my followers. Be happy about it! Be very glad! For a great reward awaits you in heaven. And remember, the ancient prophets were persecuted, too. MATTHEW 5:10-12

Look, I am sending you out as sheep among wolves. Be as wary as snakes and harmless as doves. But beware! For you will be handed over to the courts and beaten in the synagogues. And you must stand trial before governors and kings because you are my followers. This will be your opportunity to tell them about me—yes, to witness to the world. . . .

Brother will betray brother to death, fathers will betray their own children, and children will rise against their parents and cause them to be killed. And everyone will hate you because of your allegiance to me. But those who endure to the end will be saved. . . .

A student is not greater than the teacher. A servant is not greater than the master. The student shares the teacher's fate. The servant shares the master's fate. And since I, the master of the household, have been called the prince of demons, how much more will it happen to you, the members of the household!

Don't be afraid of those who want to kill you. They can only kill your body; they cannot touch your soul. Fear only God, who can destroy both soul and body in hell. Not even a sparrow, worth only half a penny, can fall to the ground without your Father knowing it. And the very hairs of your head are all numbered.
MATTHEW 10:16-25, 28-30

If you try to keep your life for yourself, you will lose it. But if you give up your life for my sake and for the sake of the Good News, you will find true life. And how do you benefit if you gain the whole world but lose your own soul in the process? Is anything worth more than your soul? MARK 8:35-37

When the world hates you, remember it hated me before it hated you. The world would love you if you belonged to it, but you don't. I chose you to come out of the world, and so it hates you. Do you remember what I told you? "A servant is not greater than the master." Since they persecuted me, naturally they will persecute you. And if they had listened to me, they would listen to you! The people of the world will hate you because you belong to me, for they don't know God who sent me. JOHN 15:18-21

Our dedication to Christ makes us look like fools. . . . To this very hour we go hungry and thirsty, without enough clothes to keep us warm. We have endured many beatings, and we have no homes of our own. We have worked wearily with our own hands to earn our living. We bless those who curse us. We are patient with those who abuse us. We respond gently when evil things are said about us. Yet we are treated like the world's garbage, like everybody's trash—right up to the present moment. 1 CORINTHIANS 4:10-13

> The apostle Paul, who knew a great deal about suffering for Christ, gave the classic statement about it in Romans 8—which is also one of the most inspiring promises made in the whole Bible:

Since we are his children, we will share his treasures—for everything God gives to his Son, Christ, is ours, too. But if we are to share his glory, we must also share his suffering.

Can anything ever separate us from Christ's love? Does it mean he no longer loves if we have trouble or calamity, or are persecuted, or are hungry or cold or in danger or threatened with death? (Even the Scriptures say, "For your sake we are killed every day; we are being slaughtered like sheep.") No, despite all these things, overwhelming victory is ours through Christ, who loved us. ROMANS 8:17, 35-37

We are pressed on every side by troubles, but we are not crushed and broken. We are perplexed, but we don't give up and quit. We are hunted down, but God never abandons us. We get knocked down, but we get up again and keep going. Through suffering, these bodies of ours constantly share in the death of Jesus so that the life of Jesus may also be seen in our bodies.

Yes, we live under constant danger of death because we serve Jesus, so that the life of Jesus will be obvious in our dying bodies.

So we live in the face of death, but it has resulted in eternal life for you. 2 CORINTHIANS 4:8-12

We have been beaten, been put in jail, faced angry mobs, worked to exhaustion, endured sleepless nights, and gone without food.

We serve God whether people honor us or despise us, whether they slander us or praise us. We are honest, but they call us impostors. We are well known, but we are treated as unknown. We live close to death, but here we are, still alive. We have been beaten within an inch of our lives. Our hearts ache, but we always have joy. We are poor, but we give spiritual riches to others. We own nothing, and yet we have everything. 2 CORINTHIANS 6:5, 8-10

If we endure hardship, we will reign with him. If we deny him, he will deny us. 2 TIMOTHY 2:12

> Does all of this mean that suffering itself is good? Hardly. Everyone suffers, and, of course, it is possible to suffer because we have done something wrong. This kind of suffering is not the "persecution of the righteous," as Peter's first letter makes plain:

You get no credit for being patient if you are beaten for doing wrong. But if you suffer for doing right and are patient beneath the blows, God is pleased with you.

This suffering is all part of what God has called you to. Christ, who suffered for you, is your example. Follow in his steps.
1 PETER 2:20-21

> Peter's letter was apparently addressed to people who were enduring persecution. This was not the official persecution that the Roman emperors staged a few years later. Rather, it was something that still happens in our own time: people slandering Christians, accusing them of wrong, mocking their faith, even discriminating against them in a work setting.

If you suffer for doing what is right, God will reward you for it. So don't be afraid and don't worry. Instead, you must worship Christ as Lord of your life. And if you are asked about your Christian hope, always be ready to explain it. But you must do this in a gentle and respectful way. Keep your conscience clear. Then if people speak evil against you, they will be ashamed when they see what a good life you live because you belong to Christ.
1 PETER 3:14-16

Dear friends, don't be surprised at the fiery trials you are going through, as if something strange were happening to you. Instead, be very glad—because these trials will make you partners with Christ in his suffering, and afterward you will have the wonderful joy of sharing his glory when it is displayed to all the world.

Be happy if you are insulted for being a Christian, for then the glorious Spirit of God will come upon you. . . . But it is no shame to suffer for being a Christian. Praise God for the privilege of being called by his wonderful name! 1 PETER 4:12-16

See also Enemies, Hope, Perseverance.

Perseverance

Perseverance isn't quite the same as stubbornness, but the two are similar. Winston Churchill, tough-minded and obstinate, claimed that we should "never, never, never, never give in, except to convictions of honor and good sense." He had a point. The Bible's view is similar, but it adds that when our own strength fails, God's strength does not.

Remain in me, and I will remain in you. For a branch cannot produce fruit if it is severed from the vine, and you cannot be fruitful apart from me.

Yes, I am the vine; you are the branches. Those who remain in me, and I in them, will produce much fruit. For apart from me you can do nothing. Anyone who parts from me is thrown away like a useless branch and withers. Such branches are gathered into a pile to be burned. But if you stay joined to me and my words remain in you, you may ask any request you like, and it will be granted! JOHN 15:4-7

Can anything ever separate us from Christ's love? Does it mean he no longer loves if we have trouble or calamity, or are persecuted, or are hungry or cold or in danger or threatened with death? (Even the Scriptures say, "For your sake we are killed every day; we are being slaughtered like sheep.") No, despite all these things, overwhelming victory is ours through Christ, who loved us.

And I am convinced that nothing can ever separate us from his love. Death can't, and life can't. The angels can't, and the demons can't. Our fears for today, our worries about tomorrow, and even the powers of hell can't keep God's love away. Whether we are high above the sky or in the deepest ocean, nothing in all creation will ever be able to separate us from the love of God that is revealed in Christ Jesus our Lord.   ROMANS 8:35-39

He died for everyone so that those who receive his new life will no longer live to please themselves. Instead, they will live to please Christ, who died and was raised for them.
2 CORINTHIANS 5:15

Don't get tired of doing what is good. Don't get discouraged and give up, for we will reap a harvest of blessing at the appropriate time.   GALATIANS 6:9

Don't drift away from the assurance you received when you heard the Good News. The Good News has been preached all over the world, and I, Paul, have been appointed by God to proclaim it.
COLOSSIANS 1:23

I am suffering here in prison. But I am not ashamed of it, for I know the one in whom I trust, and I am sure that he is able to guard what I have entrusted to him until the day of his return.
2 TIMOTHY 1:12

If we endure hardship, we will reign with him. If we deny him, he will deny us. If we are unfaithful, he remains faithful, for he cannot deny himself.   2 TIMOTHY 2:12-13

The Bible promises us that we *will* endure, for we were made for life that endures forever. It not only makes the promise, but it is filled with stories of people who bore up under great trials. In some cases their faithfulness to God led to their death—look at the case of Jesus himself. But God promises us that we will endure beyond death.

The LORD loves justice, and he will never abandon the godly.
    He will keep them safe forever, but the children of the wicked will perish. PSALM 37:28

The LORD will work out his plans for my life—for your faithful love, O LORD, endures forever. Don't abandon me, for you made me. PSALM 138:8

Those who endure to the end will be saved. MATTHEW 24:13

I give them eternal life, and they will never perish. No one will snatch them away from me, for my Father has given them to me, and he is more powerful than anyone else. So no one can take them from me. JOHN 10:28-29

There is going to come a day of judgment when God, the just judge of all the world, will judge all people according to what they have done. He will give eternal life to those who persist in doing what is good, seeking after the glory and honor and immortality that God offers. ROMANS 2:5-7

The Lord will deliver me from every evil attack and will bring me safely to his heavenly Kingdom. To God be the glory forever and ever. Amen. 2 TIMOTHY 4:18

If we are faithful to the end, trusting God just as firmly as when we first believed, we will share in all that belongs to Christ.
HEBREWS 3:14

God blesses the people who patiently endure testing. Afterward they will receive the crown of life that God has promised to those who love him. JAMES 1:12

Anyone who is willing to hear should listen to the Spirit and understand what the Spirit is saying to the churches. Everyone who is victorious will eat from the tree of life in the paradise of God. REVELATION 2:7

All who are victorious will be clothed in white. I will never erase their names from the Book of Life, but I will announce before my Father and his angels that they are mine. REVELATION 3:5

All who are victorious will inherit all these blessings, and I will be their God, and they will be my children. REVELATION 21:7

See also God's Love for Us, Patience, Temptation.

Personal Growth

You won't find the phrase *personal growth* in the Bible. It does, however, have a lot to say about the subject. One of the most important things it says is that we can't grow unless we're first planted, and we have to be planted in something besides ourselves. We have to be rooted in Christ, and nothing in the world can make us right, though Christ can.

People can read the Bible and learn much from it. It is full of good advice, particularly in the book of Proverbs. But *self-improvement* isn't the Bible's real aim. It aims to make us people who have begun a new life, a completely new direction, by uniting with Christ. Only with this new beginning, this "planting," can growth occur.

In other words, the Bible promises growth—real growth—only for the Christian. It is growth in grace, in learning to love God and our neighbor more dearly. All growing things have a dormant season now and then. But they are not dead—not so long as Christ lives in them.

Yes, I am the vine; you are the branches. Those who remain in me, and I in them, will produce much fruit. For apart from me you can do nothing. Anyone who parts from me is thrown away like a useless branch and withers. Such branches are gathered into a pile to be burned. But if you stay joined to me and my words remain in you, you may ask any request you like, and it will be granted! My true disciples produce much fruit. This brings great glory to my Father.

I have loved you even as the Father has loved me. Remain in my love. JOHN 15:5-9

We will no longer be like children, forever changing our minds about what we believe because someone has told us something different or because someone has cleverly lied to us and made the lie sound like the truth. Instead, we will hold to the truth in love, becoming more and more in every way like Christ, who is the head of his body, the church. Under his direction, the whole body is fitted together perfectly. As each part does its own special work, it helps the other parts grow, so that the whole body is healthy and growing and full of love. EPHESIANS 4:14-16

As we know Jesus better, his divine power gives us everything we need for living a godly life. He has called us to receive his own glory and goodness! And by that same mighty power, he has given us all of his rich and wonderful promises. He has promised that you will escape the decadence all around you caused by evil desires and that you will share in his divine nature.

So make every effort to apply the benefits of these promises to your life. Then your faith will produce a life of moral excellence. A life of moral excellence leads to knowing God better. Knowing God leads to self-control. Self-control leads to patient endurance, and patient endurance leads to godliness. Godliness leads to love for other Christians, and finally you will grow to have genuine love for everyone. . . . But those who fail to develop these virtues are blind or, at least, very shortsighted. They have already forgotten that God has cleansed them from their old life of sin.

So, dear friends, work hard to prove that you really are among those God has called and chosen. Doing this, you will never stumble or fall away. And God will open wide the gates of heaven for you to enter into the eternal Kingdom of our Lord and Savior Jesus Christ. 2 PETER 1:3-11

> Can we grow without trying? Children certainly do. But we all know that personal growth (inner growth, which is surely more important than strong bones and teeth) can occur only when we encourage it. In the words of the apostle Paul, we should crave it.

You must crave pure spiritual milk so that you can grow into the fullness of your salvation. Cry out for this nourishment as a baby cries for milk, now that you have had a taste of the Lord's kindness. 1 PETER 2:2-3

> You might guess from perusing all the self-help and personal-growth books that morality isn't too important. What counts (so the world tells us) is our physical health and achieving our career goals. But the booming business in psychotherapy (not to mention sleeping pills and antidepressants) proves that people pursuing the health-and-career agenda aren't finding real personal peace. Maybe we need to recall the wisdom of the Bible: We can't be the people God intended us to be until we really care about our moral health. In the Bible's view, our morals are more important than our cholesterol level.

With the Lord's authority let me say this: Live no longer as the ungodly do, for they are hopelessly confused. Their closed minds are full of darkness; they are far away from the life of God because they have shut their minds and hardened their hearts against him. They don't care anymore about right and wrong, and they have given themselves over to immoral ways. Their lives are filled with all kinds of impurity and greed.

But that isn't what you were taught when you learned about Christ. Since you have heard all about him and have learned the truth that is in Jesus, throw off your old evil nature and your former way of life, which is rotten through and through, full of lust and deception. Instead, there must be a spiritual renewal of your thoughts and attitudes. You must display a new nature because you are a new person, created in God's likeness—righteous, holy, and true. EPHESIANS 4:17-24

Dear brothers and sisters, we urge you in the name of the Lord Jesus to live in a way that pleases God, as we have taught you. You are doing this already, and we encourage you to do so more and more. For you remember what we taught you in the name of the Lord Jesus. God wants you to be holy, so you should keep clear of all sexual sin. Then each of you will control your body and live in holiness and honor—not in lustful passion as the pagans do, in their ignorance of God and his ways.

Never cheat another Christian in this matter by taking his wife, for the Lord avenges all such sins, as we have solemnly warned you before. God has called us to be holy, not to live impure lives. Anyone who refuses to live by these rules is not disobeying human rules but is rejecting God, who gives his Holy Spirit to you. 1 THESSALONIANS 4:1-8

Dear Christian friends, I plead with you to give your bodies to God. Let them be a living and holy sacrifice—the kind he will accept. When you think of what he has done for you, is this too much to ask? Don't copy the behavior and customs of this world, but let God transform you into a new person by changing the way you think. Then you will know what God wants you to do, and you will know how good and pleasing and perfect his will really is.

As God's messenger, I give each of you this warning: Be honest in your estimate of yourselves, measuring your value by how much faith God has given you. ROMANS 12:1-3

You may have seen the bumper sticker that says, "Please be patient, God isn't finished with me yet." That's a solid biblical idea. As long

as we're breathing, we're "works in progress," growing inwardly if
not outwardly.

We will fail at times—fail ourselves and fail God and others. But it
is a mark of living things that they heal. If we are "alive in Christ,"
our inner wounds and hurts need not be permanent.

I am sure that God, who began the good work within you, will
continue his work until it is finally finished on that day when
Christ Jesus comes back again.

I pray that your love for each other will overflow more and more,
and that you will keep on growing in your knowledge and
understanding. For I want you to understand what really matters
so that you may live pure and blameless lives until Christ returns.
May you always be filled with the fruit of your salvation—those
good things that are produced in your life by Jesus Christ—for this
will bring much glory and praise to God. PHILIPPIANS 1:6, 9-11

No, dear friends, I am still not all I should be, but I am focusing all
my energies on this one thing: Forgetting the past and looking
forward to what lies ahead, I strain to reach the end of the race
and receive the prize for which God, through Christ Jesus, is
calling us up to heaven.

I hope all of you who are mature Christians will agree on these
things. If you disagree on some point, I believe God will make it
plain to you. But we must be sure to obey the truth we have
learned already. PHILIPPIANS 3:13-16

You are looking forward to the joys of heaven—as you have been
ever since you first heard the truth of the Good News. This same
Good News that came to you is going out all over the world. It is
changing lives everywhere, just as it changed yours that very first
day you heard and understood the truth about God's great
kindness to sinners. COLOSSIANS 1:5-6

Dear brothers and sisters, we always thank God for you, as is right, for we are thankful that your faith is flourishing and you are all growing in love for each other. 2 THESSALONIANS 1:3

See also Ambition, Repentance, Self-Esteem, Success.

Politics and Government

What does the life of faith have to do with politics? Plenty! Maybe it's because we live in two nations: here, and the Kingdom of God. While heaven is our priority, we are still citizens here and now. Christians argue about just how much we ought to be involved in the political world. Some say the world is a lost cause, so don't get involved. Others say that this is God's world, and he cares for it, and so should we. Which is true? Both, perhaps?

Yes, God does love the world, even the people who ignore him. And yes, the Kingdom of Heaven has first claim on our loyalties. Both are true, but perhaps the key fact is this: This world and its institutions are not permanent. God is. Not surprisingly, the Bible does not have a high opinion of the world of politics—or of politicians. The Bible authors were painfully aware—especially when they were being persecuted—that governments are often guilty of pretending to be gods themselves.

Why do the nations rage? Why do the people waste their time with futile plans? The kings of the earth prepare for battle; the rulers plot together against the LORD and against his anointed one. "Let us break their chains," they cry, "and free ourselves from this slavery."

But the one who rules in heaven laughs. The Lord scoffs at them. PSALM 2:1-4

The nations have fallen into the pit they dug for others. They have been caught in their own trap.

Arise, O LORD! Do not let mere mortals defy you! Let the nations be judged in your presence! Make them tremble in fear, O LORD. Let them know they are merely human. PSALM 9:15, 19-20

The LORD shatters the plans of the nations and thwarts all their schemes. But the LORD's plans stand firm forever; his intentions can never be shaken.

The LORD looks down from heaven and sees the whole human race. From his throne he observes all who live on the earth. He made their hearts, so he understands everything they do. The best-equipped army cannot save a king, nor is great strength enough to save a warrior. PSALM 33:10-11, 13-16

"Be silent, and know that I am God! I will be honored by every nation. I will be honored throughout the world."

The LORD Almighty is here among us; the God of Israel is our fortress. PSALM 46:10-11

The gods of other nations are merely idols, but the LORD made the heavens! Honor and majesty surround him; strength and beauty are in his sanctuary.

O nations of the world, recognize the LORD; recognize that the LORD is glorious and strong. PSALM 96:5-7

Fearing people is a dangerous trap, but to trust the LORD means safety. PROVERBS 29:25

The LORD will settle international disputes. All the nations will beat their swords into plowshares and their spears into pruning

hooks. All wars will stop, and military training will come to an
end. ISAIAH 2:4

All the nations of the world are nothing in comparison with him.
They are but a drop in the bucket, dust on the scales. He picks up
the islands as though they had no weight at all.
  The nations of the world are as nothing to him. In his eyes they
are less than nothing—mere emptiness and froth.
  It is God who sits above the circle of the earth. The people below
must seem to him like grasshoppers! He is the one who spreads
out the heavens like a curtain and makes his tent from them. He
judges the great people of the world and brings them all to
nothing. ISAIAH 40:15, 17, 22-23

> During Jesus' temptation, the Devil offered him something many
> people would kill for: great political power. He declined it, and his
> answer to the Devil assures that political power is often just
> another form of idolatry. His answer also suggests something else:
> Many of the people attracted to politics are people easily tempted
> by power.

Jesus, full of the Holy Spirit, left the Jordan River. He was led by
the Spirit to go out into the wilderness, where the Devil tempted
him for forty days.
  The Devil took him up and revealed to him all the kingdoms of
the world in a moment of time. The Devil told him, "I will give
you the glory of these kingdoms and authority over
them—because they are mine to give to anyone I please. I will
give it all to you if you will bow down and worship me."
  Jesus replied, "The Scriptures say, 'You must worship the Lord
your God; serve only him.'" LUKE 4:1-2, 5-8

> Do you distrust people in authority? Many people do, and with
> good reason: Those in authority often abuse it. Even in a society
> where public officials can be voted out of office, we get cynical,

believing (correctly) that when we vote out one flawed human being, we vote in another flawed human being.

Yet in spite of all the cynicism about politicians, many people still get enthusiastic for (or against) a particular candidate or issue. It's still possible to whip people into a frenzy over politics. But the Bible warns against this with a sobering truth: Politicians, even good ones, are not the source of the good life. Only God is.

Jesus called them together and said, "You know that in this world kings are tyrants, and officials lord it over the people beneath them. But among you it should be quite different. Whoever wants to be a leader among you must be your servant, and whoever wants to be first must become your slave. For even I, the Son of Man, came here not to be served but to serve others, and to give my life as a ransom for many." MATTHEW 20:25-28

Don't put your confidence in powerful people; there is no help for you there. When their breathing stops, they return to the earth, and in a moment all their plans come to an end. But happy are those who have the God of Israel as their helper, whose hope is in the LORD their God. He is the one who made heaven and earth, the sea, and everything in them. He is the one who keeps every promise forever, who gives justice to the oppressed and food to the hungry. The LORD frees the prisoners. The LORD opens the eyes of the blind. The LORD lifts the burdens of those bent beneath their loads. The LORD loves the righteous. PSALM 146:3-8

It is better to trust the LORD than to put confidence in people. It is better to trust the LORD than to put confidence in princes. PSALM 118:8-9

Oh, the joys of those who trust the LORD, who have no confidence in the proud, or in those who worship idols. PSALM 40:4

This is what the LORD says: "Cursed are those who put their trust in mere humans and turn their hearts away from the LORD. They are like stunted shrubs in the desert, with no hope for the future. They will live in the barren wilderness, on the salty flats where no one lives.

"But blessed are those who trust in the LORD and have made the LORD their hope and confidence." JEREMIAH 17:5-7

The most unpleasant—and maybe the most realistic—view of government is given in the book of Revelation. Its final chapters depict the ultimate downfall of an immoral government noted for persecuting the righteous. Some Bible scholars say the Babylon depicted in Revelation represents the Roman Empire, which was persecuting Christians. Others feel that these chapters are a prophecy of what will yet come. Still others say it could even be both. Either way, the words seem to apply to any society riddled with immorality and cruelty. And the message is clear: No human government, no matter how powerful, endures forever. Only God and his people endure.

I saw another angel come down from heaven with great authority, and the earth grew bright with his splendor. He gave a mighty shout, "Babylon is fallen—that great city is fallen! She has become the hideout of demons and evil spirits, a nest for filthy buzzards, and a den for dreadful beasts. For all the nations have drunk the wine of her passionate immorality. The rulers of the world have committed adultery with her, and merchants throughout the world have grown rich as a result of her luxurious living."

Then I heard another voice calling from heaven, "Come away from her, my people. Do not take part in her sins, or you will be punished with her. For her sins are piled as high as heaven, and God is ready to judge her for her evil deeds. . . . Therefore, the sorrows of death and mourning and famine will overtake her in a single day. She will be utterly consumed by fire, for the Lord God who judges her is mighty."

And the rulers of the world who took part in her immoral acts and enjoyed her great luxury will mourn for her as they see the smoke rising from her charred remains. They will stand at a distance, terrified by her great torment. They will cry out, "How terrible, how terrible for Babylon, that great city! In one single moment God's judgment came on her."

The merchants of the world will weep and mourn for her, for there is no one left to buy their goods. . . . They will weep as they watch the smoke ascend, and they will say, "Where in all the world is there another city like this?" And they will throw dust on their heads to show their great sorrow. And they will say, "How terrible, how terrible for the great city! She made us all rich from her great wealth. And now in a single hour it is all gone."

But you, O heaven, rejoice over her fate. And you also rejoice, O holy people of God and apostles and prophets! For at last God has judged her on your behalf. REVELATION 18:1-20

See also Citizenship.

Prayer

Prayer is a popular subject among religious people. Many books have been written on the subject, and you can even attend seminars and workshops on prayer. The odd thing, most people *do not pray regularly.* If they do, it is rare and often only in times of real stress. While it is not good to only pray in times of need, we are fortunate that God still hears our heartfelt prayers, no matter how rare.

The LORD is close to all who call on him, yes, to all who call on him sincerely. He fulfills the desires of those who fear him; he hears their cries for help and rescues them.   PSALM 145:18-19

The eyes of the LORD watch over those who do right; his ears are open to their cries for help.
  The LORD hears his people when they call to him for help. He rescues them from all their troubles.   PSALM 34:15, 17

Trust me in your times of trouble, and I will rescue you, and you will give me glory.   PSALM 50:15

I will call on God, and the LORD will rescue me. Morning, noon, and night I plead aloud in my distress, and the LORD hears my voice. PSALM 55:16-17

The LORD says, "I will rescue those who love me. I will protect those who trust in my name. When they call on me, I will answer; I will be with them in trouble. I will rescue them and honor them. I will satisfy them with a long life and give them my salvation." PSALM 91:14-16

He will listen to the prayers of the destitute. He will not reject their pleas.

Let this be recorded for future generations, so that a nation yet to be created will praise the LORD. Tell them the LORD looked down from his heavenly sanctuary. He looked to the earth from heaven to hear the groans of the prisoners, to release those condemned to die. PSALM 102:17-20

I will answer them before they even call to me. While they are still talking to me about their needs, I will go ahead and answer their prayers! ISAIAH 65:24

Let us come boldly to the throne of our gracious God. There we will receive his mercy, and we will find grace to help us when we need it. HEBREWS 4:16

Odd, isn't it, that people spend hours playing sports, working out, practicing a musical instrument, learning to use a computer—always assuming that anything worthwhile takes time and practice? And yet communication and communion with God is seldom practiced and often neglected. There are centuries of testimonies from faithful people who told of how often they prayed and how it transformed their lives. Even a hard-boiled character like J. Edgar Hoover stated that "prayer is man's greatest means of tapping the infinite resources of God." We hear these things and are still skeptical.

But the Bible is brimming over with promises: Prayer brings us into God's presence. Prayer changes people. Prayer changes the world.

Ask me and I will tell you some remarkable secrets about what is going to happen here.   JEREMIAH 33:3

"I know the plans I have for you," says the LORD. "They are plans for good and not for disaster, to give you a future and a hope. In those days when you pray, I will listen. If you look for me in earnest, you will find me when you seek me. I will be found by you," says the LORD.   JEREMIAH 29:11-14

In our instant gratification society, prayer seems out of place. We pray for something and expect it to happen immediately—or soon, anyway. The Bible promises answers but not immediate ones, and not always the answers we want. The two following passages from the Gospels depict Jesus recommending *perseverance* in prayer.

One day Jesus told his disciples a story to illustrate their need for constant prayer and to show them that they must never give up. "There was a judge in a certain city," he said, "who was a godless man with great contempt for everyone. A widow of that city came to him repeatedly, appealing for justice against someone who had harmed her. The judge ignored her for a while, but eventually she wore him out. 'I fear neither God nor man,' he said to himself, 'but this woman is driving me crazy. I'm going to see that she gets justice, because she is wearing me out with her constant requests!'"

Then the Lord said, "Learn a lesson from this evil judge. Even he rendered a just decision in the end, so don't you think God will surely give justice to his chosen people who plead with him day and night? Will he keep putting them off? I tell you, he will grant justice to them quickly! But when I, the Son of Man, return, how many will I find who have faith?"   LUKE 18:1-8

Keep on asking, and you will be given what you ask for. Keep on
looking, and you will find. Keep on knocking, and the door will
be opened. For everyone who asks, receives. Everyone who seeks,
finds. And the door is opened to everyone who knocks. You
parents—if your children ask for a loaf of bread, do you give them
a stone instead? Or if they ask for a fish, do you give them a
snake? Of course not! If you sinful people know how to give good
gifts to your children, how much more will your heavenly Father
give good gifts to those who ask him. MATTHEW 7:7-11

> Some people claim that prayer is selfish, that people are too
> concerned about their own needs. They say we ought to pray only
> to thank God and adore him, forgetting ourselves completely. Such
> people have a point: We do need to think more about God and less
> about ourselves. But the Bible makes it clear that we *ought* to bring
> our own requests to God. How else can we forget them, except by
> laying them at God's feet? Such prayers aren't selfish at all.

Don't worry about anything; instead, pray about everything. Tell
God what you need, and thank him for all he has done. If you do
this, you will experience God's peace, which is far more wonderful
than the human mind can understand. His peace will guard your
hearts and minds as you live in Christ Jesus. PHILIPPIANS 4:6-7

Are any among you suffering? They should keep on praying
about it. And those who have reason to be thankful should
continually sing praises to the Lord.

Are any among you sick? They should call for the elders of the
church and have them pray over them, anointing them with oil in
the name of the Lord. And their prayer offered in faith will heal
the sick, and the Lord will make them well. And anyone who has
committed sins will be forgiven.

Confess your sins to each other and pray for each other so that
you may be healed. The earnest prayer of a righteous person has
great power and wonderful results. Elijah was as human as we

are, and yet when he prayed earnestly that no rain would fall, none fell for the next three and a half years! Then he prayed for rain, and down it poured. The grass turned green, and the crops began to grow again. JAMES 5:13-18

I urge you, first of all, to pray for all people. As you make your requests, plead for God's mercy upon them, and give thanks. 1 TIMOTHY 2:1

> The Bible tells us to pray for ourselves and, of course, for those close to us. It also tells us to do something that seems to go against our natural instincts:

Pray for the happiness of those who curse you. Pray for those who hurt you. LUKE 6:28

> Jesus understood the importance of prayer. But he also understood that some people like to make a show out of it, trying to impress others with their long and flowery prayers. He assured his followers that this kind of prayer has no influence with God, who understands our motives.

When you pray, go away by yourself, shut the door behind you, and pray to your Father secretly. Then your Father, who knows all secrets, will reward you.

When you pray, don't babble on and on as people of other religions do. They think their prayers are answered only by repeating their words again and again. Don't be like them, because your Father knows exactly what you need even before you ask him! MATTHEW 6:6-8

> Jesus also knew that there are obstacles to prayer—like holding a grudge. He made it clear that we should not approach God while we are harboring contempt for another person.

Listen to me! You can pray for anything, and if you believe, you will have it. But when you are praying, first forgive anyone you are holding a grudge against, so that your Father in heaven will forgive your sins, too. MARK 11:24-25

> Doubt must be one of the key reasons people don't pray—and why they receive nothing when they do pray. The Bible promises something wonderful for people who approach God without any doubts about his power:

I assure you, if you have faith and don't doubt, you can do things like this and much more. You can even say to this mountain, "May God lift you up and throw you into the sea," and it will happen. If you believe, you will receive whatever you ask for in prayer. MATTHEW 21:21-22

If you need wisdom—if you want to know what God wants you to do—ask him, and he will gladly tell you. He will not resent your asking. But when you ask him, be sure that you really expect him to answer, for a doubtful mind is as unsettled as a wave of the sea that is driven and tossed by the wind. People like that should not expect to receive anything from the Lord. JAMES 1:5-7

> Some people claim they don't know *how* to pray. The Bible is full of examples, including the famous Lord's Prayer (Matthew 6:9-13 and Luke 11:2-4). But the Bible also promises that our awkwardness at praying does not need to hold us back. God has given us a "prayer partner," the Spirit.

The Holy Spirit helps us in our distress. For we don't even know what we should pray for, nor how we should pray. But the Holy Spirit prays for us with groanings that cannot be expressed in words. ROMANS 8:26

Now all of us . . . may come to the Father through the same Holy Spirit because of what Christ has done for us. EPHESIANS 2:18

Does God hear every prayer? Of course—God hears everything. Still, the Bible assures us that not all prayers are equal. Our attitude toward God when we pray is very important—certainly more important than the words themselves, which need not be eloquent or grammatically correct. Far more important than our verbal cleverness is our desire to submit ourselves to God's will.

Get to know the God of your ancestors. Worship and serve him with your whole heart and with a willing mind. For the LORD sees every heart and understands and knows every plan and thought. If you seek him, you will find him. But if you forsake him, he will reject you forever. 1 CHRONICLES 28:9

The LORD is far from the wicked, but he hears the prayers of the righteous. PROVERBS 15:29

If you stay joined to me and my words remain in you, you may ask any request you like, and it will be granted! JOHN 15:7

The eyes of the Lord watch over those who do right, and his ears are open to their prayers. But the Lord turns his face against those who do evil. 1 PETER 3:12

Dear friends, if our conscience is clear, we can come to God with bold confidence. And we will receive whatever we request because we obey him and do the things that please him. 1 JOHN 3:21-22

We can be confident that he will listen to us whenever we ask him for anything in line with his will. And if we know he is listening when we make our requests, we can be sure that he will give us what we ask for. 1 JOHN 5:14-15

See also Confessing Sin, Fellowship with God, Thankfulness.

Pride and Conceit

People take pride in practically anything—their looks, possessions, intelligence, job, sophistication, family connections, even religion.

Does God deny us the enjoyment of being attractive, of owning a home or car, of having a good education, of having some achievements in life? Of course not. None of these things are wrong in themselves. When the Bible talks about pride and arrogance, it is talking about those who make an idol—a god—of these things. It is talking about thinking of ourselves so highly that God has no place in our life. We aren't supposed to worship our achievements. We aren't supposed to worship ourselves, either. Contrary to worldly wisdom, we are *not* God.

This chapter addresses pride, but it also deals with the flip side: humility, which God loves to see. Humility doesn't involve being negative about ourselves, hating ourselves. It means seeing ourselves as we are: created in the image of God and dependent on him, both in this life and afterward.

Stop acting so proud and haughty! Don't speak with such arrogance! The LORD is a God who knows your deeds; and he will judge you for what you have done.   1 SAMUEL 2:3

You rescue those who are humble, but your eyes are on the proud to humiliate them.   2 SAMUEL 22:28

May the LORD bring their flattery to an end and silence their proud tongues.   PSALM 12:3

You rescue those who are humble, but you humiliate the proud.
PSALM 18:27

You rebuke those cursed proud ones who wander from your commands.   PSALM 119:21

Though the LORD is great, he cares for the humble, but he keeps his distance from the proud.   PSALM 138:6

The LORD mocks at mockers, but he shows favor to the humble.
PROVERBS 3:34

Pride leads to disgrace, but with humility comes wisdom.
PROVERBS 11:2

Pride leads to arguments; those who take advice are wise.
PROVERBS 13:10

The LORD destroys the house of the proud, but he protects the property of widows.   PROVERBS 15:25

The LORD despises pride; be assured that the proud will be punished.
  Pride goes before destruction, and haughtiness before a fall.

It is better to live humbly with the poor than to share plunder with the proud. PROVERBS 16:5, 18-19

Haughty eyes, a proud heart, and evil actions are all sin. PROVERBS 21:4

There is more hope for fools than for people who think they are wise. PROVERBS 26:12

Don't praise yourself; let others do it! PROVERBS 27:2

Pride ends in humiliation, while humility brings honor. PROVERBS 29:23

The day is coming when your pride will be brought low and the LORD alone will be exalted. In that day the LORD Almighty will punish the proud, bringing them down to the dust. ISAIAH 2:11-12

In that day the arrogant will be brought down to the dust; the proud will be humbled.
Destruction is certain for those who say that evil is good and good is evil; that dark is light and light is dark; that bitter is sweet and sweet is bitter.
Destruction is certain for those who think they are wise and consider themselves to be clever. ISAIAH 5:15, 20-21

I, the LORD, will punish the world for its evil and the wicked for their sin. I will crush the arrogance of the proud and the haughtiness of the mighty. ISAIAH 13:11

Look at the proud! They trust in themselves, and their lives are crooked; but the righteous will live by their faith. HABAKKUK 2:4

Jesus prayed this prayer: "O Father, Lord of heaven and earth, thank you for hiding the truth from those who think themselves

so wise and clever, and for revealing it to the childlike."
MATTHEW 11:25

The world offers only the lust for physical pleasure, the lust for everything we see, and pride in our possessions. These are not from the Father. They are from this evil world. 1 JOHN 2:16

Look here, you people who say, "Today or tomorrow we are going to a certain town and will stay there a year. We will do business there and make a profit." How do you know what will happen tomorrow? For your life is like the morning fog—it's here a little while, then it's gone. What you ought to say is, "If the Lord wants us to, we will live and do this or that." JAMES 4:13-15

> Perhaps the worst kind of pride is spiritual pride. Jesus understood this, knowing that people who appear religious can be incredibly vain. One of his classic parables looks at this problem, promising a blessing, not on the spiritually proud, but on those who humble themselves before God.

Jesus told this story to some who had great self-confidence and scorned everyone else: "Two men went to the Temple to pray. One was a Pharisee, and the other was a dishonest tax collector. The proud Pharisee stood by himself and prayed this prayer: 'I thank you, God, that I am not a sinner like everyone else, especially like that tax collector over there! For I never cheat, I don't sin, I don't commit adultery, I fast twice a week, and I give you a tenth of my income.'

"But the tax collector stood at a distance and dared not even lift his eyes to heaven as he prayed. Instead, he beat his chest in sorrow, saying, 'O God, be merciful to me, for I am a sinner.' I tell you, this sinner, not the Pharisee, returned home justified before God. For the proud will be humbled, but the humble will be honored." LUKE 18:9-14

339

Does God really accept all people as they are? In one sense, yes. We're all sinners, and God accepts us even in our sin. However, the Bible also shows that, no—God doesn't accept us while we're clinging to our own pride. We must come to him humbly. God sends no one away except those who are full of themselves.

Then he said to [the Pharisees], "You like to look good in public, but God knows your evil hearts. What this world honors is an abomination in the sight of God." LUKE 16:15

The Scriptures say, "The person who wishes to boast should boast only of what the Lord has done." When people boast about themselves, it doesn't count for much. But when the Lord commends someone, that's different! 2 CORINTHIANS 10:17-18

A proud person is always looking down on someone else. As long as we are looking down, we can't very well see someone who is above us—like God. This idea is repeated again and again in the Bible. And our own experience proves it is true: We gain more real personal satisfaction by admiring and loving someone—God, above all—than by looking down on others.

Love the LORD, all you faithful ones! For the LORD protects those who are loyal to him, but he harshly punishes all who are arrogant. PSALM 31:23

Don't be impressed with your own wisdom. Instead, fear the LORD and turn your back on evil. Then you will gain renewed health and vitality. PROVERBS 3:7-8

The LORD Almighty says, "The day of judgment is coming, burning like a furnace. The arrogant and the wicked will be burned up like straw on that day. They will be consumed like a tree—roots and all.

"But for you who fear my name, the Sun of Righteousness will rise with healing in his wings. And you will go free, leaping with joy like calves let out to pasture." MALACHI 4:1-2

God blesses those who realize their need for him, for the Kingdom of Heaven is given to them.

God blesses those who are gentle and lowly, for the whole earth will belong to them. MATTHEW 5:3, 5

Anyone who wants to be the first must take last place and be the servant of everyone else. MARK 9:35

Love is not jealous or boastful or proud or rude. Love does not demand its own way. Love is not irritable, and it keeps no record of when it has been wronged. 1 CORINTHIANS 13:4-5

If you think you are too important to help someone in need, you are only fooling yourself. You are really a nobody. GALATIANS 6:3

Anyone who claims to know all the answers doesn't really know very much. But the person who loves God is the one God knows and cares for. 1 CORINTHIANS 8:2-3

See also Hypocrisy; Meekness, Humility, Gentleness; Money; Self-Esteem; Self-Righteousness.

Repentance

This word has gone out of style, although the word *change* is certainly popular. Change is part of repentance, of course. In fact, it is the forgotten part. We have the strange idea that repentance simply means saying to God, with tears in our eyes, "I'm sorry." Well, that is Step One. Step Two, more important than the tears, is change. Martin Luther put it this way: "To do so no more is the truest repentance." In other words, if we are gossiping, cheating, committing some sexual sin, being just plain selfish, the response to God is "I'm truly sorry," followed by "I won't do it again."

The good news is, God accepts this—joyfully, in fact. He and his angels rejoice when an unbeliever turns his life over to God. And he rejoices when a believer, caught up in some wrong, turns to his Father and says, "I'd like a new beginning." God's response always is "You shall have it."

If my people who are called by my name will humble themselves and pray and seek my face and turn from their wicked ways, I will hear from heaven and will forgive their sins and heal their land. 2 CHRONICLES 7:14

People who cover over their sins will not prosper. But if they confess and forsake them, they will receive mercy. PROVERBS 28:13

If we confess our sins to him, he is faithful and just to forgive us and to cleanse us from every wrong. 1 JOHN 1:9

The LORD is close to the brokenhearted; he rescues those who are crushed in spirit. PSALM 34:18

> The Bible's great song of repentance is Psalm 51, written by King David himself. It expresses the desire—and the expectation—that God will forgive the believer's sin and restore the broken relationship.

Have mercy on me, O God, because of your unfailing love. Because of your great compassion, blot out the stain of my sins. Wash me clean from my guilt. Purify me from my sin.

For I recognize my shameful deeds—they haunt me day and night. Against you, and you alone, have I sinned; I have done what is evil in your sight. You will be proved right in what you say, and your judgment against me is just.

For I was born a sinner—yes, from the moment my mother conceived me. But you desire honesty from the heart, so you can teach me to be wise in my inmost being.

Purify me from my sins, and I will be clean; wash me, and I will be whiter than snow. Oh, give me back my joy again; you have broken me—now let me rejoice. Don't keep looking at my sins. Remove the stain of my guilt. Create in me a clean heart, O God. Renew a right spirit within me. Do not banish me from your presence, and don't take your Holy Spirit from me. Restore to me again the joy of your salvation, and make me willing to obey you. Then I will teach your ways to sinners, and they will return to you.

Forgive me for shedding blood, O God who saves; then I will joyfully sing of your forgiveness. Unseal my lips, O Lord, that I may praise you.

You would not be pleased with sacrifices, or I would bring them.

If I brought you a burnt offering, you would not accept it. The sacrifice you want is a broken spirit. A broken and repentant heart, O God, you will not despise.   PSALM 51:1-17

> Our repentance won't mean much to us unless we are sure that it means something to God. According to the Bible, it means everything to him. The Bible overflows with images of the Father gladly embracing people who abandon their self-trust and turn to him.

He is our God. We are the people he watches over, the sheep under his care.
  Oh, that you would listen to his voice today!   PSALM 95:7

He heals the brokenhearted, binding up their wounds.
PSALM 147:3

I have swept away your sins like the morning mists. I have scattered your offenses like the clouds. Oh, return to me, for I have paid the price to set you free.   ISAIAH 44:22

Seek the LORD while you can find him. Call on him now while he is near. Let the people turn from their wicked deeds. Let them banish from their minds the very thought of doing wrong! Let them turn to the LORD that he may have mercy on them. Yes, turn to our God, for he will abundantly pardon.   ISAIAH 55:6-7

If wicked people turn away from all their sins and begin to obey my laws and do what is just and right, they will surely live and not die. All their past sins will be forgotten, and they will live because of the righteous things they have done.
  Do you think, asks the Sovereign LORD, that I like to see wicked people die? Of course not! I only want them to turn from their wicked ways and live.
  Put all your rebellion behind you, and get for yourselves a new heart and a new spirit. For why should you die, O people of

Israel? I don't want you to die, says the Sovereign LORD. Turn
back and live! EZEKIEL 18:21-23, 31-32

Many people like to think of Jesus as a great teacher, full of advice
about love and peace. Well, Jesus *was* a great teacher, no doubt.
But Jesus was aware that the world needed more than just good
advice and sweet sayings about love and kindness. As the opening
of Mark's Gospel makes clear, Jesus insisted that people turn away
from their immorality and their self-reliance and put their trust in
God alone. In other words, they must repent. Without this, there is
no life of faith and no salvation.

Jesus went to Galilee to preach God's Good News. "At last the
time has come!" he announced. "The Kingdom of God is near!
Turn from your sins and believe this Good News!" MARK 1:14-15

Healthy people don't need a doctor—sick people do. I have come
to call sinners to turn from their sins, not to spend my time with
those who think they are already good enough. LUKE 5:31-32

Is God some coldhearted cosmic tyrant, eager to punish people who
don't repent? The Bible presents us with something quite different from
that: the God who actually rejoices when a repentant person turns to him.
Joy is not just something a repentant person feels at being in a right
relationship with God. Joy is something God himself feels.

If you had one hundred sheep, and one of them strayed away and
was lost in the wilderness, wouldn't you leave the ninety-nine
others to go and search for the lost one until you found it? And
then you would joyfully carry it home on your shoulders. When
you arrived, you would call together your friends and neighbors
to rejoice with you because your lost sheep was found. In the
same way, heaven will be happier over one lost sinner who
returns to God than over ninety-nine others who are righteous
and haven't strayed away!

Or suppose a woman has ten valuable silver coins and loses one. Won't she light a lamp and look in every corner of the house and sweep every nook and cranny until she finds it? And when she finds it, she will call in her friends and neighbors to rejoice with her because she has found her lost coin. In the same way, there is joy in the presence of God's angels when even one sinner repents. LUKE 15:4-10

> All of us like to speculate about other people's spiritual condition. Jesus knew this. And, he knew that a lot of religious people overlook the fact that the real question is not "Is Tom living the way he ought to?" but rather "Am *I* living the way I ought to?"

And why worry about a speck in your friend's eye when you have a log in your own? How can you think of saying, "Friend, let me help you get rid of that speck in your eye," when you can't see past the log in your own eye? Hypocrite! First get rid of the log from your own eye; then perhaps you will see well enough to deal with the speck in your friend's eye. MATTHEW 7:3-5; LUKE 6:41-42

Jesus was informed that Pilate had murdered some people from Galilee as they were sacrificing at the Temple in Jerusalem. "Do you think those Galileans were worse sinners than other people from Galilee?" he asked. "Is that why they suffered? Not at all! And you will also perish unless you turn from your evil ways and turn to God." LUKE 13:1-3

God overlooked people's former ignorance about these things, but now he commands everyone everywhere to turn away from idols and turn to him. For he has set a day for judging the world with justice by the man he has appointed, and he proved to everyone who this is by raising him from the dead. ACTS 17:30-31

I am the one who corrects and disciplines everyone I love. Be diligent and turn from your indifference. REVELATION 3:19

[John the Baptist:] "I baptize with water those who turn from their sins and turn to God. But someone is coming soon who is far greater than I am—so much greater that I am not even worthy to be his slave. He will baptize you with the Holy Spirit and with fire." MATTHEW 3:11

Peter replied, "Each of you must turn from your sins and turn to God, and be baptized in the name of Jesus Christ for the forgiveness of your sins. Then you will receive the gift of the Holy Spirit. This promise is to you and to your children, and even to the Gentiles— all who have been called by the Lord our God." ACTS 2:38-39

Now turn from your sins and turn to God, so you can be cleansed of your sins. Then wonderful times of refreshment will come from the presence of the Lord, and he will send Jesus your Messiah to you again. ACTS 3:19-20

> Feeling bad about our sins is not enough. Sometimes this sorrow can lead to—well, sadness, but nothing else. Feeling bad is a start, but the Bible makes it clear that sorrow can either drive us toward God or toward despair.

God can use sorrow in our lives to help us turn away from sin and seek salvation. We will never regret that kind of sorrow. But sorrow without repentance is the kind that results in death. 2 CORINTHIANS 7:10

The Lord isn't really being slow about his promise to return, as some people think. No, he is being patient for your sake. He does not want anyone to perish, so he is giving more time for everyone to repent. 2 PETER 3:9

The Sovereign LORD, the Holy One of Israel, says, "Only in returning to me and waiting for me will you be saved. In quietness and confidence is your strength." ISAIAH 30:15

Get to know the God of your ancestors. Worship and serve him with your whole heart and with a willing mind. For the LORD sees every heart and understands and knows every plan and thought. If you seek him, you will find him. But if you forsake him, he will reject you forever. 1 CHRONICLES 28:9

You, O LORD, have never abandoned anyone who searches for you. PSALM 9:10

I confessed all my sins to you and stopped trying to hide them. I said to myself, "I will confess my rebellion to the LORD." And you forgave me! All my guilt is gone.

 Therefore, let all the godly confess their rebellion to you while there is time, that they may not drown in the floodwaters of judgment. PSALM 32:5-6

God blesses those who mourn, for they will be comforted. MATTHEW 5:4

If you confess with your mouth that Jesus is Lord and believe in your heart that God raised him from the dead, you will be saved. For it is by believing in your heart that you are made right with God, and it is by confessing with your mouth that you are saved. As the Scriptures tell us, "Anyone who believes in him will not be disappointed."

 For "Anyone who calls on the name of the Lord will be saved." ROMANS 10:9-11, 13

> One of Jesus' most famous parables is the parable of the Prodigal Son. It would be more accurate to call it the parable of the repentant son, or, even better, the parable of the forgiving father. Nowhere else in the Bible are repentance and the promise of God's forgiveness made more vivid.

A man had two sons. The younger son told his father, "I want my share of your estate now, instead of waiting until you die." So his father agreed to divide his wealth between his sons.

A few days later this younger son packed all his belongings and took a trip to a distant land, and there he wasted all his money on wild living. About the time his money ran out, a great famine swept over the land, and he began to starve. He persuaded a local farmer to hire him to feed his pigs. The boy became so hungry that even the pods he was feeding the pigs looked good to him. But no one gave him anything.

When he finally came to his senses, he said to himself, "At home even the hired men have food enough to spare, and here I am, dying of hunger! I will go home to my father and say, 'Father, I have sinned against both heaven and you, and I am no longer worthy of being called your son. Please take me on as a hired man.'"

So he returned home to his father. And while he was still a long distance away, his father saw him coming. Filled with love and compassion, he ran to his son, embraced him, and kissed him. His son said to him, "Father, I have sinned against both heaven and you, and I am no longer worthy of being called your son."

But his father said to the servants, "Quick! Bring the finest robe in the house and put it on him. Get a ring for his finger, and sandals for his feet. And kill the calf we have been fattening in the pen. We must celebrate with a feast, for this son of mine was dead and has now returned to life. He was lost, but now he is found." So the party began. LUKE 15:11-24

See also Confessing Sin; Justification; New Birth, New Life.

Revenge

R evenge is sweet"—in the world's view. It seems human—all *too* human—to retaliate when someone injures us. People gain pleasure sometimes from just planning revenge, even if they never carry it out.

This is not only a waste of time and mental energy, but, more important, downright wrong.

Never seek revenge or bear a grudge against anyone, but love your neighbor as yourself. I am the LORD. LEVITICUS 19:18

If you set a trap for others, you will get caught in it yourself. If you roll a boulder down on others, it will roll back and crush you. PROVERBS 26:27

The classic statement on revenge is found in Jesus' famous words in the Sermon on the Mount:

You have heard that the law of Moses says, "If an eye is injured, injure the eye of the person who did it. If a tooth gets knocked out, knock out the tooth of the person who did it." But I say, don't

resist an evil person! If you are slapped on the right cheek, turn
the other, too. If you are ordered to court and your shirt is taken
from you, give your coat, too. If a soldier demands that you carry
his gear for a mile, carry it two miles. Give to those who ask, and
don't turn away from those who want to borrow.

You have heard that the law of Moses says, "Love your
neighbor" and hate your enemy. But I say, love your enemies!
Pray for those who persecute you! In that way, you will be acting
as true children of your Father in heaven. For he gives his sunlight
to both the evil and the good, and he sends rain on the just and on
the unjust, too. MATTHEW 5:38-45

> On one occasion, Jesus had to rein in his own disciples who were
> bent on vengeance:

He sent messengers ahead to a Samaritan village to prepare for his
arrival. But they were turned away. The people of the village
refused to have anything to do with Jesus because he had resolved
to go to Jerusalem. When James and John heard about it, they said
to Jesus, "Lord, should we order down fire from heaven to burn
them up?" But Jesus turned and rebuked them. So they went on to
another village. LUKE 9:52-56

> Christians have been persecuted from the New Testament days until
> now. It is hard to keep from hating the persecutors. But Paul, who
> had endured persecution himself, told the Christians to endure it
> patiently, without wanting vengeance.

God will use this persecution to show his justice. For he will make
you worthy of his Kingdom, for which you are suffering, and in
his justice he will punish those who persecute you. And God will
provide rest for you who are being persecuted and also for us
when the Lord Jesus appears from heaven. He will come with his
mighty angels, in flaming fire, bringing judgment on those who

don't know God and on those who refuse to obey the Good News of our Lord Jesus. 2 THESSALONIANS 1:5-8

> Sometimes our offended sense of justice leads us to take revenge. After all, we ask, shouldn't someone step in and correct this unjust situation? The Bible answers, yes, someone should. But that someone is God, not us.

Don't say, "I will get even for this wrong." Wait for the LORD to handle the matter. PROVERBS 20:22

Never pay back evil for evil to anyone. Do things in such a way that everyone can see you are honorable. Do your part to live in peace with everyone, as much as possible.

Dear friends, never avenge yourselves. Leave that to God. For it is written, "I will take vengeance; I will repay those who deserve it," says the Lord. ROMANS 12:17-19

See also Anger, Enemies, Envy, Forgiving Others, Hate.

Righteousness

What happened to the word *righteousness?* It went out of style. Now people like to be thought of as concerned or compassionate, not righteous.

Well, the word may seem old-fashioned, but the concept is eternally up-to-date. The key idea is being *right*—in a right relationship with God and with other people. It is more than acting concerned, for it describes a state in which we are what we should be. In fact, the Bible makes it clear that before we can make the world right, we must be made right within ourselves.

Don't confuse righteousness with self-righteousness. (There's a separate chapter on that subject, by the way.) Righteousness is not something we draw out of ourselves. It comes from God. And God rewards those whose hearts—and actions—are right with him.

It is better to be godly and have little than to be evil and possess much.

The godly will inherit the land and will live there forever.

PSALM 37:16, 29

The LORD watches over the path of the godly, but the path of the wicked leads to destruction. PSALM 1:6

You bless the godly, O LORD, surrounding them with your shield of love. PSALM 5:12

The LORD examines both the righteous and the wicked. He hates everyone who loves violence. PSALM 11:5

The righteous face many troubles, but the LORD rescues them from each and every one.
Calamity will surely overtake the wicked, and those who hate the righteous will be punished. PSALM 34:19, 21

Give your burdens to the LORD, and he will take care of you. He will not permit the godly to slip and fall. PSALM 55:22

Wicked people are an abomination to the LORD, but he offers his friendship to the godly.
The curse of the LORD is on the house of the wicked, but his blessing is on the home of the upright. PROVERBS 3:32-33

The way of the righteous is like the first gleam of dawn, which shines ever brighter until the full light of day. PROVERBS 4:18

The LORD will not let the godly starve to death, but he refuses to satisfy the craving of the wicked. PROVERBS 10:3

Trouble chases sinners, while blessings chase the righteous!
PROVERBS 13:21

It is better to be poor and godly than rich and dishonest.
PROVERBS 16:8

The godly know the rights of the poor; the wicked don't care to know. PROVERBS 29:7

God blesses those who are hungry and thirsty for justice, for they will receive it in full.
God blesses those who are persecuted because they live for God, for the Kingdom of Heaven is theirs. MATTHEW 5:6, 10

How exactly do we get to be righteous? The answer is both simple and complex. Righteousness is a simple matter of obedience to God—both his commands as well as his leading in our life. However, being sinful, self-centered human beings automatically renders this a complex undertaking. Fortunately, God knows this. All he asks is that we try.

We are righteous when we obey all the commands the LORD our God has given us. DEUTERONOMY 6:25

Will those who do evil never learn? They eat up my people like bread; they wouldn't think of praying to the LORD. Terror will grip them, for God is with those who obey him. PSALM 14:4-5

No good thing will the LORD withhold from those who do what is right. PSALM 84:11

In his Sermon on the Mount, Jesus gave a harsh warning to people who try to *appear* righteous:

Take care! Don't do your good deeds publicly, to be admired, because then you will lose the reward from your Father in heaven. MATTHEW 6:1

Jesus also made it clear that he did not come to earth to save people who were already satisfied with themselves. He preached the

Kingdom of God to people who knew their inadequacies and wanted to be better.

Healthy people don't need a doctor—sick people do. I have come to call sinners, not those who think they are already good enough. MARK 2:17

Now you are free from sin, your old master, and you have become slaves to your new master, righteousness. ROMANS 6:18

Since you have heard all about him and have learned the truth that is in Jesus, throw off your old evil nature and your former way of life, which is rotten through and through, full of lust and deception. Instead, there must be a spiritual renewal of your thoughts and attitudes. You must display a new nature because you are a new person, created in God's likeness—righteous, holy, and true. EPHESIANS 4:21-24

> Does *righteous* ever mean totally sinless? Not according to the Bible. The best people fail, but they have a promise of mercy and a new start.

Righteous people will be rewarded for their own goodness, and wicked people will be punished for their own wickedness. But if wicked people turn away from all their sins and begin to obey my laws and do what is just and right, they will surely live and not die. All their past sins will be forgotten, and they will live because of the righteous things they have done.

Do you think, asks the Sovereign LORD, that I like to see wicked people die? Of course not! I only want them to turn from their wicked ways and live. EZEKIEL 18:20-23

If we confess our sins to him, he is faithful and just to forgive us and to cleanse us from every wrong. 1 JOHN 1:9

"Righteousness is its own reward" goes the old cliché. This
particular cliché happens to be true. We ought to do right simply
because . . . well, because right is right. But according to the Bible,
God does reward the righteous in other ways, in this world and,
more important, in the next world.

There truly is a reward for those who live for God; surely there is
a God who judges justly here on earth. PSALM 58:11

The fears of the wicked will all come true; so will the hopes of the
godly. PROVERBS 10:24

The godly will shine like the sun in their Father's Kingdom.
MATTHEW 13:43

Now the prize awaits me—the crown of righteousness that the
Lord, the righteous Judge, will give me on that great day of his
return. And the prize is not just for me but for all who eagerly
look forward to his glorious return. 2 TIMOTHY 4:8

Those who are peacemakers will plant seeds of peace and reap a
harvest of goodness. JAMES 3:18

See also Justification, Obeying God, Self-Righteousness.

The Sabbath

People under the age of forty may not remember the "blue laws" that kept most businesses (including most stores) from operating on Sundays. Strange as it seems, a generation ago people still saw Sunday as a day for churchgoing and recreation—not transacting business. But the Bible makes it clear that one day out of seven is a special day, a day to remember that just as we honor God with our work throughout the week, so on the Sabbath we honor him with our worship and our recreation. It reminds us that we are God's people. It was such an important belief in the Bible that it is one of the Ten Commandments.

Remember to observe the Sabbath day by keeping it holy. Six days a week are set apart for your daily duties and regular work, but the seventh day is a day of rest dedicated to the LORD your God. On that day no one in your household may do any kind of work. This includes you, your sons and daughters, your male and female servants, your livestock, and any foreigners living among you. For in six days the LORD made the heavens, the earth, the sea, and everything in them; then he rested on the seventh day. That is

why the LORD blessed the Sabbath day and set it apart as holy.
EXODUS 20:8-11

Tell the people of Israel to keep my Sabbath day, for the Sabbath is
a sign of the covenant between me and you forever. It helps you to
remember that I am the LORD, who makes you holy. Yes, keep the
Sabbath day, for it is holy. . . . Anyone who works on that day will
be cut off from the community. Work six days only, but the
seventh day must be a day of total rest. I repeat: Because the LORD
considers it a holy day, anyone who works on the Sabbath must be
put to death. The people of Israel must keep the Sabbath day
forever. It is a permanent sign of my covenant with them.
EXODUS 31:13-17

Blessed are those who are careful to do this. Blessed are those who
honor my Sabbath days of rest by refusing to work. And blessed
are those who keep themselves from doing wrong. ISAIAH 56:2

Keep my Sabbath days holy, for they are a sign to remind you that
I am the LORD your God. EZEKIEL 20:20

Jesus took the Sabbath commands seriously but added a human
touch that had been forgotten:

He said to them, "The Sabbath was made to benefit people, and
not people to benefit the Sabbath. And I, the Son of Man, am
master even of the Sabbath!" MARK 2:27-28

See also Work.

Salvation

Self-improvement" and "self-help" are popular concepts
today. They would have been totally meaningless to the authors of
the Bible. They made no promises at all about *learning* to be children
of God or *working* to be the right kind of people. The message of
salvation is that there is no *improvement*—there is *transformation*.
We are changed—by God—from being sinners into being God's
children. We are changed from being alienated from him to being
reconciled to him. This isn't accomplished by reading books or
attending seminars or joining a twelve-step program. It occurs by first
recognizing that we *need* saving, not just improving.

This goes against the grain. We like to think we've discovered
another way to achieve our personal goals. But the salvation message
in the Bible has nothing to do with helping us—it has to do with
completely making us over. The Bible promises us that we do this by
being "born again." The old person we were, however good, noble,
attractive, and successful, won't do—not when compared to a perfect
God.

The world likes to view Jesus as only a good moral teacher. Why?
There have been good and wise moral teachers since the beginning
of time. They have benefited the world—but not saved it. Wise

advice is not what we need. We need (here's that old-fashioned word) a *Savior.* According to the Bible, it was and is Jesus.

The Old Testament writers didn't have Jesus. They looked forward to him, anticipating him. This is why so many of the Old Testament passages seem to have their fulfillment in the saving work of Jesus.

The LORD is close to the brokenhearted; he rescues those who are crushed in spirit. PSALM 34:18

The LORD protects those of childlike faith; I was facing death, and then he saved me. PSALM 116:6

"I know the plans I have for you," says the LORD. "They are plans for good and not for disaster, to give you a future and a hope. In those days when you pray, I will listen. If you look for me in earnest, you will find me when you seek me." JEREMIAH 29:11-13

I will sprinkle clean water on you, and you will be clean. Your filth will be washed away, and you will no longer worship idols. And I will give you a new heart with new and right desires, and I will put a new spirit in you. I will take out your stony heart of sin and give you a new, obedient heart. And I will put my Spirit in you so you will obey my laws and do whatever I command. . . .

You will be my people, and I will be your God. EZEKIEL 36:25-28

The virgin will conceive a child! She will give birth to a son and will call him Immanuel—"God is with us." ISAIAH 7:14

Jesus came into the world, proclaiming the Kingdom of God—not a kingdom on a map but the rule of God over those willing to be ruled by him. In other words, salvation is extended to those who are willing to say to God, "I don't rule my own life very well. You do it." According to Jesus, anyone can make this statement, but few do.

You can enter God's Kingdom only through the narrow gate. The highway to hell is broad, and its gate is wide for the many who choose the easy way. But the gateway to life is small, and the road is narrow, and only a few ever find it. MATTHEW 7:13-14

If you try to keep your life for yourself, you will lose it. But if you give up your life for me, you will find true life. And how do you benefit if you gain the whole world but lose your own soul in the process? Is anything worth more than your soul? MATTHEW 16:25-26

I, the Son of Man, have come to seek and save those like him who are lost. LUKE 19:10

Then he told them, "Go into all the world and preach the Good News to everyone, everywhere. Anyone who believes and is baptized will be saved. But anyone who refuses to believe will be condemned." MARK 16:15-16

God so loved the world that he gave his only Son, so that everyone who believes in him will not perish but have eternal life. God did not send his Son into the world to condemn it, but to save it. JOHN 3:16-17

Jesus replied, "I assure you, unless you are born again, you can never see the Kingdom of God."

"What do you mean?" exclaimed Nicodemus. "How can an old man go back into his mother's womb and be born again?"

Jesus replied, "The truth is, no one can enter the Kingdom of God without being born of water and the Spirit. Humans can reproduce only human life, but the Holy Spirit gives new life from heaven. So don't be surprised at my statement that you must be born again." JOHN 3:3-7

Yes, I am the gate. Those who come in through me will be saved.
Wherever they go, they will find green pastures. JOHN 10:9

I, the Son of Man, came here not to be served but to serve others,
and to give my life as a ransom for many. MARK 10:45

Paul, who wrote much of the New Testament, understood the
self-improvement mentality. He had been brought up to believe that
keeping the Jewish law was the way to please God. He did keep it
faithfully, then concluded it hadn't made him right in God's sight.
And no matter how diligent he was, he could not keep the law
perfectly. Again and again in his letters Paul reminds his readers that
Christ alone is the way to salvation.

No one can ever be made right in God's sight by doing what his
law commands. For the more we know God's law, the clearer it
becomes that we aren't obeying it.

But now God has shown us a different way of being right in his
sight—not by obeying the law but by the way promised in the
Scriptures long ago. We are made right in God's sight when we
trust in Jesus Christ to take away our sins. And we all can be
saved in this same way, no matter who we are or what we have
done.

For all have sinned; all fall short of God's glorious standard. Yet
now God in his gracious kindness declares us not guilty. He has
done this through Christ Jesus, who has freed us by taking away
our sins. ROMANS 3:20-24

The law of Moses could not save us, because of our sinful nature.
But God put into effect a different plan to save us. He sent his own
Son in a human body like ours, except that ours are sinful. God
destroyed sin's control over us by giving his Son as a sacrifice for
our sins. ROMANS 8:3

If you confess with your mouth that Jesus is Lord and believe in your heart that God raised him from the dead, you will be saved. For it is by believing in your heart that you are made right with God, and it is by confessing with your mouth that you are saved.
ROMANS 10:9-10

> Paul knew full well that the gospel would meet with skeptics. Do intelligent people really believe that Jesus could be the Son of God and that his being crucified could somehow make us "right with God"? Actually, many intelligent people do believe this. And many don't. Paul made it clear that the message couldn't be judged just by its popularity.

I know very well how foolish the message of the cross sounds to those who are on the road to destruction. But we who are being saved recognize this message as the very power of God. As the Scriptures say, "I will destroy human wisdom and discard their most brilliant ideas." 1 CORINTHIANS 1:18-19

God can use sorrow in our lives to help us turn away from sin and seek salvation. We will never regret that kind of sorrow. But sorrow without repentance is the kind that results in death.
2 CORINTHIANS 7:10

Once you were dead, doomed forever because of your many sins. You used to live just like the rest of the world, full of sin, obeying Satan, the mighty prince of the power of the air. He is the spirit at work in the hearts of those who refuse to obey God. All of us used to live that way, following the passions and desires of our evil nature. We were born with an evil nature, and we were under God's anger just like everyone else.

But God is so rich in mercy, and he loved us so very much, that even while we were dead because of our sins, he gave us life when he raised Christ from the dead. (It is only by God's special favor that you have been saved!) For he raised us from the dead along with Christ, and we are seated with him in the heavenly realms—all because we are one with Christ Jesus. . . .

God saved you by his special favor when you believed. And you can't take credit for this; it is a gift from God. Salvation is not a reward for the good things we have done, so none of us can boast about it. EPHESIANS 2:1-9

This is a true saying, and everyone should believe it: Christ Jesus came into the world to save sinners. 1 TIMOTHY 1:15

God our Savior . . . wants everyone to be saved and to understand the truth. For there is only one God and one Mediator who can reconcile God and people. He is the man Christ Jesus. He gave his life to purchase freedom for everyone. This is the message that God gave to the world at the proper time. 1 TIMOTHY 2:3-6

What makes us think that we can escape if we are indifferent to this great salvation that was announced by the Lord Jesus himself? It was passed on to us by those who heard him speak, and God verified the message by signs and wonders and various miracles and by giving gifts of the Holy Spirit whenever he chose to do so. HEBREWS 2:3-4

I am convinced that nothing can ever separate us from his love. Death can't, and life can't. The angels can't, and the demons can't. Our fears for today, our worries about tomorrow, and even the powers of hell can't keep God's love away. ROMANS 8:38

Because God's children are human beings—made of flesh and blood—Jesus also became flesh and blood by being born in human form. For only as a human being could he die, and only by dying could he break the power of the Devil, who had the power of death. HEBREWS 2:14

The New Testament uses the word *new* many, many times. Just as advertisers constantly offer us "new and improved" products, so the New Testament constantly offers us a new life. Wherever you see the word *salvation* in the New Testament, you will probably see the word *new* nearby.

Those who become Christians become new persons. They are not the same anymore, for the old life is gone. A new life has begun! All this newness of life is from God, who brought us back to himself through what Christ did. And God has given us the task of reconciling people to him. For God was in Christ, reconciling the world to himself, no longer counting people's sins against them. This is the wonderful message he has given us to tell others. . . . For God made Christ, who never sinned, to be the offering for our sin, so that we could be made right with God through Christ. 2 CORINTHIANS 5:17-21

You were buried with Christ when you were baptized. And with him you were raised to a new life because you trusted the mighty power of God, who raised Christ from the dead. You were dead because of your sins and because your sinful nature was not yet cut away. Then God made you alive with Christ. He forgave all our sins. COLOSSIANS 2:12-13

He saved us, not because of the good things we did, but because of his mercy. He washed away our sins and gave us a new life through the Holy Spirit. He generously poured out the Spirit upon us because of what Jesus Christ our Savior did. TITUS 3:5-6

Now we can rejoice in our wonderful new relationship with God—all because of what our Lord Jesus Christ has done for us in making us friends of God. ROMANS 5:11

Anyone can talk about salvation, and anyone can say the words "God has saved me." Words are empty, though, unless backed up by actions. Jesus made it clear that the saved person will do more than just talk about it.

Jesus said to the people who believed in him, "You are truly my disciples if you keep obeying my teachings. And you will know the truth, and the truth will set you free.

"I assure you, anyone who obeys my teaching will never die!"
JOHN 8:31-32, 51

If you love me, obey my commandments.

Those who obey my commandments are the ones who love me. And because they love me, my Father will love them, and I will love them. And I will reveal myself to each one of them.
JOHN 14:15, 21

See also Justification; New Birth, New Life; Repentance; Sin and Redemption.

Self-Control and Self-Denial

After the 1960s it appeared that self-control was as outmoded as the horse and buggy. Then it came back into style—in physical fitness and dieting, anyway. Sidewalks and parks across the country are cluttered with self-denying individuals beating their bodies into submission. And for what reason?

Is this the kind of self-control God desires from us? Maybe. The Bible has a few things to say about gluttony and excessive drinking. But the self-control the Bible applauds is a different thing: saying yes to God, saying no to any selfish urges that lead us away from God or hinder us from loving other people. In the Bible's view, this is vastly more important than counting calories or sweating on a treadmill.

A person without self-control is as defenseless as a city with broken-down walls. PROVERBS 25:28

An evil man is held captive by his own sins; they are ropes that catch and hold him. He will die for lack of self-control; he will be lost because of his incredible folly. PROVERBS 5:22-23

Jesus said to the disciples, "If any of you wants to be my follower, you must put aside your selfish ambition, shoulder your cross, and follow me. If you try to keep your life for yourself, you will lose it. But if you give up your life for me, you will find true life. And how do you benefit if you gain the whole world but lose your own soul in the process? Is anything worth more than your soul? For I, the Son of Man, will come in the glory of my Father with his angels and will judge all people according to their deeds." MATTHEW 16:24-27

I assure you, everyone who has given up house or wife or brothers or parents or children, for the sake of the Kingdom of God, will be repaid many times over in this life, as well as receiving eternal life in the world to come. LUKE 18:29-30

He will pour out his anger and wrath on those who live for themselves, who refuse to obey the truth and practice evil deeds. ROMANS 2:8

Our old sinful selves were crucified with Christ so that sin might lose its power in our lives. We are no longer slaves to sin. ROMANS 6:6

Dear Christian friends, you have no obligation whatsoever to do what your sinful nature urges you to do. For if you keep on following it, you will perish. But if through the power of the Holy Spirit you turn from it and its evil deeds, you will live. ROMANS 8:12-13

When the Holy Spirit controls our lives, he will produce this kind of fruit in us: love, joy, peace, patience, kindness, goodness, faithfulness, gentleness, and self-control. Here there is no conflict with the law.

Those who belong to Christ Jesus have nailed the passions and desires of their sinful nature to his cross and crucified them there.

If we are living now by the Holy Spirit, let us follow the Holy Spirit's leading in every part of our lives. GALATIANS 5:22-25

> Self-control involves more than abstaining from certain sinful behaviors. It also means resisting our natural impulse to retaliate, as Jesus made clear:

Don't resist an evil person! If you are slapped on the right cheek, turn the other, too. If you are ordered to court and your shirt is taken from you, give your coat, too. If a soldier demands that you carry his gear for a mile, carry it two miles. Give to those who ask, and don't turn away from those who want to borrow. MATTHEW 5:39-42

> Strangely, the current taboos about eating certain foods are nothing new. In the New Testament days the Christians encountered people—some claiming to be Christians—who laid down restrictive rules about eating or handling certain things. Then, as now, people liked to give the appearance of being smart or disciplined—someone "in control." The apostle Paul realized these restrictions had no place in a life devoted to God.

You have died with Christ, and he has set you free from the evil powers of this world. So why do you keep on following rules of the world, such as, "Don't handle, don't eat, don't touch." Such rules are mere human teaching about things that are gone as soon as we use them. These rules may seem wise because they require strong devotion, humility, and severe bodily discipline. But they have no effect when it comes to conquering a person's evil thoughts and desires. COLOSSIANS 2:20-23

> "Just say no" is easy to say, harder to do. In fact, the world always poses an obvious question to us: Why deny yourself anything? We only have to switch on the evening news to see where this attitude has led us. According to the Bible, we can, with God's help, live

well in this me-first world. Self-control is something God is happy to supply us with, if we only ask.

God has not given us a spirit of fear and timidity, but of power, love, and self-discipline. 2 TIMOTHY 1:7

Knowing God leads to self-control. Self-control leads to patient endurance, and patient endurance leads to godliness. 2 PETER 1:6

We are instructed to turn from godless living and sinful pleasures. We should live in this evil world with self-control, right conduct, and devotion to God, while we look forward to that wonderful event when the glory of our great God and Savior, Jesus Christ, will be revealed. TITUS 2: 12-13

See also Anger, Hate, Obeying God, Revenge, Selfishness, Temptation.

Self-Esteem

Flip on the TV or radio and you'll find a thousand ways to enhance your self-esteem—losing weight, working out, having cosmetic surgery, getting a degree, meditating, whatever. If all these ways were successful, we'd have the healthiest self-esteem of any people on earth. Somehow, though, we don't. And why should we? The person who loses fifty pounds can look in the mirror and say, "Wow, I'm thinner." But can the person say, "Yes, I'm really the kind of person I should be"? Or is the answer to the self-esteem problem something that can't be attained through exercise or education or any other popular method? Solomon grappled with the very same question:

As I looked at everything I had worked so hard to accomplish, it was all so meaningless. It was like chasing the wind. There was nothing really worthwhile anywhere. ECCLESIASTES 2:11

I observed that most people are motivated to success by their envy of their neighbors. But this, too, is meaningless, like chasing the wind. ECCLESIASTES 4:4

There is another serious problem I have seen in the world. Riches are sometimes hoarded to the harm of the saver, or they are put into risky investments that turn sour, and everything is lost. In the end, there is nothing left to pass on to one's children. People who live only for wealth come to the end of their lives as naked and empty-handed as on the day they were born.

And this, too, is a very serious problem. As people come into this world, so they depart. All their hard work is for nothing. They have been working for the wind, and everything will be swept away. Throughout their lives, they live under a cloud—frustrated, discouraged, and angry. ECCLESIASTES 5:13-17

Enjoy what you have rather than desiring what you don't have. Just dreaming about nice things is meaningless; it is like chasing the wind. ECCLESIASTES 6:9

> The Bible doesn't use the term *self-esteem,* but the concept is there. What the Bible promises is not enhanced self-esteem but something even better: knowing we are right with God, with other people, and with ourselves. There is no better means of enhancing self-esteem. And, strangely enough, those who feel themselves to be right with God probably don't give much thought to their self-esteem at all. Like happiness, it isn't attained by those who are breathlessly pursuing it.

Oh, the joys of those who trust the LORD, who have no confidence in the proud, or in those who worship idols. PSALM 40:4

I trust in God, so why should I be afraid? What can mere mortals do to me? PSALM 56:4

Trust in the LORD with all your heart; do not depend on your own understanding. Seek his will in all you do, and he will direct your paths. Don't be impressed with your own wisdom. Instead, fear the LORD and turn your back on evil. Then you will gain renewed health and vitality. PROVERBS 3:5-8

You will keep in perfect peace all who trust in you, whose thoughts are fixed on you! ISAIAH 26:3

He gives power to those who are tired and worn out; he offers strength to the weak. Even youths will become exhausted, and young men will give up. But those who wait on the LORD will find new strength. They will fly high on wings like eagles. They will run and not grow weary. They will walk and not faint. ISAIAH 40:29-31

"I know the plans I have for you," says the LORD. "They are plans for good and not for disaster, to give you a future and a hope." JEREMIAH 29:11

> Jesus assured his followers that we are important, not because of anything we do ourselves, but because we are part of the new Kingdom of God. As ambassadors for this Kingdom, we have a noble position.

Not even a sparrow, worth only half a penny, can fall to the ground without your Father knowing it. And the very hairs on your head are all numbered. So don't be afraid; you are more valuable to him than a whole flock of sparrows.

   If you cling to your life, you will lose it; but if you give it up for me, you will find it. MATTHEW 10:29-31, 39

> The expression "salt of the earth" has passed from the Bible into everyday language. It is one of many images Jesus used to remind people that they have an important role to play in this world. This, more than all the self-esteem books and videos in the world, should give meaning and purpose to our life.

You are the salt of the earth. But what good is salt if it has lost its flavor? Can you make it useful again? It will be thrown out and trampled underfoot as worthless. You are the light of the world— like a city on a mountain, glowing in the night for all to see. Don't hide your light under a basket! Instead, put it on a stand and let it shine for all. In the same way, let your good deeds shine out for all to see, so that everyone will praise your heavenly Father.
MATTHEW 5:13-16

He [God] will give you all you need from day to day if you live for him and make the Kingdom of God your primary concern.

So don't worry about tomorrow, for tomorrow will bring its own worries. Today's trouble is enough for today. MATTHEW 6:33-34

Have you ever considered what an incredible *burden* it is, always worrying about self-esteem and personal growth? For some people it's like having a second full-time job, pursuing one self-esteem boost after another. Jesus gives a comforting promise to those who feel their lives aren't quite right.

Jesus said, "Come to me, all of you who are weary and carry heavy burdens, and I will give you rest. Take my yoke upon you. Let me teach you, because I am humble and gentle, and you will find rest for your souls. For my yoke fits perfectly, and the burden I give you is light." MATTHEW 11:28-30

Jesus said to the disciples, "If any of you wants to be my follower, you must put aside your selfish ambition, shoulder your cross, and follow me. If you try to keep your life for yourself, you will lose it. But if you give up your life for me, you will find true life. And how do you benefit if you gain the whole world but lose your own soul in the process? Is anything worth more than your soul?" MATTHEW 16:24-26

Those who love their life in this world will lose it. Those who despise their life in this world will keep it for eternal life.
JOHN 12:25

> The Bible could be called the Book of Being Realistic about Ourselves. It reminds us again and again of something that each of us knows instinctively: Whatever our achievements are, they don't bring complete happiness. Genuine happiness can only be had when we learn to rely on God, not on our own accomplishments, however great they may seem. The greatest achievement in any human life is becoming aware that God is in charge.

If God is for us, who can ever be against us? ROMANS 8:31

As God's messenger, I give each of you this warning: Be honest in your estimate of yourselves, measuring your value by how much faith God has given you. Just as our bodies have many parts and each part has a special function, so it is with Christ's body. We are all parts of his one body, and each of us has different work to do. And since we are all one body in Christ, we belong to each other, and each of us needs all the others.
God has given each of us the ability to do certain things well.
ROMANS 12:3-6

As the Scriptures say, "The person who wishes to boast should boast only of what the Lord has done." When people boast about themselves, it doesn't count for much. But when the Lord commends someone, that's different! 2 CORINTHIANS 10:17-18

What about me? Have I been faithful? Well, it matters very little what you or anyone else thinks. I don't even trust my own judgment on this point. My conscience is clear, but that isn't what matters. It is the Lord himself who will examine me and decide.
1 CORINTHIANS 4:3-4

I have received wonderful revelations from God. But to keep me from getting puffed up, I was given a thorn in my flesh, a messenger from Satan to torment me and keep me from getting proud.

Three different times I begged the Lord to take it away. Each time he said, "My gracious favor is all you need. My power works best in your weakness." So now I am glad to boast about my weaknesses, so that the power of Christ may work through me. Since I know it is all for Christ's good, I am quite content with my weaknesses and with insults, hardships, persecutions, and calamities. For when I am weak, then I am strong.
2 CORINTHIANS 12:7-10

I once thought all these things were so very important, but now I consider them worthless because of what Christ has done. Yes, everything else is worthless when compared with the priceless gain of knowing Christ Jesus my Lord. I have discarded everything else, counting it all as garbage, so that I may have Christ and become one with him. I no longer count on my own goodness or my ability to obey God's law, but I trust Christ to save me. For God's way of making us right with himself depends on faith.
PHILIPPIANS 3:7-9

You are a chosen people. You are a kingdom of priests, God's holy nation, his very own possession. This is so you can show others the goodness of God, for he called you out of the darkness into his wonderful light.

"Once you were not a people; now you are the people of God. Once you received none of God's mercy; now you have received his mercy." 1 PETER 2:9-10

The ever popular musical comedy *The Fantasticks* has the teenage heroine repeating to herself, "I am special, I am special." The audience is expected to laugh at this and rightly so. Words can't change reality, and if we don't really know, deep down, that we're special, the words are hollow. The Bible continually emphasizes walking the walk, not just talking the talk. If we are really God's people, our actions will show it.

It is by our actions that we know we are living in the truth, so we will be confident when we stand before the Lord, even if our hearts condemn us. For God is greater than our hearts, and he knows everything. 1 JOHN 3:19-20

If you think you are too important to help someone in need, you are only fooling yourself. You are really a nobody.

Be sure to do what you should, for then you will enjoy the personal satisfaction of having done your work well, and you won't need to compare yourself to anyone else. For we are each responsible for our own conduct. GALATIANS 6:3-5

> Psalm 139 could almost be called the "Self-Esteem Psalm." But it isn't an ego builder in the usual sense. It is a song of praise to a God who watches over our life, who loved us and cared for us even before we were born. The psalm restates a promise that occurs again and again in the Bible: Our worth isn't based on our own accomplishments, however impressive they are, but on the fact that God cares for us.

O LORD, you have examined my heart and know everything about me. You know when I sit down or stand up. You know my every thought when far away. You chart the path ahead of me and tell me where to stop and rest. Every moment you know where I am. You know what I am going to say even before I say it, LORD. You both precede and follow me. You place your hand of blessing on my head. Such knowledge is too wonderful for me, too great for me to know!

I can never escape from your spirit! I can never get away from your presence! If I go up to heaven, you are there; if I go down to the place of the dead, you are there. If I ride the wings of the morning, if I dwell by the farthest oceans, even there your hand will guide me, and your strength will support me. I could ask the darkness to hide me and the light around me to become night—but even in darkness I cannot hide from you. To you the night shines as bright as day. Darkness and light are both alike to you.

You made all the delicate, inner parts of my body and knit me together in my mother's womb. Thank you for making me so wonderfully complex! Your workmanship is marvelous—and how well I know it. You watched me as I was being formed in utter seclusion, as I was woven together in the dark of the womb. You saw me before I was born. Every day of my life was recorded in your book. Every moment was laid out before a single day had passed.

How precious are your thoughts about me, O God! They are innumerable! I can't even count them; they outnumber the grains of sand! And when I wake up in the morning, you are still with me! . . .

Search me, O God, and know my heart; test me and know my thoughts. Point out anything in me that offends you, and lead me along the path of everlasting life. PSALM 139

See also Ambition, The Body, Contentment, Worldly Cares, Worry and Anxiety.

Selfishness

Selfishness has been described as "the only real atheism." This makes sense: If we worship ourselves, we can't worship God also. If we act as if we ourselves are the center of the universe, it must mean God is not there at the center. Most of us are not *totally* selfish, of course. We are sometimes very selfish, less so at other times. The more we focus on ourselves, the less we focus on God and other people. The book of Proverbs provides a vivid picture of the selfish person.

A recluse is self-indulgent, snarling at every sound principle of conduct. PROVERBS 18:1

Normally we think of a recluse as someone who lives by himself. But you could apply the verse above to anyone who lives *for* himself, as so many people do. The Bible continually warns of the dangers of living this way. It is not something God takes lightly.

He will pour out his anger and wrath on those who live for themselves, who refuse to obey the truth and practice evil deeds.

There will be trouble and calamity for everyone who keeps on sinning. ROMANS 2:8-9

When you follow the desires of your sinful nature, your lives will produce these evil results: sexual immorality, impure thoughts, eagerness for lustful pleasure, idolatry, participation in demonic activities, hostility, quarreling, jealousy, outbursts of anger, selfish ambition, divisions, the feeling that everyone is wrong except those in your own little group, envy, drunkenness, wild parties, and other kinds of sin. Let me tell you again, as I have before, that anyone living that sort of life will not inherit the Kingdom of God. GALATIANS 5:19-21

Wherever there is jealousy and selfish ambition, there you will find disorder and every kind of evil. JAMES 3:16

> In New Testament days, as in ours, many people practiced certain forms of self-denial (usually avoiding certain foods—does this sound familiar?). The apostle Paul understood that these practices had no effect whatever on human selfishness.

You have died with Christ, and he has set you free from the evil powers of this world. So why do you keep on following rules of the world, such as, "Don't handle, don't eat, don't touch." Such rules are mere human teaching about things that are gone as soon as we use them. These rules may seem wise because they require strong devotion, humility, and severe bodily discipline. But they have no effect when it comes to conquering a person's evil thoughts and desires. COLOSSIANS 2:20-23

> "Me first" could well be the motto for our society today—or maybe for any day, because history shows that selfishness is nothing new. But the person who lives for God is expected to look beyond history, toward the return of Christ and eternal life in heaven. Our life in this world is kind of a training ground for that ultimate

destination. We prepare ourselves for it daily by little acts of
kindness and consideration for others.

We are instructed to turn from godless living and sinful pleasures.
We should live in this evil world with self-control, right conduct,
and devotion to God, while we look forward to that wonderful
event when the glory of our great God and Savior, Jesus Christ,
will be revealed.   TITUS 2:12-13

Jesus himself pretty well summarized the best antidote to
selfishness: Love God, love other people.

"Of all the commandments, which is the most important?"
  Jesus replied, "The most important commandment is this: 'Hear,
O Israel! The Lord our God is the one and only Lord. And you
must love the Lord your God with all your heart, all your soul, all
your mind, and all your strength.' The second is equally
important: 'Love your neighbor as yourself.' No other
commandment is greater than these."   MARK 12:28-31

See also Ambition, Self-Control and Self-Denial, Self-Esteem.

Self-Righteousness

Religious people have a reputation—partly deserved—for being self-righteous. Of course, there are plenty of self-righteous people in the world who aren't religious at all. How often have you met someone crowing about his latest diet, exercise plan, self-esteem booster, "spiritual technique," whatever? People who criticize Christians for self-righteousness often commit the same sin. And the fact is, what they call our "self-righteousness" may simply be our concern for morality—a concern that has never been popular.

Still, self-righteousness is wrong, as the Bible makes plain. Nothing is hidden from God. We are promised real righteousness if we pursue it. We are promised something else if we put ourselves on a moral pedestal.

There is a path before each person that seems right, but it ends in death. PROVERBS 14:12

Fools think they need no advice, but the wise listen to others. PROVERBS 12:15

People may be pure in their own eyes, but the LORD examines their motives. PROVERBS 16:2

People may think they are doing what is right, but the LORD examines the heart. PROVERBS 21:2

There is more hope for fools than for people who think they are wise. PROVERBS 26:12

Trusting oneself is foolish, but those who walk in wisdom are safe. PROVERBS 28:26

Some people curse their father and do not thank their mother. They feel pure, but they are filthy and unwashed. They are proud beyond description and disdainful. PROVERBS 30:11-13

Destruction is certain for those who say that evil is good and good is evil; that dark is light and light is dark; that bitter is sweet and sweet is bitter.
   Destruction is certain for those who think they are wise and consider themselves to be clever. ISAIAH 5:20-21

> The Bible makes it plain that all people—even the most moral—are sinners. This is one reason that self-righteousness is never right. Being self-righteous means we have lost sight of our own continued moral failure. The prophet Isaiah reminds us that *no one* is completely pure in God's eyes:

We are all infected and impure with sin. When we proudly display our righteous deeds, we find they are but filthy rags. Like autumn leaves, we wither and fall. And our sins, like the wind, sweep us away. ISAIAH 64:6

Jesus often spoke against self-righteousness. He was keenly aware of people's tendency to focus on other people's failures, ignoring their own:

Stop judging others, and you will not be judged. For others will treat you as you treat them. Whatever measure you use in judging others, it will be used to measure how you are judged. And why worry about a speck in your friend's eye when you have a log in your own? How can you think of saying, "Friend, let me help you get rid of that speck in your eye," when you can't see past the log in your own eye? Hypocrite! First get rid of the log from your own eye; then perhaps you will see well enough to deal with the speck in your friend's eye. MATTHEW 7:1-5

Matthew invited Jesus and his disciples to be his dinner guests, along with his fellow tax collectors and many other notorious sinners. The Pharisees were indignant. "Why does your teacher eat with such scum?" they asked his disciples.

When he heard this, Jesus replied, "Healthy people don't need a doctor—sick people do." Then he added, "Now go and learn the meaning of this Scripture: 'I want you to be merciful; I don't want your sacrifices.' For I have come to call sinners, not those who think they are already good enough." MATTHEW 9:10-13

One of the world's most beautiful stories about self-righteousness is Jesus' parable of the tax collector and the Pharisee. The story is both a promise of mercy to people who are humble, and a stern warning to people who are proud of their own morality.

Jesus told this story to some who had great self-confidence and scorned everyone else: "Two men went to the Temple to pray. One was a Pharisee, and the other was a dishonest tax collector. The proud Pharisee stood by himself and prayed this prayer: 'I thank you, God, that I am not a sinner like everyone else, especially like that tax collector over there! For I never cheat, I don't sin, I don't commit adultery, I fast twice a week, and I give you a tenth of my income.'

"But the tax collector stood at a distance and dared not even lift his eyes to heaven as he prayed. Instead, he beat his chest in sorrow, saying, 'O God, be merciful to me, for I am a sinner.' I tell you, this sinner, not the Pharisee, returned home justified before God. For the proud will be humbled, but the humble will be honored." LUKE 18:9-14

He said to [the Pharisees], "You like to look good in public, but God knows your evil hearts. What this world honors is an abomination in the sight of God." LUKE 16:15

Jesus told him, "I have come to judge the world. I have come to give sight to the blind and to show those who think they see that they are blind."

The Pharisees who were standing there heard him and asked, "Are you saying we are blind?"

"If you were blind, you wouldn't be guilty," Jesus replied. "But you remain guilty because you claim you can see." JOHN 9:39-41

> The apostle Paul was just the right person to speak on the subject of self-righteousness. He had been, all his life, a moral and religious Jew, taking care to observe the Jewish law. But when he turned to Christ, he realized that his moral life was no reason for him to boast or to put on airs. Nothing matters except placing our faith in Christ and the mercy of God. The way to heaven is not through our own moral efforts but through the righteousness of the Son of God.

Can we boast, then, that we have done anything to be accepted by God? No, because our acquittal is not based on our good deeds. It is based on our faith. ROMANS 3:27

The Scriptures say, "The person who wishes to boast should boast only of what the Lord has done." When people boast about themselves, it doesn't count for much. But when the Lord commends someone, that's different! 2 CORINTHIANS 10:17-18

If you think you are too important to help someone in need, you are only fooling yourself. You are really a nobody. GALATIANS 6:3

See also Hypocrisy, Judging Others, Righteousness, Self-Esteem.

Sexuality

The world generally takes a more—and less—serious view of sex than the Bible does. Its view is *more* serious because it seems obsessed with it—discussing it and presenting it in screaming detail in television, films, songs, and books. Adultery and casual sex are rampant. The world seems to have little else on its mind.

Its view is *less* serious because it so often fails to make the connection between sex and committed love. We get the impression that the world is filled with people gloating over their sexual experiences but puzzled why they don't find them more satisfying. Could it be because they've forgotten that sex is part—not the whole—of a lifelong commitment between one man and one woman? Could it be they've also forgotten that sex is not the only way—perhaps not even the best way—for a husband and wife to enjoy each other?

One thing the world seems to be certain about: Christianity is a killjoy, antisex religion. But this is a lie. Nothing in the Bible says that sex is wrong. The Bible does hold the view that sex is such a mysterious and powerful thing that it ought to be subject to certain boundaries—like marriage. The Bible views the body as something important—something to be taken care of and used In God's service, not used as a sexual toy.

God wants you to be holy, so you should keep clear of all sexual sin. Then each of you will control your body and live in holiness and honor—not in lustful passion as the pagans do, in their ignorance of God and his ways.

Never cheat another Christian in this matter by taking his wife, for the Lord avenges all such sins, as we have solemnly warned you before. God has called us to be holy, not to live impure lives. Anyone who refuses to live by these rules is not disobeying human rules but is rejecting God, who gives his Holy Spirit to you. 1 THESSALONIANS 4:3-8

> Many people have harmed themselves as well others through sexual irresponsibility. For these people the Bible has some wonderful promises: God accepts all sorrowing sinners, including sexual sinners.

Put to death the sinful, earthly things lurking within you. Have nothing to do with sexual sin, impurity, lust, and shameful desires. Don't be greedy for the good things of this life, for that is idolatry. God's terrible anger will come upon those who do such things. You used to do them when your life was still part of this world. But now is the time to get rid of anger, rage, malicious behavior, slander, and dirty language. Don't lie to each other, for you have stripped off your old evil nature and all its wicked deeds. In its place you have clothed yourselves with a brand-new nature that is continually being renewed as you learn more and more about Christ, who created this new nature within you. COLOSSIANS 3:5-10

> Did you notice in the preceding passage the words "You used to do them . . ."? There is the promise of forgiveness for people who once dabbled in sexual sin but are now right with God. Note in the following selection the passage beginning "There was a time when some of you were just like that. . . ."

Don't you know that those who do wrong will have no share in the Kingdom of God? Don't fool yourselves. Those who indulge in sexual sin, who are idol worshipers, adulterers, male prostitutes, homosexuals, thieves, greedy people, drunkards, abusers, and swindlers—none of these will have a share in the Kingdom of God. There was a time when some of you were just like that, but now your sins have been washed away, and you have been set apart for God. You have been made right with God because of what the Lord Jesus Christ and the Spirit of our God have done for you.

Don't you realize that your bodies are actually parts of Christ? Should a man take his body, which belongs to Christ, and join it to a prostitute? Never! And don't you know that if a man joins himself to a prostitute, he becomes one body with her? For the Scriptures say, "The two are united into one." But the person who is joined to the Lord becomes one spirit with him.

Run away from sexual sin! No other sin so clearly affects the body as this one does. For sexual immorality is a sin against your own body. 1 CORINTHIANS 6:9-11, 15-18

> Even the most self-controlled person still faces sexual temptation from time to time. How can we avoid it, with sex being a constant theme in TV, movies, and popular songs? Unlike the media's constant celebration of selfish sex, though, the Bible shows the flip side: Sex outside of marriage does harm to ourselves and to others.

Give honor to marriage, and remain faithful to one another in marriage. God will surely judge people who are immoral and those who commit adultery. HEBREWS 13:4

A prostitute will bring you to poverty, and sleeping with another man's wife may cost you your very life. PROVERBS 6:26

A prostitute is a deep pit; an adulterous woman is treacherous. She hides and waits like a robber, looking for another victim who will be unfaithful to his wife. PROVERBS 23:27-28

The man who loves wisdom brings joy to his father, but if he hangs around with prostitutes, his wealth is wasted. PROVERBS 29:3

When you follow the desires of your sinful nature, your lives will produce these evil results: sexual immorality, impure thoughts, eagerness for lustful pleasure, idolatry, participation in demonic activities, hostility, quarreling, jealousy, outbursts of anger, selfish ambition, divisions, the feeling that everyone is wrong except those in your own little group, envy, drunkenness, wild parties, and other kinds of sin. Let me tell you again, as I have before, that anyone living that sort of life will not inherit the Kingdom of God. GALATIANS 5:19-21

Let there be no sexual immorality, impurity, or greed among you. Such sins have no place among God's people. Obscene stories, foolish talk, and coarse jokes—these are not for you. Instead, let there be thankfulness to God. You can be sure that no immoral, impure, or greedy person will inherit the Kingdom of Christ and of God. For a greedy person is really an idolater who worships the things of this world. Don't be fooled by those who try to excuse these sins, for the terrible anger of God comes upon all those who disobey him. Don't participate in the things these people do. For though your hearts were once full of darkness, now you are full of light from the Lord, and your behavior should show it!

Take no part in the worthless deeds of evil and darkness; instead, rebuke and expose them. It is shameful even to talk about the things that ungodly people do in secret. But when the light shines on them, it becomes clear how evil these things are. And where your light shines, it will expose their evil deeds. This is why it is said, "Awake, O sleeper, rise up from the dead, and Christ will give you light." EPHESIANS 5:3-8, 11-14

Don't forget the cities of Sodom and Gomorrah and their neighboring towns, which were filled with sexual immorality and every kind of sexual perversion. Those cities were

destroyed by fire and are a warning of the eternal fire that will
punish all who are evil. JUDE 7

Those who are dominated by the sinful nature think about sinful
things, but those who are controlled by the Holy Spirit think
about things that please the Spirit. If your sinful nature controls
your mind, there is death. But if the Holy Spirit controls your
mind, there is life and peace. For the sinful nature is always
hostile to God. It never did obey God's laws, and it never will.
That's why those who are still under the control of their sinful
nature can never please God.

   But you are not controlled by your sinful nature. You are
controlled by the Spirit if you have the Spirit of God living in you.
(And remember that those who do not have the Spirit of Christ
living in them are not Christians at all.)

   For if you keep on following it, you will perish. But if through
the power of the Holy Spirit you turn from it and its evil deeds,
you will live. ROMANS 8:5-9, 13

Because there is so much sexual immorality, each man should
have his own wife, and each woman should have her own
husband. 1 CORINTHIANS 7:2

I advise you to live according to your new life in the Holy Spirit.
Then you won't be doing what your sinful nature craves.

   Those who belong to Christ Jesus have nailed the passions and
desires of their sinful nature to his cross and crucified them there.
GALATIANS 5:16, 24

Those who live only to satisfy their own sinful desires will
harvest the consequences of decay and death. But those who live
to please the Spirit will harvest everlasting life from the Spirit.
GALATIANS 6:8

The Letter to the Hebrews gives a consoling promise to anyone who has endured sexual temptation: Jesus himself, our Savior, was human just as we are. Instead of some airy spirit, we have a Lord who experienced the full range of human life, so he understands us.

Since he himself has gone through suffering and temptation, he is able to help us when we are being tempted.

This High Priest of ours understands our weaknesses, for he faced all of the same temptations we do, yet he did not sin.

HEBREWS 2:18; 4:15

The first Christians lived in a culture as sex-saturated as our own. Yet the apostles didn't see this as a reason to lower their moral standards. Paul, writing to the Christians at Corinth (a notoriously immoral city), instructed them that their biggest concern should not be the immorality of unbelievers but the immorality of those claiming to be Christians.

When I wrote to you before, I told you not to associate with people who indulge in sexual sin. But I wasn't talking about unbelievers who indulge in sexual sin, or who are greedy or are swindlers or idol worshipers. You would have to leave this world to avoid people like that. What I meant was that you are not to associate with anyone who claims to be a Christian yet indulges in sexual sin, or is greedy, or worships idols, or is abusive, or a drunkard, or a swindler. Don't even eat with such people.

1 CORINTHIANS 5:9-11

See also Adultery, The Body, Self-Control and Self-Denial, Temptation.

Sickness

Ged cares about our spiritual life *and* our physical life. He created the human body, and he is pleased when we enjoy health and vigor. But in this world our bodies endure sickness, pain, decay. Sometimes we abuse our own bodies, but often our ailments occur because—well, we don't always know why, nor does God promise that we will understand why.

Healing occurs—sometimes dramatically, as in the work of Jesus and his disciples. The Gospels overflow with stories of Jesus healing every kind of bodily affliction. So did his disciples, whom he promised would do the same works that he did.

Dramatic healings, in fact, still occur today, and many Christians testify to healings that, according to the medical experts, could not have happened. God still works to heal people in ways that defy medical knowledge. It is never wrong to pray for healing, either for ourselves or others. The Bible tells us to pray for whatever we need, and that surely includes freedom from sickness and pain.

But healing does not always occur, even to the most loving, God-centered people. So why doesn't healing happen more often today? We don't know. But the Bible does promise us that if we are not healed in this life, there is something greater awaiting us afterward.

O LORD, you alone can heal me; you alone can save. My praises are for you alone! JEREMIAH 17:14

I will give you back your health and heal your wounds, says the LORD. JEREMIAH 30:17

Remember your promise to me, for it is my only hope. Your promise revives me; it comforts me in all my troubles. PSALM 119:49-50

Jesus called his twelve disciples to him and gave them authority to cast out evil spirits and to heal every kind of disease and illness. MATTHEW 10:1

Paul's first letter to the Corinthians tells about spiritual gifts, one of which is healing. It is clear that the gift of healing did not end with Jesus and his disciples.

There are different ways God works in our lives, but it is the same God who does the work through all of us. A spiritual gift is given to each of us as a means of helping the entire church.

To one person the Spirit gives the ability to give wise advice; to another he gives the gift of special knowledge. The Spirit gives special faith to another, and to someone else he gives the power to heal the sick. . . . It is the one and only Holy Spirit who distributes these gifts. He alone decides which gift each person should have.

Now all of you together are Christ's body, and each one of you is a separate and necessary part of it. Here is a list of some of the members that God has placed in the body of Christ: first are apostles, second are prophets, third are teachers, then those who do miracles, those who have the gift of healing, those who can help others, those who can get others to work together, those who speak in unknown languages.

1 CORINTHIANS 12:6-11, 27-28

Are any among you suffering? They should keep on praying about it. And those who have reason to be thankful should continually sing praises to the Lord.

Are any among you sick? They should call for the elders of the church and have them pray over them, anointing them with oil in the name of the Lord. And their prayer offered in faith will heal the sick, and the Lord will make them well. JAMES 5:13-15

> In one of Paul's letters he talks about a "thorn in the flesh," perhaps some kind of physical ailment. Paul was certainly a man of faith, yet he was not healed of it. Why? Nobody knows. Paul did the obvious thing in the situation. He accepted it:

Three different times I begged the Lord to take it away. Each time he said, "My gracious favor is all you need. My power works best in your weakness." So now I am glad to boast about my weaknesses, so that the power of Christ may work through me. Since I know it is all for Christ's good, I am quite content with my weaknesses and with insults, hardships, persecutions, and calamities. For when I am weak, then I am strong. 2 CORINTHIANS 12:8-10

> Healing has its part in the work of Christians. Something less dramatic, but just as important, is the attitude we show toward the sick. Jesus told a parable of the Last Judgment, in which he promised eternal benefits toward those who had shown compassion toward the sick and other suffering people.

When the Son of Man comes in his glory, and all the angels with him, then he will sit upon his glorious throne. All the nations will be gathered in his presence, and he will separate them as a shepherd separates the sheep from the goats. He will place the sheep at his right hand and the goats at his left. Then the King will say to those on the right, "Come, you who are blessed by my Father, inherit the Kingdom prepared for you from the foundation of the world. For I was hungry, and you fed me. I was thirsty, and you gave me a drink. I was a stranger, and you invited me into your home. I was naked, and you gave me clothing. I was sick, and you cared for me. I was in prison, and you visited me."

Then these righteous ones will reply, "Lord, when did we ever see you hungry and feed you? Or thirsty and give you something to drink? Or a stranger and show you hospitality? Or naked and give you clothing? When did we ever see you sick or in prison, and visit you?" And the King will tell them, "I assure you, when you did it to one of the least of these my brothers and sisters, you were doing it to me!"

Then the King will turn to those on the left and say, "Away with you, you cursed ones, into the eternal fire prepared for the Devil and his demons! For I was hungry, and you didn't feed me. I was thirsty, and you didn't give me anything to drink. I was a stranger, and you didn't invite me into your home. I was naked, and you gave me no clothing. I was sick and in prison, and you didn't visit me."

Then they will reply, "Lord, when did we ever see you hungry or thirsty or a stranger or naked or sick or in prison, and not help you?" And he will answer, "I assure you, when you refused to help the least of these my brothers and sisters, you were refusing to help me." And they will go away into eternal punishment, but the righteous will go into eternal life. MATTHEW 25:31-46

> Every person who has ever been healed has died. Even Lazarus, the friend Jesus raised from the dead, died again. The Bible makes no promise that our present bodies, whatever their condition, will stay healthy or last forever. In fact, the Bible promises something much more glorious: a new body, like our present ones but also different, a body made for eternity.

We know that when this earthly tent we live in is taken down—when we die and leave these bodies—we will have a home in heaven, an eternal body made for us by God himself and not by human hands. We grow weary in our present bodies, and

we long for the day when we will put on our heavenly bodies like new clothing. For we will not be spirits without bodies, but we will put on new heavenly bodies. Our dying bodies make us groan and sigh, but it's not that we want to die and have no bodies at all. We want to slip into our new bodies so that these dying bodies will be swallowed up by everlasting life.
2 CORINTHIANS 5:1-4

Though our bodies are dying, our spirits are being renewed every day. 2 CORINTHIANS 4:16

See also The Body, Comfort in Times of Trouble, Eternal Life, God's Love for Us, Patience.

Sin and Redemption

Are there any sinners around anymore? People are called dysfunctional or not in touch with themselves or negative or uptight or immature—but never *sinful*. Odd that we've discarded the word *sin,* since it includes all these other categories, and more. It also covers all of us—not just the cruelest and most criminal, but even people who seem well adjusted. The Bible assures us that we all sin. Our sin—seeking our own selfish way instead of God's way, making ourselves the center of the universe—separates us from God. It mars our relationships with others. None of this has changed, even if we threw out the word *sin* because it seemed too old-fashioned.

We need to bring it back into fashion. We need to remind people that *sin* doesn't just refer to blatantly criminal behavior. It refers to a universal condition: focusing on ourselves instead of on God and other people. The condition, according to the Bible, isn't remedied by reading self-improvement books or thinking positive thoughts or trying to do better. It is such a serious matter that we need something—someone—to reconcile us to God. The Bible is the story of that Someone.

The human heart is most deceitful and desperately wicked. Who really knows how bad it is? But I know! I, the LORD, search all hearts and examine secret motives. I give all people their due rewards, according to what their actions deserve. JEREMIAH 17:9-10

The LORD looks down from heaven on the entire human race; he looks to see if there is even one with real understanding, one who seeks for God. But no, all have turned away from God; all have become corrupt. No one does good, not even one! PSALM 14:2-3

Can an Ethiopian change the color of his skin? Can a leopard take away its spots? Neither can you start doing good, for you always do evil. JEREMIAH 13:23

There is not a single person in all the earth who is always good and never sins. ECCLESIASTES 7:20

God shows his anger from heaven against all sinful, wicked people who push the truth away from themselves. For the truth about God is known to them instinctively. God has put this knowledge in their hearts. From the time the world was created, people have seen the earth and sky and all that God made. They can clearly see his invisible qualities—his eternal power and divine nature. So they have no excuse whatsoever for not knowing God.

Yes, they knew God, but they wouldn't worship him as God or even give him thanks. And they began to think up foolish ideas of what God was like. The result was that their minds became dark and confused. Claiming to be wise, they became utter fools instead. And instead of worshiping the glorious, ever-living God, they worshiped idols made to look like mere people, or birds and animals and snakes.

So God let them go ahead and do whatever shameful things their hearts desired. As a result, they did vile and degrading things with each other's bodies. Instead of believing what they knew was the truth about God, they deliberately chose to believe lies. So they worshiped the things God made but not the Creator himself, who is to be praised forever. Amen. ROMANS 1:18-25

The New Testament presents Jesus as the one who solves the sin problem. The image used is the one of sacrifice, based on the Old Testament idea of sacrificing an innocent animal as a "sin offering" to make peace with God. In the New Testament, Jesus is the final "offering," the one completely innocent person who let himself be offered up—sacrificed—to save sinners once and for all. In both Old and New Testaments, the key idea is that our many moral failures deserve punishment, but God allowed an innocent sacrifice to take the punishment we deserve. Our response to the death of the innocent is to say, "That punishment should have been mine. Thank you, God, for showing me how serious my offenses are. And thank you for the innocent party you allowed to take my place. Out of gratitude to you, I turn my back on my sins and commit my life to you."

This way of thinking offends some people, yet it makes perfect sense: Our sins, our selfishness, separate us from God, so something serious has to be done to restore the broken relationship. Sin is a serious problem. A perfectly innocent man dying on a cross is the serious remedy. The New Testament presents Jesus' crucifixion as the ultimate sacrifice. Our sin is forgiven because a sinless man took the punishment we ourselves deserved. This is what the Bible calls our redemption. We are *redeemed*—set free from—our sins.

John saw Jesus coming toward him and said, "Look! There is the Lamb of God who takes away the sin of the world!" JOHN 1:29

God was in Christ, reconciling the world to himself, no longer counting people's sins against them. This is the wonderful message he has given us to tell others.

God made Christ, who never sinned, to be the offering for our sin, so that we could be made right with God through Christ.
2 CORINTHIANS 5:19, 21

This is a true saying, and everyone should believe it: Christ Jesus came into the world to save sinners—and I was the worst of them all. But that is why God had mercy on me, so that Christ Jesus could use me as a prime example of his great patience with even the worst sinners. Then others will realize that they, too, can believe in him and receive eternal life. 1 TIMOTHY 1:15-16

We are made right in God's sight when we trust in Jesus Christ to take away our sins. And we all can be saved in this same way, no matter who we are or what we have done.

For all have sinned; all fall short of God's glorious standard. Yet now God in his gracious kindness declares us not guilty. He has done this through Christ Jesus, who has freed us by taking away our sins. For God sent Jesus to take the punishment for our sins and to satisfy God's anger against us. We are made right with God when we believe that Jesus shed his blood, sacrificing his life for us. ROMANS 3:22-25

He was handed over to die because of our sins, and he was raised from the dead to make us right with God. ROMANS 4:25

Our old sinful selves were crucified with Christ so that sin might lose its power in our lives. We are no longer slaves to sin.

Sin is no longer your master, for you are no longer subject to the law, which enslaves you to sin. Instead, you are free by God's grace.

Now you are free from sin, your old master, and you have become slaves to your new master, righteousness. ROMANS 6:6, 14, 18

When we were utterly helpless, Christ came at just the right time and died for us sinners. Now, no one is likely to die for a good person, though someone might be willing to die for a person who is especially good. But God showed his great love for us by sending Christ to die for us while we were still sinners. ROMANS 5:6-8

When Adam sinned, sin entered the entire human race. Adam's sin brought death, so death spread to everyone, for everyone sinned.

What a contrast between Adam and Christ, who was yet to come! And what a difference between our sin and God's generous gift of forgiveness. For this one man, Adam, brought death to many through his sin. But this other man, Jesus Christ, brought forgiveness to many through God's bountiful gift.

Yes, Adam's one sin brought condemnation upon everyone, but Christ's one act of righteousness makes all people right in God's sight and gives them life.   ROMANS 5:12, 14-15, 18

When you were slaves of sin, you weren't concerned with doing what was right. And what was the result? It was not good, since now you are ashamed of the things you used to do, things that end in eternal doom. But now you are free from the power of sin and have become slaves of God. Now you do those things that lead to holiness and result in eternal life. For the wages of sin is death, but the free gift of God is eternal life through Christ Jesus our Lord.   ROMANS 6:20-23

> Jesus made it clear that his mission was not to form a club of the world's sinless people. He came to bestow kindness on those who had become painfully aware of their own failings.

Jesus . . . told them, "Healthy people don't need a doctor—sick people do. I have come to call sinners, not those who think they are already good enough."   MARK 2:17

Jesus told this story to some who had great self-confidence and scorned everyone else: "Two men went to the Temple to pray. One was a Pharisee, and the other was a dishonest tax collector. The proud Pharisee stood by himself and prayed this prayer: 'I thank you, God, that I am not a sinner like everyone else, especially like that tax collector over there! For I never cheat, I don't sin, I don't commit adultery, I fast twice a week, and I give you a tenth of my income.'

"But the tax collector stood at a distance and dared not even lift his eyes to heaven as he prayed. Instead, he beat his chest in sorrow, saying, 'O God, be merciful to me, for I am a sinner.' I tell you, this sinner, not the Pharisee, returned home justified before God. For the proud will be humbled, but the humble will be honored." LUKE 18:9-14

> Are Christians sinless? No way! We are, after all, still human. The Bible promises that our ongoing relationship with God will make us better and better—but never completely sin-free in this world. But the Bible also promises that we need not fret over sin. Since we strive to be in a right relationship with God, he forgives.

If we are living in the light of God's presence, just as Christ is, then we have fellowship with each other, and the blood of Jesus, his Son, cleanses us from every sin.

If we say we have no sin, we are only fooling ourselves and refusing to accept the truth. But if we confess our sins to him, he is faithful and just to forgive us and to cleanse us from every wrong. If we claim we have not sinned, we are calling God a liar and showing that his word has no place in our hearts. 1 JOHN 1:7-10

Confess your sins to each other and pray for each other so that you may be healed. The earnest prayer of a righteous person has great power and wonderful results.

You can be sure that the one who brings that person back will save that sinner from death and bring about the forgiveness of many sins. JAMES 5:16, 20

See also Confessing Sin, Justification, Repentance, Righteousness, Salvation, Self-Righteousness.

Spiritual Power

We associate *power* with military might, political clout, financial pull, or at least physical brawn. The Bible, on the other hand, takes little interest in these forms of power, except to note that they will all pass away. The power that the Bible tells of and promises is spiritual power, something the world thinks is unimportant. Perhaps the world underestimates such power because it works in ways no one expects. Even so, people of faith have understood it for many centuries. It is sad that so many Christians neglect the power at their disposal.

The Kingdom of God is not just fancy talk; it is living by God's power. 1 CORINTHIANS 4:20

God has not given us a spirit of fear and timidity, but of power, love, and self-discipline. 2 TIMOTHY 1:7

To those called by God to salvation, both Jews and Gentiles, Christ is the mighty power of God and the wonderful wisdom of God. This "foolish" plan of God is far wiser than the wisest of human plans, and God's weakness is far stronger than the greatest of human strength.

Remember, dear brothers and sisters, that few of you were wise in the world's eyes, or powerful, or wealthy when God called you. Instead, God deliberately chose things the world considers foolish in order to shame those who think they are wise. And he chose those who are powerless to shame those who are powerful. God chose things despised by the world, things counted as nothing at all, and used them to bring to nothing what the world considers important, so that no one can ever boast in the presence of God. 1 CORINTHIANS 1:24-29

I know very well how foolish the message of the cross sounds to those who are on the road to destruction. But we who are being saved recognize this message as the very power of God. As the Scriptures say, "I will destroy human wisdom and discard their most brilliant ideas." 1 CORINTHIANS 1:18-19

My message and my preaching were very plain. I did not use wise and persuasive speeches, but the Holy Spirit was powerful among you. I did this so that you might trust the power of God rather than human wisdom. 1 CORINTHIANS 2:4-5

> The Bible authors understood the human tendency toward pride. Again and again in the Bible the people who benefit most from the power of God are quick to point out that it was God's, not their own.

This precious treasure—this light and power that now shine within us—is held in perishable containers, that is, in our weak bodies. So everyone can see that our glorious power is from God and is not our own. 2 CORINTHIANS 4:7

We are human, but we don't wage war with human plans and methods. We use God's mighty weapons, not mere worldly weapons, to knock down the Devil's strongholds. With these weapons we break down every proud argument that keeps people from knowing God. With these weapons we conquer

their rebellious ideas, and we teach them to obey Christ.
2 CORINTHIANS 10:3-5

When we brought you the Good News, it was not only with
words but also with power, for the Holy Spirit gave you full
assurance that what we said was true. And you know that the
way we lived among you was further proof of the truth of our
message. 1 THESSALONIANS 1:5

The earnest prayer of a righteous person has great power and
wonderful results. JAMES 5:16

> Often we think of power as causing major changes in the world. In
> fact, as the Second Letter of Peter promises, spiritual power is also
> an everyday thing, the power the believer needs to live right.

As we know Jesus better, his divine power gives us everything we
need for living a godly life. He has called us to receive his own glory
and goodness! And by that same mighty power, he has given us all
of his rich and wonderful promises. He has promised that you will
escape the decadence all around you caused by evil desires and that
you will share in his divine nature.

So make every effort to apply the benefits of these promises to
your life. Then your faith will produce a life of moral excellence. A
life of moral excellence leads to knowing God better. 2 PETER 1:3-5

When the apostles were with Jesus, they kept asking him, "Lord,
are you going to free Israel now and restore our kingdom?"

"The Father sets those dates," he replied, "and they are not for
you to know. But when the Holy Spirit has come upon you, you
will receive power and will tell people about me everywhere—in
Jerusalem, throughout Judea, in Samaria, and to the ends of the
earth." ACTS 1:6-8

A deep sense of awe came over them all, and the apostles performed many miraculous signs and wonders. ACTS 2:43

You know that God anointed Jesus of Nazareth with the Holy Spirit and with power. Then Jesus went around doing good and healing all who were oppressed by the Devil, for God was with him. ACTS 10:38

> Life can be a burden, not only in times of crisis but sometimes just on a day-to-day level. To anyone feeling worn out by the world, God's promises of spiritual power are like water in a desert.

He gives power to those who are tired and worn out; he offers strength to the weak. Even youths will become exhausted, and young men will give up. But those who wait on the LORD will find new strength. They will fly high on wings like eagles. They will run and not grow weary. They will walk and not faint.
ISAIAH 40:29-31

Each time [God] said, "My gracious favor is all you need. My power works best in your weakness." So now I am glad to boast about my weaknesses, so that the power of Christ may work through me. 2 CORINTHIANS 12:9

See also Angels, God's Guidance, The Holy Spirit.

Success

Norman Vincent Peale defined success as "the development of a mature and constructive personality." This is certainly closer to the Bible's view than most people's. We usually define success in terms of money, power, influence—and being envied, of course. This is not the view of the Bible. In fact, the New Testament assures Jesus' followers that they may endure hardship but not necessarily success in the usual, worldly sense.

Don't let this discourage you. Our Lord did not tell us to give up all pleasure in this life. He merely told us that there are higher, better things—things that will last forever, and things that make worldly success seem trivial.

Jesus proved this at the beginning of his earthly ministry, when Satan tempted him with worldly success.

Jesus was led out into the wilderness by the Holy Spirit to be tempted there by the Devil.

The Devil took him to the peak of a very high mountain and showed him the nations of the world and all their glory. "I will give it all to you," he said, "if you will only kneel down and worship me."

"Get out of here, Satan," Jesus told him. "For the Scriptures say, 'You must worship the Lord your God; serve only him.'"
MATTHEW 4:1, 8-10

> The Bible's values are like the world's values turned upside down. While the Bible never says that worldly success is always a bad thing, it does say—many, many times—that our ultimate concern is not success as the world views it.

Jesus answered, "I am not an earthly king. . . . My Kingdom is not of this world." JOHN 18:36

How do you benefit if you gain the whole world but lose your own soul in the process? Is anything worth more than your soul?
MATTHEW 16:26

What sorrows await you who are rich, for you have your only happiness now. What sorrows await you who are satisfied and prosperous now, for a time of awful hunger is before you. What sorrows await you who laugh carelessly, for your laughing will turn to mourning and sorrow. LUKE 6:24-25

The world would love you if you belonged to it, but you don't. I chose you to come out of the world, and so it hates you.
JOHN 15:19

> Can we live a life of devotion to God *and* be a worldly success? It's a rare thing but possible. Jesus numbered some successful people among his followers. Like other people, the successful person should remind himself that all good things are a gift from God—and all good things in this world will pass away, for the greatest good lies beyond this life.

Those in frequent contact with the things of the world should make good use of them without becoming attached to them, for this world and all it contains will pass away. 1 CORINTHIANS 7:31

It is a good thing to receive wealth from God and the good health to enjoy it. To enjoy your work and accept your lot in life—that is indeed a gift from God. ECCLESIASTES 5:19

How happy are those who fear the LORD—all who follow his ways! You will enjoy the fruit of your labor. How happy you will be! How rich your life! PSALM 128:1-2

> Success is not fame nor wealth nor power. Real success is ours when we seek and love and obey God. Doing this naturally involves looking at life from a radically different perspective from most people.

Don't copy the behavior and customs of this world, but let God transform you into a new person by changing the way you think. Then you will know what God wants you to do, and you will know how good and pleasing and perfect his will really is. ROMANS 12:2

We have stopped evaluating others by what the world thinks about them. Once I mistakenly thought of Christ that way, as though he were merely a human being. How differently I think about him now! What this means is that those who become Christians become new persons. They are not the same anymore, for the old life is gone. A new life has begun!

All this newness of life is from God, who brought us back to himself through what Christ did. And God has given us the task of reconciling people to him. 2 CORINTHIANS 5:16-18

God forbid that I should boast about anything except the cross of our Lord Jesus Christ. Because of that cross, my interest in this world died long ago, and the world's interest in me is also long dead. . . . What counts is whether we really have been changed into new and different people. May God's mercy and peace be upon all those who live by this principle. They are the new people of God. GALATIANS 6:14-16

> The Bible continually mentions wisdom as something we should desire. But this isn't wisdom as the world usually understands it. The wisdom God promises is not know-how that leads to wealth and power. It's something much more important: the wisdom to do right, to live the way God intended.

[Wisdom is speaking:] "My gifts are better than the purest gold, my wages better than sterling silver! I walk in righteousness, in paths of justice." PROVERBS 8:19-20

Where does this leave the philosophers, the scholars, and the world's brilliant debaters? God has made them all look foolish and has shown their wisdom to be useless nonsense.

Instead, God deliberately chose things the world considers foolish in order to shame those who think they are wise. And he chose those who are powerless to shame those who are powerful. God chose things despised by the world, things counted as nothing at all, and used them to bring to nothing what the world considers important, so that no one can ever boast in the presence of God. 1 CORINTHIANS 1:20, 27-29

Stop fooling yourselves. If you think you are wise by this world's standards, you will have to become a fool so you can become wise by God's standards. For the wisdom of this world is foolishness to God. As the Scriptures say, "God catches those who think they are wise in their own cleverness." And again, "The Lord knows the thoughts of the wise, that they are worthless." 1 CORINTHIANS 3:18-20

> Religious people are often portrayed in movies and TV as peculiar people. The Bible does the same. How could it be otherwise? When our values are different from other people's, naturally we will get

some criticism—maybe even blatant hostility. The world may like to think of people of faith as strange or losers or both. The Bible tells us how to deal with this: Forget it. We value something more enduring than what the world values.

God purchased you at a high price. Don't be enslaved by the world. 1 CORINTHIANS 7:23

Our dedication to Christ makes us look like fools. . . . To this very hour we go hungry and thirsty, without enough clothes to keep us warm. We have endured many beatings, and we have no homes of our own. We have worked wearily with our own hands to earn our living. We bless those who curse us. We are patient with those who abuse us. We respond gently when evil things are said about us. Yet we are treated like the world's garbage, like everybody's trash—right up to the present moment. 1 CORINTHIANS 4:10-13

Tell those who are rich in this world not to be proud and not to trust in their money, which will soon be gone. But their trust should be in the living God, who richly gives us all we need for our enjoyment. 1 TIMOTHY 6:17

Listen to me, dear brothers and sisters. Hasn't God chosen the poor in this world to be rich in faith? Aren't they the ones who will inherit the kingdom God promised to those who love him? JAMES 2:5

Don't you realize that friendship with this world makes you an enemy of God? I say it again, that if your aim is to enjoy this world, you can't be a friend of God. JAMES 4:4

Stop loving this evil world and all that it offers you, for when you love the world, you show that you do not have the love of the Father in you. For the world offers only the lust for physical pleasure, the lust for everything we see, and pride in our

possessions. These are not from the Father. They are from this evil world. And this world is fading away, along with everything it craves. But if you do the will of God, you will live forever.
1 JOHN 2:15-17

Those who love their life in this world will lose it. Those who despise their life in this world will keep it for eternal life.
JOHN 12:25

As we know Jesus better, his divine power gives us everything we need for living a godly life. He has called us to receive his own glory and goodness! And by that same mighty power, he has given us all of his rich and wonderful promises. He has promised that you will escape the decadence all around you caused by evil desires and that you will share in his divine nature.

So make every effort to apply the benefits of these promises to your life. Then your faith will produce a life of moral excellence. A life of moral excellence leads to knowing God better. 2 PETER 1:3-5

> The Bible ends with a vision of heaven, something so overwhelming that none of God's people could ever be sorry to have missed success in this present world.

I saw the holy city, the new Jerusalem, coming down from God out of heaven like a beautiful bride prepared for her husband.

I heard a loud shout from the throne saying, "Look, the home of God is now among his people! He will live with them, and they will be his people. God himself will be with them. He will remove all of their sorrows, and there will be no more death or sorrow or crying or pain. For the old world and its evils are gone forever."

And the one sitting on the throne said, "Look, I am making all things new!" REVELATION 21:2-5

See also Ambition, Laziness, Self-Esteem, Work, Worry and Anxiety.

Temptation

A character in an Oscar Wilde play says, "I can resist everything except temptation." Following Wilde's philosophy, the modern world doesn't take temptation too seriously. Listening to radio and TV, you might think the only temptations worth resisting are temptations to eat fat and cholesterol. (Is it because the only sin we can think of is overeating?) The media bombard us with images of food and drink, then suggest we ought to look like supermodels. The message is this: Indulge your desires to the hilt, then feel guilty because you yielded to the temptation. Does our body-fixated society believe that the only serious temptation is the temptation to let our bodies get out of shape? It seems that way, and it also seems that all other sins and temptations are treated lightly. The word *temptation* is considered as old-fashioned as the word *sin*.

But in fact, temptation *is* serious. It doesn't take a rocket scientist to see that humans are more inclined to do wrong than to do right. And everything around us says, "Go ahead, give in—everyone else is." It is easy to accept the world's idea that the upright person is uptight, repressed, frustrated, and unhappy.

But the Bible portrays temptation as serious—so serious that God gives us what we need to resist it.

Wisdom will enter your heart, and knowledge will fill you with joy. Wise planning will watch over you. Understanding will keep you safe.

Wisdom will save you from evil people, from those whose speech is corrupt. PROVERBS 2:10-12

Fear of the LORD is a life-giving fountain; it offers escape from the snares of death. PROVERBS 14:27

Sin is no longer your master, for you are no longer subject to the law, which enslaves you to sin. Instead, you are free by God's grace. ROMANS 6:14

Humble yourselves before God. Resist the Devil, and he will flee from you. JAMES 4:7

The Lord knows how to rescue godly people from their trials, even while punishing the wicked right up until the day of judgment. 2 PETER 2:9

> As these passages make clear, God himself is our rescuer. It is never appropriate to ask why God is tempting us, for God, as James explained, is never the source of anything evil.

No one who wants to do wrong should ever say, "God is tempting me." God is never tempted to do wrong, and he never tempts anyone else either. Temptation comes from the lure of our own evil desires. These evil desires lead to evil actions, and evil actions lead to death. So don't be misled, my dear brothers and sisters.

Whatever is good and perfect comes to us from God above, who created all heaven's lights. Unlike them, he never changes or casts shifting shadows. JAMES 1:13-17

One problem Christians face is the false security of being free of temptation. The apostle Paul makes it plain that none of us—not in this life, anyway—is ever free of temptation.

If you think you are standing strong, be careful, for you, too, may fall into the same sin. But remember that the temptations that come into your life are no different from what others experience. And God is faithful. He will keep the temptation from becoming so strong that you can't stand up against it. When you are tempted, he will show you a way out so that you will not give in to it. 1 CORINTHIANS 10:12-13

The old sinful nature loves to do evil, which is just opposite from what the Holy Spirit wants. And the Spirit gives us desires that are opposite from what the sinful nature desires. These two forces are constantly fighting each other, and your choices are never free from this conflict. GALATIANS 5:17

God allows us to be tempted. Why? Wouldn't it be better if he just removed all temptation from our life? Easier, perhaps, but not better. Just as our muscles gain from a physical workout—being stressed, tested—so we gain spiritually from resisting temptation, as this passage from James says so beautifully:

Dear brothers and sisters, whenever trouble comes your way, let it be an opportunity for joy. For when your faith is tested, your endurance has a chance to grow. So let it grow, for when your endurance is fully developed, you will be strong in character and ready for anything.

God blesses the people who patiently endure testing. Afterward they will receive the crown of life that God has promised to those who love him. And remember, no one who wants to do wrong should ever say, "God is tempting me." God is never tempted to do wrong, and he never tempts anyone else either. Temptation comes from the lure of our own evil desires.

These evil desires lead to evil actions, and evil actions lead to death. JAMES 1:2-4, 12-15

> Those who endure have a promise: heaven.

The ones who can live here are those who are honest and fair, who reject making a profit by fraud, who stay far away from bribes, who refuse to listen to those who plot murder, who shut their eyes to all enticement to do wrong. These are the ones who will dwell on high. ISAIAH 33:15-16

> What about tempting or leading other people to sin? The American legal system calls it soliciting when someone tries to lead someone else to commit a crime, and soliciting itself is a crime. The Bible takes the same attitude toward those who deliberately lead others to sin.

Those who lead the upright into sin will fall into their own trap, but the honest will inherit good things. PROVERBS 28:10

If anyone causes one of these little ones who trusts in me to lose faith, it would be better for that person to be thrown into the sea with a large millstone tied around the neck. MATTHEW 18:6

> Rather than leading others into sin, we are to lead others *away* from temptation. As members of Christ's body, we should look out for each other's spiritual welfare, not just our own.

Dear friends, if a Christian is overcome by some sin, you who are godly should gently and humbly help that person back onto the right path. And be careful not to fall into the same temptation yourself. Share each other's troubles and problems, and in this way obey the law of Christ. GALATIANS 6:1-2

One of the joys of Christianity is that Jesus, its key figure, is both God and human. While faith is spiritual, we have the comfort of knowing that the founder of our faith was a physical human being like us, someone who understands our temptations because he experienced them himself.

Since [Jesus] himself has gone through suffering and temptation, he is able to help us when we are being tempted.

This High Priest of ours understands our weaknesses, for he faced all of the same temptations we do, yet he did not sin.

HEBREWS 2:18; 4:15

See also Sin and Redemption.

Thankfulness

Mark Twain claimed that "if you pick up a starving dog and make him prosperous, he will not bite you. That is the principal difference between a dog and a man." Twain understood something about human nature: We are often ingrates, accepting something good from someone but never bothering to feel or express gratitude.

This is the way of the world, but it has no place in the life of faith. "A true Christian is a man who never for a moment forgets what God has done for him in Christ." This statement by author John Baillie sums up the Bible's view of thankfulness toward God and toward Christ. Gratitude is something we can't be without. A constant consciousness of how lucky we are, of how much God loves us and does for us, keeps us from false self-pity. Just as human children owe their parents gratitude, so children of God owe him the same, but much more.

The Bible reminds us of something we often forget in our hurried lives: Gratitude is important to happiness. With the "me first" mentality so common, we forget that there is satisfaction, joy, and contentment in feeling—and showing—thankfulness to those who have been kind to us.

Praise the LORD! Give thanks to the LORD, for he is good! His faithful love endures forever. PSALM 106:1

May you be filled with joy, always thanking the Father, who has enabled you to share the inheritance that belongs to God's holy people, who live in the light. COLOSSIANS 1:11-12

Since everything God created is good, we should not reject any of it. We may receive it gladly, with thankful hearts. For we know it is made holy by the word of God and prayer. 1 TIMOTHY 4:4-5

Yes, you will be enriched so that you can give even more generously. And when we take your gifts to those who need them, they will break out in thanksgiving to God. 2 CORINTHIANS 9:11

Since we are receiving a kingdom that cannot be destroyed, let us be thankful and please God by worshiping him with holy fear and awe. HEBREWS 12:28

How we thank God, who gives us victory over sin and death through Jesus Christ our Lord! 1 CORINTHIANS 15:57

Thanks be to God, who made us his captives and leads us along in Christ's triumphal procession. Now wherever we go he uses us to tell others about the Lord and to spread the Good News like a sweet perfume. 2 CORINTHIANS 2:14

Let the peace that comes from Christ rule in your hearts. For as members of one body you are all called to live in peace. And always be thankful.
Let the words of Christ, in all their richness, live in your hearts and make you wise. Use his words to teach and counsel each other. Sing psalms and hymns and spiritual songs to God with thankful hearts. COLOSSIANS 3:15-16

Don't worry about anything; instead, pray about everything. Tell God what you need, and thank him for all he has done. If you do this, you will experience God's peace, which is far more wonderful than the human mind can understand. His peace will guard your hearts and minds as you live in Christ Jesus.
PHILIPPIANS 4:6-7

You will sing psalms and hymns and spiritual songs among yourselves, making music to the Lord in your hearts. And you will always give thanks for everything to God the Father in the name of our Lord Jesus Christ. EPHESIANS 5:19-20

Always be joyful. Keep on praying. No matter what happens, always be thankful, for this is God's will for you who belong to Christ Jesus. 1 THESSALONIANS 5:16-18

See also Fellowship with God, Obeying God, Prayer.

The Tongue

This section could have been titled "Gossip" or "Slander" or "Criticism." The key idea here is that words can heal, but words can also do great harm. And it doesn't require an outright lie to harm another person. A little insinuation, a hint, is often enough. Once a bit of information starts on the gossip grapevine, it rarely improves.

The Bible has much to say about our use—or abuse—of the tongue. We may be tempted to write gossip off as a relatively minor sin, but the Word of God takes a different view. Just as we are expected to restrain our hands from hitting everyone with whom we feel angry, so we're expected to restrain our tongues from doing harm also. Not all violence leads to bruising and bleeding.

Do any of you want to live a life that is long and good? Then watch your tongue! Keep your lips from telling lies! Turn away from evil and do good. Work hard at living in peace with others.

The eyes of the LORD watch over those who do right; his ears are open to their cries for help. PSALM 34:12-15

It is foolish to belittle a neighbor; a person with good sense remains silent.

A gossip goes around revealing secrets, but those who are trustworthy can keep a confidence. PROVERBS 11:12-13

Some people make cutting remarks, but the words of the wise bring healing. PROVERBS 12:18

A troublemaker plants seeds of strife; gossip separates the best of friends. PROVERBS 16:28

What dainty morsels rumors are—but they sink deep into one's heart. PROVERBS 18:8

A gossip tells secrets, so don't hang around with someone who talks too much. PROVERBS 20:19

I will not tolerate people who slander their neighbors. I will not endure conceit and pride. PSALM 101:5

As surely as a wind from the north brings rain, so a gossiping tongue causes anger! PROVERBS 25:23

Fire goes out for lack of fuel, and quarrels disappear when gossip stops.
A quarrelsome person starts fights as easily as hot embers light charcoal or fire lights wood. PROVERBS 26:20-21

> Jesus had much to say about the tongue. He was aware that people who are outwardly "religious" could abstain from the "big" sins like adultery and drunkenness. Yet these same people could do immense harm through their speech.

A tree is identified by its fruit. Make a tree good, and its fruit will be good. Make a tree bad, and its fruit will be bad. You brood of snakes! How could evil men like you speak what is good and right? For whatever is in your heart determines what you say. A

good person produces good words from a good heart, and an evil
person produces evil words from an evil heart. And I tell you this,
that you must give an account on judgment day of every idle
word you speak. The words you say now reflect your fate then;
either you will be justified by them or you will be condemned.
MATTHEW 12:33-37

Evil words come from an evil heart and defile the person who
says them. For from the heart come evil thoughts, murder,
adultery, all other sexual immorality, theft, lying, and slander.
These are what defile you. MATTHEW 15:18-20

Following Jesus' lead, the New Testament authors have a lot to say
about controlling the tongue. They were aware—as all of us should
be—of the damage that can be done by words.

If you claim to be religious but don't control your tongue, you are
just fooling yourself, and your religion is worthless. JAMES 1:26

Get rid of all bitterness, rage, anger, harsh words, and slander, as
well as all types of malicious behavior. Instead, be kind to each
other, tenderhearted, forgiving one another, just as God through
Christ has forgiven you. EPHESIANS 4:31-32

Now is the time to get rid of anger, rage, malicious behavior, slander,
and dirty language. Don't lie to each other, for you have stripped off
your old evil nature and all its wicked deeds. In its place you have
clothed yourselves with a brand-new nature that is continually being
renewed as you learn more and more about Christ, who created this
new nature within you. COLOSSIANS 3:8-10

The classic passage on controlling the tongue is in the book of
James. It ought to be posted on every Christian's bathroom mirror so
that it could be read every morning.

Those who control their tongues can also control themselves in every other way. We can make a large horse turn around and go wherever we want by means of a small bit in its mouth. And a tiny rudder makes a huge ship turn wherever the pilot wants it to go, even though the winds are strong. So also, the tongue is a small thing, but what enormous damage it can do. A tiny spark can set a great forest on fire. And the tongue is a flame of fire. It is full of wickedness that can ruin your whole life. It can turn the entire course of your life into a blazing flame of destruction, for it is set on fire by hell itself.

People can tame all kinds of animals and birds and reptiles and fish, but no one can tame the tongue. It is an uncontrollable evil, full of deadly poison. Sometimes it praises our Lord and Father, and sometimes it breaks out into curses against those who have been made in the image of God. And so blessing and cursing come pouring out of the same mouth. Surely, my brothers and sisters, this is not right! JAMES 3:2-10

How much gossip and verbal cruelty occur under the name of "constructive criticism"? In his letter, James makes it plain that criticizing fellow Christians—either to their face or behind their back—is unchristian behavior.

Don't speak evil against each other, my dear brothers and sisters. If you criticize each other and condemn each other, then you are criticizing and condemning God's law. But you are not a judge who can decide whether the law is right or wrong. Your job is to obey it. God alone, who made the law, can rightly judge among us. He alone has the power to save or to destroy. So what right do you have to condemn your neighbor? JAMES 4:11-12

Get rid of all malicious behavior and deceit. Don't just pretend to be good! Be done with hypocrisy and jealousy and backstabbing.
1 PETER 2:1

What about the other side of the coin? Even when we control our own tongues, how do we respond to the damage done to us by someone else's? Remember that God will defend us. The Bible assures us we have nothing to fear in the long run.

Listen to me, you who know right from wrong and cherish my law in your hearts. Do not be afraid of people's scorn or their slanderous talk. . . . The worm will eat away at them as it eats wool. But my righteousness will last forever. My salvation will continue from generation to generation.   ISAIAH 51:7-8

God blesses you when you are mocked and persecuted and lied about because you are my followers. Be happy about it! Be very glad! For a great reward awaits you in heaven. And remember, the ancient prophets were persecuted, too.   MATTHEW 5:11-12

See also Anger, Envy, Hate, Judging Others, Self-Righteousness.

Trusting God

Trust, like commitment, has become an evasive commodity in our world. People everywhere express a lack of trust in things they once considered dependable—government, schools, the media, even their own family members and friends. So who can we trust? The message of the Bible is clear: no one, except God. This doesn't mean we walk through the world feeling and acting paranoid and suspicious. It means we hold a realistic view of human beings and institutions, not being too shocked when they fail us. It means we can feel secure anyway, knowing that God is faithful when no one else is.

Trust in the LORD and do good. Then you will live safely in the land and prosper. Take delight in the LORD, and he will give you your heart's desires. Commit everything you do to the LORD. Trust him, and he will help you. PSALM 37:3-5

Oh, the joys of those who trust the LORD, who have no confidence in the proud, or in those who worship idols. PSALM 40:4

God is our refuge and strength, always ready to help in times of trouble. So we will not fear, even if earthquakes come and the mountains crumble into the sea. PSALM 46:1-2

The LORD God is our light and protector. He gives us grace and glory. No good thing will the LORD withhold from those who do what is right. O LORD Almighty, happy are those who trust in you. PSALM 84:11-12

Trust in the LORD with all your heart; do not depend on your own understanding. Seek his will in all you do, and he will direct your paths. PROVERBS 3:5-6

Fearing people is a dangerous trap, but to trust the LORD means safety. PROVERBS 29:25

Look at the proud! They trust in themselves, and their lives are crooked; but the righteous will live by their faith. HABAKKUK 2:4

Why worry about your clothes? Look at the lilies and how they grow. They don't work or make their clothing, yet Solomon in all his glory was not dressed as beautifully as they are. And if God cares so wonderfully for flowers that are here today and gone tomorrow, won't he more surely care for you? You have so little faith!

So don't worry about having enough food or drink or clothing. Why be like the pagans who are so deeply concerned about these things? Your heavenly Father already knows all your needs, and he will give you all you need from day to day if you live for him and make the Kingdom of God your primary concern.
MATTHEW 6:28-33

Don't be afraid, little flock. For it gives your Father great happiness to give you the Kingdom. LUKE 12:32

See also Faith, God's Guidance, Hope, Obeying God.

Wisdom and Discernment

The word *wisdom* isn't used much today. People prefer *knowledge,* which means information, data, facts. People acquire knowledge to get ahead in their jobs—or to be a contestant on *Jeopardy!* There is nothing wrong with knowledge—but in the Bible's view, it is less important than wisdom.

Wisdom is understanding things as they are—ourselves, God, the way the world works. Knowledge creates scientists and scholars. Wisdom creates people who move through life with a clear view of God's purpose for them. And it creates something that knowledge by itself can't: goodness. In the Bible, goodness and wisdom are never separated. In simple terms, wisdom is gained by trusting God.

True wisdom and power are with God; counsel and understanding are his. JOB 12:13

The law of the LORD is perfect, reviving the soul. The decrees of the LORD are trustworthy, making wise the simple. PSALM 19:7

Reverence for the LORD is the foundation of true wisdom. The rewards of wisdom come to all who obey him.

Praise his name forever! PSALM 111:10

Your commands make me wiser than my enemies, for your commands are my constant guide. Yes, I have more insight than my teachers, for I am always thinking of your decrees.
PSALM 119:98-99

The LORD grants wisdom! From his mouth come knowledge and understanding. He grants a treasure of good sense to the godly. He is their shield, protecting those who walk with integrity.
PROVERBS 2:6-7

Don't be impressed with your own wisdom. Instead, fear the LORD and turn your back on evil. Then you will gain renewed health and vitality. PROVERBS 3:7-8

The wise are glad to be instructed, but babbling fools fall flat on their faces. PROVERBS 10:8

To acquire wisdom is to love oneself; people who cherish understanding will prosper. PROVERBS 19:8

Wisdom is far more valuable than rubies. Nothing you desire can be compared with it. PROVERBS 8:11

He has showered his kindness on us, along with all wisdom and understanding. EPHESIANS 1:8

Let the words of Christ, in all their richness, live in your hearts and make you wise. Use his words to teach and counsel each other. Sing psalms and hymns and spiritual songs to God with thankful hearts. COLOSSIANS 3:16

Solomon, the Bible's great role model of human wisdom, is famous for the humble prayer he made when he became king of Israel. This beautiful prayer, which God answered bountifully, shows the value of wisdom above all other possessions. Solomon also shows us that wisdom is not for our own selfish use but to benefit others.

"LORD my God, now you have made me king instead of my father, David, but I am like a little child who doesn't know his way around. . . . Give me an understanding mind so that I can govern your people well and know the difference between right and wrong. For who by himself is able to govern this great nation of yours?"

The Lord was pleased with Solomon's reply and was glad that he had asked for wisdom. So God replied, "Because you have asked for wisdom in governing my people and have not asked for a long life or riches for yourself or the death of your enemies— I will give you what you asked for! I will give you a wise and understanding mind such as no one else has ever had or ever will have!" 1 KINGS 3:7-12

The quiet words of a wise person are better than the shouts of a foolish king. ECCLESIASTES 9:17

Anyone who listens to my teaching and obeys me is wise, like a person who builds a house on solid rock. MATTHEW 7:24

The apostle Paul, an educated man, had to remind Christians that the wisdom that comes from God might appear foolish to unbelievers. In fact, Paul realized that all his learning was insignificant compared with the true wisdom from heaven. His words are a comfort to the person without much education and a warning to people vain about their own intelligence.

As the Scriptures say, "I will destroy human wisdom and discard their most brilliant ideas."

So where does this leave the philosophers, the scholars, and the world's brilliant debaters? God has made them all look foolish and has shown their wisdom to be useless nonsense. Since God in his wisdom saw to it that the world would never find him through human wisdom, he has used our foolish preaching to save all who believe.

This "foolish" plan of God is far wiser than the wisest of human plans, and God's weakness is far stronger than the greatest of human strength.

Remember, dear brothers and sisters, that few of you were wise in the world's eyes, or powerful, or wealthy when God called you. Instead, God deliberately chose things the world considers foolish in order to shame those who think they are wise. And he chose those who are powerless to shame those who are powerful.

For the wisdom of this world is foolishness to God. As the Scriptures say, "God catches those who think they are wise in their own cleverness." And again, "The Lord knows the thoughts of the wise, that they are worthless."

1 CORINTHIANS 1:19-21, 25-27; 3:19-20

> Paul reminded Christians that the Holy Spirit—God as an active force in our life—gives us discernment, the ability to see and understand things that unbelievers are blind to.

God has actually given us his Spirit (not the world's spirit) so we can know the wonderful things God has freely given us. When we tell you this, we do not use words of human wisdom. We speak words given to us by the Spirit, using the Spirit's words to explain spiritual truths. But people who aren't Christians can't understand these truths from God's Spirit. It all sounds foolish to them because only those who have the Spirit can understand what the Spirit means. 1 CORINTHIANS 2:12-14

> Paul also reminds us that some Christians are particularly gifted with discernment. In our day, with many people confused about right

beliefs (and also confused about whether belief even matters), this gift ought to be highly valued.

A spiritual gift is given to each of us as a means of helping the entire church.

To one person the Spirit gives the ability to give wise advice; to another he gives the gift of special knowledge. . . . He gives someone else the ability to know whether it is really the Spirit of God or another spirit that is speaking. . . . It is the one and only Holy Spirit who distributes these gifts. He alone decides which gift each person should have. 1 CORINTHIANS 12:7-11

> God is constantly spoken of in the Bible as a *giving* God. Wisdom is something he happily gives to those who ask. The greatest benefit of this wisdom is that it enables us to walk the walk of faith in this world.

If you need wisdom—if you want to know what God wants you to do—ask him, and he will gladly tell you. He will not resent your asking. JAMES 1:5

If you are wise and understand God's ways, live a life of steady goodness so that only good deeds will pour forth. And if you don't brag about the good you do, then you will be truly wise! But if you are bitterly jealous and there is selfish ambition in your hearts, don't brag about being wise. That is the worst kind of lie. For jealousy and selfishness are not God's kind of wisdom. Such things are earthly, unspiritual, and motivated by the Devil. For wherever there is jealousy and selfish ambition, there you will find disorder and every kind of evil.

But the wisdom that comes from heaven is first of all pure. It is also peace loving, gentle at all times, and willing to yield to others. It is full of mercy and good deeds. It shows no partiality and is always sincere. JAMES 3:13-17

See also False Teachings.

Witnessing

Who would have thought, as this century drew to its close, how "evangelistic" people would become? People are evangelists—sometimes loud and violent ones—for animal rights, for abortion, against nuclear weapons, etc. Having a cause has become trendy.

In the Bible, the only cause is the great Cause, God himself. The Bible has much to say about being a witness for this God and his goodness. Witnessing for God is sometimes confrontational but never violent and never cruel.

How beautiful on the mountains are the feet of those who bring good news of peace and salvation, the news that the God of Israel reigns! ISAIAH 52:7

The Spirit of the Sovereign LORD is upon me, because the LORD has appointed me to bring good news to the poor. He has sent me to comfort the brokenhearted and to announce that captives will be released and prisoners will be freed. He has sent me to tell those who mourn that the time of the LORD's favor has come, and with it, the day of God's anger against their enemies. ISAIAH 61:1-2

Jesus spoke often about the matter of witnessing on behalf of God's Kingdom. According to him, there is no such thing as a completely private faith. A child of God could never keep his beliefs to himself.

You are the salt of the earth. But what good is salt if it has lost its flavor? Can you make it useful again? It will be thrown out and trampled underfoot as worthless. You are the light of the world—like a city on a mountain, glowing in the night for all to see. Don't hide your light under a basket! Instead, put it on a stand and let it shine for all. In the same way, let your good deeds shine out for all to see, so that everyone will praise your heavenly Father. MATTHEW 5:13-16

If anyone acknowledges me publicly here on earth, I will openly acknowledge that person before my Father in heaven. But if anyone denies me here on earth, I will deny that person before my Father in heaven. MATTHEW 10:32-33

The Good News about the Kingdom will be preached throughout the whole world, so that all nations will hear it; and then, finally, the end will come. MATTHEW 24:14

When the Holy Spirit has come upon you, you will receive power and will tell people about me everywhere—in Jerusalem, throughout Judea, in Samaria, and to the ends of the earth. ACTS 1:8

After the Gospels, the New Testament could be called the "Book of Witnesses," as the story unfolds of the apostles and their witnessing about the Good News of Christ. This often brought persecution, but Jesus' followers knew they could not keep the news of salvation to themselves, no matter what the world might think or do.

You are to take his message everywhere, telling the whole world what you have seen and heard. ACTS 22:15

God was in Christ, reconciling the world to himself, no longer counting people's sins against them. This is the wonderful message he has given us to tell others. We are Christ's ambassadors, and God is using us to speak to you. We urge you, as though Christ himself were here pleading with you, "Be reconciled to God!" 2 CORINTHIANS 5:19-20

God has not given us a spirit of fear and timidity, but of power, love, and self-discipline. So you must never be ashamed to tell others about our Lord. And don't be ashamed of me, either, even though I'm in prison for Christ. With the strength God gives you, be ready to suffer with me for the proclamation of the Good News. 2 TIMOTHY 1:7-8

One of Jesus' sternest warnings was against believers who chose to hide their belief. He stated that such people's belief was a sham.

If a person is ashamed of me and my message, I, the Son of Man, will be ashamed of that person when I return in my glory and in the glory of the Father and the holy angels. LUKE 9:26

Witnessing, according to the New Testament, involves much more than talking about Christ. Witnessing means we live in such a way that our life would not make sense unless there was a God at work in us. It means that our life forces people to ask the question, What do those people have? And how can I get it? If we really do put God at the center of our life, those questions will inevitably be asked.

God is working in you, giving you the desire to obey him and the power to do what pleases him.

In everything you do, stay away from complaining and arguing so that no one can speak a word of blame against you. You are to live clean, innocent lives as children of God in a dark world full of crooked and perverse people. Let your lives shine brightly before them. PHILIPPIANS 2:13-15

Whatever you do or say, let it be as a representative of the Lord Jesus, all the while giving thanks through him to God the Father. COLOSSIANS 3:17

Live wisely among those who are not Christians, and make the most of every opportunity. Let your conversation be gracious and effective so that you will have the right answer for everyone. COLOSSIANS 4:5-6

Dear brothers and sisters, you are foreigners and aliens here. So I warn you to keep away from evil desires because they fight against your very souls. Be careful how you live among your unbelieving neighbors. Even if they accuse you of doing wrong, they will see your honorable behavior, and they will believe and give honor to God when he comes to judge the world. 1 PETER 2:11-12

You must worship Christ as Lord of your life. And if you are asked about your Christian hope, always be ready to explain it. But you must do this in a gentle and respectful way. Keep your conscience clear. Then if people speak evil against you, they will be ashamed when they see what a good life you live because you belong to Christ. 1 PETER 3:15-16

This should be your ambition: to live a quiet life, minding your own business and working with your hands, just as we commanded you before. As a result, people who are not Christians will respect the way you live. 1 THESSALONIANS 4:11-12

See also Opportunities.

Work

Work has become a four-letter word for many people. Societies go through cycles—one generation works hard and plays little, another generation reverses the trend. Right now society seems to be in a pro-play, anti-work feeling. We seem to have forgotten the truth of William James's statement: "Nothing is work unless you would rather be doing something else." In other words, if you truly enjoy work, it isn't work. Maybe we've neglected this truth and fallen prey to the "can't wait till Friday" mentality. But the Bible makes no pleasant promises to people who spend their entire workweek looking forward to the weekend.

For those who regard work as some kind of abnormal burden on humankind, recall that man, even before he sinned, was given work to do by God:

So God created people in his own image; God patterned them after himself; male and female he created them.

God blessed them and told them, "Multiply and fill the earth and subdue it. Be masters over the fish and birds and all the animals."

The LORD God placed the man in the Garden of Eden to tend and care for it. GENESIS 1:27-28; 2:15

> The Bible assumes that work is a natural thing, something God ordained for the human race. Because of this, it is probably safe to assume the Bible authors would not have thought kindly of the modern welfare state and its incentives *not* to work. But the Bible also commands us to worship nothing except God—workaholics, take note. We should not take our jobs (or ourselves) *too* seriously—and that includes work done in God's service. Charles Wesley, a dutiful worker, observed that "God buries his workmen but carries on his work." In other words, God's work—and the world's work—will go on, even if one workaholic slows down a bit.

Hard work means prosperity; only fools idle away their time.
Work hard and become a leader; be lazy and become a slave.
Lazy people don't even cook the game they catch, but the diligent make use of everything they find. PROVERBS 12:11, 24, 27

An empty stable stays clean, but no income comes from an empty stable.
Work brings profit, but mere talk leads to poverty!
PROVERBS 14:4, 23

Good planning and hard work lead to prosperity, but hasty shortcuts lead to poverty. PROVERBS 21:5

Do you see any truly competent workers? They will serve kings rather than ordinary people. PROVERBS 22:29

Hard workers have plenty of food; playing around brings poverty. PROVERBS 28:19

> To balance out the "work hard and succeed" promises of the book of Proverbs, the book of Ecclesiastes assures us that human beings

cannot find their *ultimate* satisfaction in work. Only God can
provide that kind of satisfaction:

As I looked at everything I had worked so hard to accomplish, it
was all so meaningless. It was like chasing the wind. There was
nothing really worthwhile anywhere. ECCLESIASTES 2:11

People who work hard sleep well, whether they eat little or much.
But the rich are always worrying and seldom get a good night's
sleep. ECCLESIASTES 5:12

> Paul, a hard worker in the Lord's service, had no patience with
> laziness. He knew that idleness not only displeased God but also
> gave unbelievers a low opinion of Christians.

This should be your ambition: to live a quiet life, minding your own
business and working with your hands, just as we commanded you
before. As a result, people who are not Christians will respect the
way you live, and you will not need to depend on others to meet
your financial needs. 1 THESSALONIANS 4:11-12

Those who won't care for their own relatives, especially those
living in the same household, have denied what we believe. Such
people are worse than unbelievers. 1 TIMOTHY 5:8

Now, dear brothers and sisters, we give you this command with the
authority of our Lord Jesus Christ: Stay away from any Christian
who lives in idleness and doesn't follow the tradition of hard work
we gave you. For you know that you ought to follow our example.
We were never lazy when we were with you. We never accepted
food from anyone without paying for it. We worked hard day and
night so that we would not be a burden to any of you. It wasn't that
we didn't have the right to ask you to feed us, but we wanted to
give you an example to follow. Even while we were with you, we
gave you this rule: "Whoever does not work should not eat."

Yet we hear that some of you are living idle lives, refusing to work and wasting time meddling in other people's business. In the name of the Lord Jesus Christ we appeal to such people—no, we command them: Settle down and get to work. Earn your own living. 2 THESSALONIANS 3:6-12

If you are a thief, stop stealing. Begin using your hands for honest work, and then give generously to others in need. EPHESIANS 4:28

I have never coveted anyone's money or fine clothing. You know that these hands of mine have worked to pay my own way, and I have even supplied the needs of those who were with me. And I have been a constant example of how you can help the poor by working hard. You should remember the words of the Lord Jesus: "It is more blessed to give than to receive." ACTS 20:33-35

> Paul promised Christians something that we often forget: Work does not need to be humdrum, because we can do it to the glory of God. Like any part of ourselves, our work—whatever it may be—can honor the Lord.

Work hard, but not just to please your masters when they are watching. As slaves of Christ, do the will of God with all your heart. Work with enthusiasm, as though you were working for the Lord rather than for people. EPHESIANS 6:6-7

Whatever you eat or drink or whatever you do, you must do all for the glory of God. 1 CORINTHIANS 10:31

Never be lazy in your work, but serve the Lord enthusiastically.
ROMANS 12:11

> People forget that the Old Testament is full of moral commands concerning work and business. It is easy to neglect reading the Old Testament law books, but, in fact, its commands regarding honesty

and fairness should still apply. Also worth remembering are the Ten
Commandments, one of which specifically addresses the issue of
not worshiping one's work.

Remember to observe the Sabbath day by keeping it holy. Six days
a week are set apart for your daily duties and regular work, but
the seventh day is a day of rest dedicated to the LORD your God.
On that day no one in your household may do any kind of work.
This includes you, your sons and daughters, your male and
female servants, your livestock, and any foreigners living among
you. For in six days the LORD made the heavens, the earth, the sea,
and everything in them; then he rested on the seventh day. That is
why the LORD blessed the Sabbath day and set it apart as holy.
EXODUS 20:8-11

Do not cheat or rob anyone. Always pay your hired workers
promptly. LEVITICUS 19:13

Never take advantage of poor laborers, whether fellow Israelites
or foreigners living in your towns. Pay them their wages each day
before sunset because they are poor and are counting on it.
Otherwise they might cry out to the LORD against you, and it
would be counted against you as sin. DEUTERONOMY 24:14-15

See also Laziness, Money, The Sabbath, Success.

Worldly Cares

Are "spiritual" people totally without worldly concerns? Hardly. Have you known a religious person who voluntarily starved to death or didn't come in from a thunderstorm? No, even spiritual people take care of themselves. Christianity is "otherworldly" because we fix our attention on heaven. But it is also "this worldly," for God cares about our physical needs and wants us to be content and comfortable.

In fact, some of the most comforting promises in the Bible are the ones in this chapter. God promises that our basic needs will be taken care of, so we need not let these concerns dominate our thoughts.

It is useless for you to work so hard from early morning until late at night, anxiously working for food to eat; for God gives rest to his loved ones. PSALM 127:2

So I tell you, don't worry about everyday life—whether you have enough food, drink, and clothes. Doesn't life consist of more than food and clothing? Look at the birds. They don't need to plant or harvest or put food in barns because your heavenly Father feeds them. And you are far more valuable to him than they are. Can all your worries add a single moment to your life? Of course not.

And why worry about your clothes? Look at the lilies and how they grow. They don't work or make their clothing, yet Solomon in all his glory was not dressed as beautifully as they are. And if God cares so wonderfully for flowers that are here today and gone tomorrow, won't he more surely care for you? You have so little faith!

So don't worry about having enough food or drink or clothing. Why be like the pagans who are so deeply concerned about these things? Your heavenly Father already knows all your needs, and he will give you all you need from day to day if you live for him and make the Kingdom of God your primary concern.

So don't worry about tomorrow, for tomorrow will bring its own worries. Today's trouble is enough for today.   MATTHEW 6:25-34

Watch out! Don't let me find you living in careless ease and drunkenness, and filled with the worries of this life. Don't let that day catch you unaware, as in a trap. For that day will come upon everyone living on the earth. Keep a constant watch. And pray that, if possible, you may escape these horrors and stand before the Son of Man.   LUKE 21:34-36

Jesus said, "Come to me, all of you who are weary and carry heavy burdens, and I will give you rest. Take my yoke upon you. Let me teach you, because I am humble and gentle, and you will find rest for your souls. For my yoke fits perfectly, and the burden I give you is light."   MATTHEW 11:28-30

Have you noticed that one of the biggest-selling medicines today is the acid blocker? Does anyone seriously believe that the medicines are for problems related to food? Isn't the real problem usually our load of stress and worry? And isn't it ironic that our affluent society, so convinced that our material comforts assure us of a good life, is so dependent on acid blockers and antidepressants? According to the Bible, the best medicine for worldly care is our awareness of God's care.

Don't worry about anything; instead, pray about everything. Tell God what you need and thank him for all he has done. If you do this, you will experience God's peace, which is far more wonderful than the human mind can understand. His peace will guard your hearts and minds as you live in Christ Jesus.
PHILIPPIANS 4:6-7

As Christ's soldier, do not let yourself become tied up in the affairs of this life, for then you cannot satisfy the one who has enlisted you in his army. 2 TIMOTHY 2:4

Stay away from the love of money; be satisfied with what you have. For God has said, "I will never fail you. I will never forsake you." HEBREWS 13:5

Don't worry about food—what to eat and drink. Don't worry whether God will provide it for you. These things dominate the thoughts of most people, but your Father already knows your needs. He will give you all you need from day to day if you make the Kingdom of God your primary concern.
So don't be afraid, little flock. For it gives your Father great happiness to give you the Kingdom. LUKE 12:29-32

True religion with contentment is great wealth. After all, we didn't bring anything with us when we came into the world, and we certainly cannot carry anything with us when we die. So if we have enough food and clothing, let us be content. 1 TIMOTHY 6:6-8

This same God who takes care of me will supply all your needs from his glorious riches, which have been given to us in Christ Jesus. PHILIPPIANS 4:19

See also Contentment, Eternal Life, Hope, Worry and Anxiety.

Worldly Pleasures

A re religious people killjoys? Maybe some are. Non-Christians often like to portray us that way. Perhaps the world has forgotten the meaning of the words *good clean fun* and has concluded that you can't be a Christian and enjoy life in this world.

It's not so. People of faith are not gloomy souls who deny themselves innocent pleasures. They are simply people with their eyes on the next world as well as this one. And the Bible makes one thing plain: Some of this world's pleasures are just not good for us—particularly if they distract us from loving God and loving other people.

The Bible also makes it plain that worldly pleasure just doesn't *satisfy* in the deepest sense.

I hoped to experience the only happiness most people find during their brief life in this world.

I also tried to find meaning by building huge homes for myself and by planting beautiful vineyards. I made gardens and parks, filling them with all kinds of fruit trees. I built reservoirs to collect the water to irrigate my many flourishing groves. . . . I also owned great herds and flocks, more than any of the kings who lived in

Jerusalem before me. I collected great sums of silver and gold, the treasure of many kings and provinces. I hired wonderful singers, both men and women, and had many beautiful concubines. I had everything a man could desire!

So I became greater than any of the kings who ruled in Jerusalem before me. And with it all, I remained clear-eyed so that I could evaluate all these things. Anything I wanted, I took. I did not restrain myself from any joy. . . . But as I looked at everything I had worked so hard to accomplish, it was all so meaningless. It was like chasing the wind. ECCLESIASTES 2:3-11

There is another serious problem I have seen in the world. Riches are sometimes hoarded to the harm of the saver, or they are put into risky investments that turn sour, and everything is lost. In the end, there is nothing left to pass on to one's children. People who live only for wealth come to the end of their lives as naked and empty-handed as on the day they were born.

And this, too, is a very serious problem. As people come into this world, so they depart. All their hard work is for nothing. They have been working for the wind, and everything will be swept away. Throughout their lives, they live under a cloud—frustrated, discouraged, and angry. ECCLESIASTES 5:13-17

> As you can see, Ecclesiastes confronts the double-edged problem of worldly pleasure. People yearn for what they don't have, and when they do have it, it doesn't satisfy them.

Enjoy what you have rather than desiring what you don't have. Just dreaming about nice things is meaningless; it is like chasing the wind. ECCLESIASTES 6:9

> Regardless of how unfulfilling such pleasures are, people pursue them anyway. Both the Old and New Testaments have harsh warnings against making an idol of pleasure.

Foolishness brings joy to those who have no sense; a sensible person stays on the right path. PROVERBS 15:21

Destruction is certain for you who get up early to begin long drinking bouts that last late into the night. You furnish lovely music and wine at your grand parties; the harps, lyres, tambourines, and flutes are superb! But you never think about the LORD or notice what he is doing. ISAIAH 5:11-12

You are a pleasure-crazy kingdom, living at ease and feeling secure, bragging as if you were the greatest in the world! You say, "I'm self-sufficient and not accountable to anyone!"...
   You felt secure in all your wickedness. "No one sees me," you said. Your "wisdom" and "knowledge" have caused you to turn away from me and claim, "I am self-sufficient and not accountable to anyone!" So disaster will overtake you suddenly, and you won't be able to charm it away. Calamity will fall upon you, and you won't be able to buy your way out. A catastrophe will arise so fast that you won't know what hit you.
ISAIAH 47:8-11

Those who love their life in this world will lose it. JOHN 12:25

Their destruction is their reward for the harm they have done. They love to indulge in evil pleasures in broad daylight. They are a disgrace and a stain among you. They revel in deceitfulness while they feast with you. 2 PETER 2:13

> The alternative—the only real alternative—to the pursuit and worship of pleasure is Christ.

We should be decent and true in everything we do, so that everyone can approve of our behavior. Don't participate in wild parties and getting drunk, or in adultery and immoral living, or in

fighting and jealousy. But let the Lord Jesus Christ take control of
you, and don't think of ways to indulge your evil desires.
ROMANS 13:13-14

Their closed minds are full of darkness; they are far away from the
life of God because they have shut their minds and hardened their
hearts against him. They don't care anymore about right and
wrong, and they have given themselves over to immoral ways.
Their lives are filled with all kinds of impurity and greed.

But that isn't what you were taught when you learned about
Christ. Since you have heard all about him and have learned the
truth that is in Jesus, throw off your old evil nature and your
former way of life, which is rotten through and through, full of
lust and deception. EPHESIANS 4:18-22

Once we, too, were foolish and disobedient. We were misled by
others and became slaves to many wicked desires and evil
pleasures. Our lives were full of evil and envy. We hated others,
and they hated us.

But then God our Savior showed us his kindness and love.
TITUS 3:3-4

> Does this mean that God's children must lead a bland, drab, boring
> life in this world? Not at all.

Your heavenly Father already knows all your needs, and he will
give you all you need from day to day if you live for him and make
the Kingdom of God your primary concern. MATTHEW 6:32-33

And if you still have doubts about the pleasure of living your life for God, see the
chapter on Joy.

Worry and Anxiety

Christian author William R. Inge defined worry as "interest paid on trouble before it becomes due." Worry is the great plague of life, both for believers and unbelievers. It crosses all educational and economic and racial boundaries. It is human to worry, to fret, to fear the future and the unknown.

Worry may be normal, but it can also be sinful. "Sinful?" you say. Definitely. The Bible is brimming over with promises to God's people. So we need not worry, because God is in control of the universe, not us.

Happy are those who fear the LORD. Yes, happy are those who delight in doing what he commands.

When darkness overtakes the godly, light will come bursting in. They are generous, compassionate, and righteous. All goes well for those who are generous, who lend freely and conduct their business fairly. Such people will not be overcome by evil circumstances. Those who are righteous will be long remembered. They do not fear bad news; they confidently trust the LORD to care for them. They are confident and fearless and can face their foes triumphantly. PSALM 112:1, 4-8

I cried out, "I'm slipping!" and your unfailing love, O LORD, supported me. When doubts filled my mind, your comfort gave me renewed hope and cheer. PSALM 94:18-19

Give your burdens to the LORD, and he will take care of you. He will not permit the godly to slip and fall. PSALM 55:22

As pressure and stress bear down on me, I find joy in your commands. PSALM 119:143

In my distress I cried out to the LORD; yes, I prayed to my God for help. He heard me from his sanctuary; my cry reached his ears. PSALM 18:6

I look for someone to come and help me, but no one gives me a passing thought! No one will help me; no one cares a bit what happens to me. Then I pray to you, O LORD. I say, "You are my place of refuge. You are all I really want in life. Hear my cry, for I am very low." PSALM 142:4-6

Worry weighs a person down; an encouraging word cheers a person up. PROVERBS 12:25

So what do people get for all their hard work? Their days of labor are filled with pain and grief; even at night they cannot rest. It is all utterly meaningless. ECCLESIASTES 2:22-23

> Jesus himself, the Son of God, spoke many times on the subject of worry. Feeling himself completely dependent on his Father, he promised his followers that they, too, can—and should—devote their lives to something more fruitful than worrying.

I tell you, don't worry about everyday life—whether you have enough food, drink, and clothes. Doesn't life consist of more than food and clothing? Look at the birds. They don't need to plant or harvest or put food in barns because your heavenly Father feeds them. And you are far more valuable to him than they are. Can all your worries add a single moment to your life? Of course not.

And why worry about your clothes? Look at the lilies and how they grow. They don't work or make their clothing, yet Solomon in all his glory was not dressed as beautifully as they are. And if God cares so wonderfully for flowers that are here today and gone tomorrow, won't he more surely care for you? You have so little faith!

So don't worry about having enough food or drink or clothing. Why be like the pagans who are so deeply concerned about these things? Your heavenly Father already knows all your needs, and he will give you all you need from day to day if you live for him and make the Kingdom of God your primary concern.

So don't worry about tomorrow, for tomorrow will bring its own worries. Today's trouble is enough for today. MATTHEW 6:25-34

Look, I am sending you out as sheep among wolves. Be as wary as snakes and harmless as doves. But beware! For you will be handed over to the courts and beaten in the synagogues. And you must stand trial before governors and kings because you are my followers. This will be your opportunity to tell them about me—yes, to witness to the world. When you are arrested, don't worry about what to say in your defense, because you will be given the right words at the right time. For it won't be you doing the talking—it will be the Spirit of your Father speaking through you. MATTHEW 10:16-20

Give all your worries and cares to God, for he cares about what happens to you. 1 PETER 5:7

> The apostle Paul, in the following passage, promised Christians that they can dispel worry by fixing their minds on good things, not on their worries. It is one of the classic Bible passages on worry, one that people should engrave on their hearts.

Don't worry about anything; instead, pray about everything. Tell
God what you need, and thank him for all he has done. If you do
this, you will experience God's peace, which is far more
wonderful than the human mind can understand. His peace will
guard your hearts and minds as you live in Christ Jesus.

And now, dear friends, let me say one more thing as I close this
letter. Fix your thoughts on what is true and honorable and right.
Think about things that are pure and lovely and admirable. Think
about things that are excellent and worthy of praise.
PHILIPPIANS 4:6-8

If God is for us, who can ever be against us? Since God did not
spare even his own Son but gave him up for us all, won't God, who
gave us Christ, also give us everything else?   ROMANS 8:31-32

See also Contentment, Joy, Peace, Trusting God, Worldly Cares.

TOPICAL INDEX

Failure 50, 108, 120, 203, 428
Faith 108
False Teachings 113
Family 42, 256, 294
Fathers 42, 256, 294
Fear 120
Fellowship with God 125
Fellowship with Other Believers 129
Fighting 61, 94, 138
Food 135
Forgiving Others 138
Freedom 141
Friends 145
Future 101, 186, 203, 428
Gay 36, 353, 380, 388
Generosity 150
Gifts of the Spirit 27
Giving 150, 232
Gloom 50, 120, 203, 428
Glossolalia 27
God 125, 156, 161, 163, 166, 170, 175,
  242, 282, 428
God as Judge 156
God's Concern for the Poor 161
God's Fairness 163
God's Guidance 166
God's Love for Us 170
God's Mercy 175
Gossip 224, 423
Government 46, 323
Grace 282, 317, 428
Gratitude 420
Grief 50, 68, 297, 313, 394, 428
Growth 282, 317, 372
Guilt 180
Happiness 65, 203, 220, 302
Hate 183
Healing 36, 50, 297, 394
Health 36, 50, 394
Heaven 186
Hell 193
Help 50, 108, 166, 170, 203
Holy Spirit, the 196
Home 42, 256, 294
Homosexuality 36, 353, 380, 388

Honesty 253
Hope 203
Humility 261, 336
Husbands 256
Hypocrisy 209
Identity 317, 372
Idleness 235
Idolatry 37, 91, 242, 282, 380, 447
Illness 394
Immorality 37, 388
Immortality 101, 186, 193, 203
Infidelity 1, 256
Inspiration 32, 196
Jealousy 97
Jesus Christ 186, 215, 360
Jesus' Second Coming 215
Joy 220
Judging Others 224
Justice 156, 163, 186, 193, 265
Justification 229
Kindness 232
Knowledge 12, 409, 430
Labor 235, 439
Laughter 65, 220
Law 46, 323
Laziness 235
Legalism 113, 141, 209
Liberty 141
Loneliness 239
Loving God 242
Loving Others 246
Lying 253
Marriage 256
Materialism 12, 268, 380, 409, 447
Maturity 6, 317
Meaning 203, 317, 372
Meekness, Humility, Gentleness 261
Mercy 265
Mission 287, 435
Money 268
Morality 282, 353, 399
Mothers 42, 256, 294
Mourning 68, 101, 203
Nature 89
New Age 113